Dying to Live

*A Theological and Practical Workbook on
Death, Dying and Bereavement*

Marian Carter

scm press

Published in 2014 by SCM Press
Editorial office
3rd Floor
Invicta House
108–114 Golden Lane,
London
EC1Y 0TG

SCM Press is an imprint of Hymns Ancient & Modern Ltd
(a registered charity)
13A Hellesdon Park Road
Norwich NR6 5DR, UK

www.scmpress.co.uk

British Library Cataloguing in Publication data

A catalogue record for this book is available
from the British Library

978 0 334 05240 1

Typeset by Regent Typesetting
Printed and bound by
CPI Group (UK) Ltd, Croydon

Contents

Acknowledgements

I owe a debt of gratitude to Dr Natalie Watson of SCM Press, who has guided my enthusiasm. My background is in teaching and later ordination as a Baptist minister, then, realizing certain strengths in Anglicanism, I worked in a parish and was ordained with the first group of women priests. An interchange of understanding between tutor and students enriched my life in teaching Pastoral Theology at the University College of St Mark and St John and the South West Ministerial Training Course. I have worked in three hospices, one for nearly six years, learning from my patients, their relatives and staff. I will always be grateful to them. The loss of my youngest sister Angie, who died in the hospice where I was chaplain, was a great challenge to my faith.

God has given me companions on the journey: Sister Angela Morris, my spiritual guide; David Newton, my mentor at the hospice; Sharon Kelly, a colleague; friends including the late Peter Fairbrother, George Neal, Jo Roberts; the Companions group; my family and Angie, my late sister, who showed me how to live and how to die.

Introduction

This book is to encourage reflective practice arising from theology associated with dying, bereavement and the afterlife. It encourages readers to interact with the contents, 'to enter into a conversation' with me, the writer. It will encourage you to reflect critically on your experience in the light of Christian faith and theology, to discern how God is calling us to minister, becoming more informed and confident in the practice of ministry: an inner journey and an outer journey. It is concerned with theology and practice – but don't be put off!

'Theology' means 'words about God'. It has been used to describe what we understand about the mystery which is God – and it is something that we are continually discovering. As Christians we do theology with God in 'listening to' words from God, through Scripture, worship, meditation, silence, and 'speaking' words to God, through prayer, bringing us into a closer walk with God and into a relationship with our brothers and sisters. How we experience God differs. God is known through the natural world; through the arts, creating or participating in painting, drama, sculpture, literature or music; catching a glimpse of God through the Church, music, liturgy, Scripture; through saintly people. Knowledge of God leads us to explore the nature and activity of God at work in our world – theology. I like to do theology together, with friends around my kitchen table. Theology is for everyone, not just for professionals.

What of the word 'practice'? As we discern through our prayers where God is at work we are led to action, that 'God's kingdom may come on earth as it is in heaven'. I am putting the words 'theology' and 'practice' together since I believe this is what Jesus did.

Who is this book for?

This book is intended for a disparate group of Christians: ordinary church members with many life skills in human caring to help their questioning neighbour; those invited to be part of a pastoral team visiting the elderly and housebound, the dying and the bereaved; those seeking; those who have received a recognized, authorized ministry as Readers and lay preachers and who lead worship; those training for ordained ministry; and clergy wanting to improve their reflective skills in care of the dying, funerals and bereavement.

What is the book about?

Each chapter follows a pattern: a summary of the chapter followed by a diagram of the method to be used, the pastoral circle. Beginning with **experience** roots the material in the reality of life; experiences in the chapters come from hospice and parish ministry – names have been changed to preserve confidentiality. **Reflection on experience** allows me to tease out theological implications of the experience. Life is embedded in a particular historical time and location so we move to reflect on the **cultural context**, much of which could be called 'secular', but Christianity is rooted in the everyday. Jesus' cultural context was his rooting in the Hebrew Scriptures, an observant Jew in rural first-century occupied Palestine. Our context is very different. We live in the developed world, influenced by the advances of medical science which have extended life expectancy and distanced ideas of mortality. Context is informed by the physical and social sciences and theology. **Scripture and the Christian tradition** give insights pertinent to the particular chapter, including some of the different ways that Scripture has been interpreted across the centuries, the tradition, and Christian denominations. There are brief indications from the insights of other faiths. The section on **cultural context in dialogue with Scripture and the tradition** considers how the insights of cultural context inform and challenge our faith formed by Scripture, and Scripture's insights challenge the knowledge emerging from our context; this **dialogue leads into theology.** Personal belief is a provisional attempt to understand God and God's call to action within our own experience, otherwise it is second-hand and defective. It takes into account the contemporary world and draws on the thinking of the Christian tradition, present and past, in which each of us is formed. This is why theology is so exciting: it is always in process. It is this theological reflection that guides and informs our **pastoral practice.** We have learnt much in the last century from other disciplines. As Christians we do not have the monopoly on knowledge, but, believing that all truth is God's, we need the humility to learn while recognizing that in some respects other disciplines are governed by understanding we would not own. Our pastoral care will always be provisional and contextual. At times I refer back to the original experience: this is called the 'spiral curriculum', since when we return we will have a deeper understanding of where God is at work in a situation.

Overview of the chapters

Chapter 1: Laying the Foundations is an introduction to the book. An experience illustrates the range of attitudes to mortality that are reflected on theologically. The context depicts reasons for changes in attitudes: the growth in the sciences, the medical model, which has dramatically changed expectations of life, marginalizing thoughts about death. For many, scientific thinking is a primary challenge to faith and religion; nevertheless the Scriptures are informative and lead to a theology of humanity, creation and salvation, which challenge and inform our practice of ministry.

Chapter 2: Care of the Dying and of Their Carers considers the history of care when faith was significant, followed by periods of doubt. Today there is a growing recognition of achieving 'a good death', with an emphasis on spirituality in government reports. Scriptural insights challenge. The critical dialogue, of cultural context and scriptural insights, leads to a theology of incarnation and presence informing our practice of ministry with the dying and their relatives.

Chapter 3: Ministry to the Bereaved explores the experience of loss, and how we respond: death is noted as the ultimate loss for ourselves and those we love. The context of the twenty-first century uses models to understand the process of bereavement derived from psychology. The Scriptures offer insights into loss, not as something to be avoided but as a source of potential inner growth. Cultural context and Scriptures lead to theologies of vulnerable incarnation and hope, which guide our pastoral responses.

Chapter 4: Another Ending – the Funeral explores the purpose and changing patterns of funerals and rituals in the twenty-first century. Denominational liturgies are briefly examined. We look at burial customs in the Scriptures. A theology of vulnerable incarnation and of hope emerges, which informs our practice of ministry and is pastoral to those of faith.

Chapter 5: Liturgy, Theology and Funerals for the Non-Churched explores funerals of those of little or no faith whose relatives nevertheless ask for the help of the Church. Scripture has insights concerning the 'outsider', in contrast to Jesus' inclusive ministry. Context and Scripture are brought together in dialogue leading to a theology of grief, vulnerable incarnation and God, a pastoral sensitivity in working with the bereaved in preparing a funeral and a theology and practice of ministry that is sensitive.

Chapter 6: Looking to the Future – Post-Funeral Support considers how ongoing care of the bereaved can be offered throughout the Christian year in a society that sometimes appears to marginalize and forget the existence of death. Scripture examines the understanding of the covenant relationship of God and people. Relationship is a reminder of the Trinitarian Godhead. Context and Scripture lead to a Trinitarian theology informing pastoral practice.

Chapter 7: Resources for Pastoral Carers recognizes the challenges to those who are involved in ministry of the dying and the bereaved. This can be an exhausting ministry in which to work, since it goes against the grain in our current culture. It begins with an example when the patient becomes the carer. The Scriptures are a rich resource of guidance to 'come apart'. The chapter suggests resources for our own physical, mental, emotional and spiritual health.

Chapter 8: Joining Up the Dots brings together the book using the model of Oden in the context of the twenty-first century, its significance vis-à-vis the advances of science and technology and the huge benefits that the latter bring; a theology emerges, raising issues of autonomy and forgiveness leading to pastoral practice.

Footnotes indicate the sources of quotations, or act as a starting point for pursuing an idea. There are reflective questions to relate my experience to that of the reader. A brief list of books follows.

Methodology

Much Christian education in the past has been didactic, doctrinal in subject content, or non-existent. Power was held by male clergy. Many educated Christians today question this style of learning so different from 'secular' styles. The content of the faith has also been an issue, with clergy lacking in trust that lay people could interpret the Scriptures for themselves. Some Christian groups believe that it is wrong to question the truths of the Bible and discourage questions, but Jesus offered stories and left his listeners to make sense of them for their own lives (Mark 4.9–13, 33–34; Matt. 13.51–53); he turned the question back to the questioner (Luke 10.25); he accompanied those who were searching for meaning, clarifying their thinking (Luke 24.13–35). The teaching of Jesus set his listeners free to respond. It is indoctrination, a fixed viewpoint, that enslaves. We have

Jesus' promise that the Spirit will lead us into all truth (John 16.13), when we are humble enough to listen and discern God's will.

Paulo Freire (1921–97) challenged traditional education methods in his book *Pedagogy of the Oppressed*. His emphasis was on dialogue, signifying respect in the pupil–teacher relationship, in contrast to what he describes as the 'banking' type of education, where the educator 'deposits' knowledge into the mind of the listener. Freire believed that the educators had to forget themselves, to die in order to be born again and to educate alongside, to teach and learn from the person being taught. He used the metaphor of Easter to explore how the power divide between teachers and learners could be transcended. Education was about praxis, it deepened understanding and made a difference to building community, leading to actions for justice and human flourishing. His is a pedagogy of hope. He wrote of conscientization, of developing a consciousness in people that has the power to transform their thinking and attitudes. His thinking is particularly applicable to the Church. Freire's learning used personal experience, narrative, the senses (objects to look at, feel and explore), the imagination (stories), different ways of learning (visual, aural, kinaesthetic) and exploring together. If we use these methods, we discover that sense is made by the reader in relating new learning to his or her existing learning and experience.

Mentoring

The method to be used in this book is one of lifelong learning. In current adult education, individuals are encouraged to have a 'buddy' or a 'mentor'. The invitation is for the reader to find someone with whom to share. The reader, or a ministry team group, will be invited to engage with this book through activities, questions and reflection, which are indicated in the text by a bullet point, and record the experience to form a diary of reflection. My hope and prayer is that you will engage and that you and your ministry will be enriched.

Marian Carter
Easter 2014

I

Laying the Foundations

Life's continual task is to build your death.
Montaigne (1533–92)

This chapter lays the foundations for the book, with the pastoral circle as method. It uses an experience of dying to reflect theologically on reactions to death. The cultural context reflects changes in attitudes to death, resulting from the rise and influence of medical science and the demise of traditional Christianity. Scriptural insights suggest the nature of humanity, God in creation, the relationship of sin and death, and the need for salvation. The dialogue between cultural context and Scripture raises the question of the relationship between science and religion, leading to theological concepts of creation, humanity and death which inform our pastoral practice. There are questions in the text for an individual or group of readers to use in a diary of reflection (see Introduction).

Pastoral circle

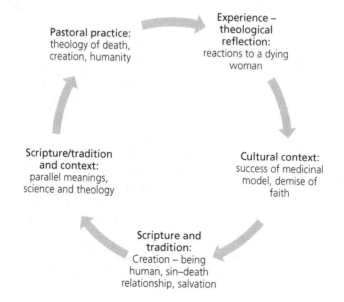

Pastoral practice: theology of death, creation, humanity

Experience – theological reflection: reactions to a dying woman

Cultural context: success of medicinal model, demise of faith

Scripture and tradition: Creation – being human, sin–death relationship, salvation

Scripture/tradition and context: parallel meanings, science and theology

Experience

Jean had been clear of breast cancer for 25 years. When the cancer recurred, in her spine and neck, it quickly became terminal. In her final weeks Jean went into hospital for symptom control. She spent time preparing the family for her death and organizing her funeral. The nurses were touched by her quiet acceptance and the way she talked and planned for death.

Jean belonged to a Christian congregation, some of whom believed the cancer to be evidence of evil or maybe sin. For some it was the devil, who needed to be exorcised. They approached the vicar. He was uncertain what to do. The vicar asked his curate about the idea of exorcism. She said, 'Look at Jean's influence in her ward; how her courage helps others. I visit her to bring her comfort and come out having been blessed. Do you think that is evidence of the devil?' The vicar decided not to exorcise. Some of the congregation held a prayer vigil in the church for her recovery.

When Jean died, many of the members of her church were perplexed, angry with God and the vicar, who had to face many challenging questions.

Reflection on experience

Understandings of death are varied in Jean's dying. It may be that those nearer to death, by longevity or terminal illness, are best able to talk about it. Many today fear the process of dying and death itself, using euphemisms such as 'he's popped his clogs' to avoid talking about it. Parents shelter their children from death by not letting them attend the funeral of a grandparent, teacher or schoolmate. Parents replace a dead pet, in the hope that a child will not notice. We fill every moment of life, ignoring mortality; we turn off media reports of war and famine in far-off places, until brought home when our troops return in coffins. Yet death is universal; at some time it will happen to each of us and those we love. Woody Allen said, 'It's not that I'm afraid of dying. I just don't want to be there when it happens.' Others believe that awareness of our mortality is central to the meaning we make of this life and that it guides our actions. Moltmann reminds us, 'to live as if there were no death is to live an illusion. Death acts as a catalyst to plunge us into more authentic life modes and it enhances our pleasure in the living of life.'[1]

Throughout the centuries humans have wrestled with death, its significance, for life and a hereafter, as did Jean and her friends.

Jean said: 'I know that I am dying. I asked the consultant, and he affirmed it. He would not say how long I had to live. It gives me time to talk to my family, to prepare for death and my funeral. I thank God for those clear years, which allowed me to look after my daughters when they were young. I am a bit frightened of dying – though it will be an adventure, something I have not done before. I have hope and know that whatever happens after death I am in the hands of a loving God.'

Jean's daughter said: 'Mum is amazing – of course I do not want to lose her, but my sister and I have time to talk and tell her how much we love her. We can laugh and cry at the funny and sad incidents from our childhood. We were shocked that she wanted to talk about her funeral; she wrote it down so that we could know what she wants.'

Jean's friend Janet said: 'Jean's cancer is because she did not care for herself, ignoring the signs of her illness, always putting others first. That might be Christian, but I don't agree with Jean – you have to look after number one. Yes, of course, others matter, but it is like they tell you on an aircraft, "If there is an incident, put on your own lifejacket first and then one on your child."'

Her friend Susan said: 'Cancer is a vicious disease, nothing to do with a good God, so it must be the devil. If the devil has got into Jean, then we must ask the vicar to get rid of it. I think they call it "exorcise".'

Jean's vicar said: 'I am not sure what to do. Is the cancer a punishment? Jean has lived a good life. Cancer is certainly "evil" but is it the devil? Perhaps I should do what Susan says and exorcise the evil. I don't know what else I can do. We can certainly put Jean's name on the prayer list.'

Her nurse said: 'Jean is amazing – I would just howl and feel angry and cheated of life if it was me. This life is all we have. When you are dead, that's it.'

The consultant said: 'I don't like telling people that their condition is terminal – usually there is a lot that, as doctors, we can do. We have the technology and the medication; death is our failure. Jean refused the morphine injection. I said it would reduce the pain, but Jean said that at the moment she could bear the pain level, wanting to stay alert to listen and talk to friends and family. Jean knows what she wants, not all patients do.'

---

1 Jürgen Moltmann, 1996, *The Coming of God: Christian Eschatology*, London: SCM Press, p. 50.

Different reactions to death are illustrated in this story – death as inevitable; an adventure; trust and hope in God beyond death; loss; punishment and evil; necessitating prayer; cheating on the only life we have; a failure.

Humans have always wondered about death

One of the earliest, extant writings is the Sumerian *Epic of Gilgamesh* (eighteenth century BCE), a poem about King Gilgamesh, who in his travels meets Utnapishtim, from whom he learns the mysteries of how to worship the gods, why there is death, what makes a king and how to live a good life. Yet he oppresses his people, who appeal to the gods for help. The gods create a primitive, wild man, Enkidu, to distract Gilgamesh. After a fight the two become friends and journey together to challenge a beast they eventually kill. The gods are angry and sentence Enkidu to death. Gilgamesh grieves his friend's death and mourns by tearing his clothes. He becomes aware of his own mortality and decides to seek the secret of immortality. To do this he crosses the Waters of Death. Utnapishtim tells him that fighting mortality, the fate of humans, is futile and diminishes life's joys. He should enjoy the simple pleasure of his mortal life, for this is man's lot. Gilgamesh still hankers for immortality, a gift of the gods.[2] Utnapishtim's wife asks that he be given a parting gift. It is the secret of a plant to make him young again. By stealth he obtains the plant but, while bathing, a snake steals it. Immortality is not to be his. Gilgamesh returns to his kingdom to look at the city he has built that will survive him and be his memorial. The story is one of learning through experience, of friendship, of death, of grieving at loss, of courage, of the dual nature of humans as both saint and sinner, the search for meaning and finally the reluctant acceptance of mortality.

Centuries later in 399 BCE Plato records in the *Phaedo* a reconstruction of Socrates' death following his trial and condemnation for heresy. He dies drinking hemlock. Socrates welcomes death since it frees his immortal soul from the imprisonment of his body. For Gilgamesh, life is to be enjoyed now, for there is nothing else; for Socrates, death is welcome as a freeing of his immortal spirit from the limitations of his body.

---

2 Andrew R. George (trans. and ed.), 1999, *The Epic of Gilgamesh*, London, Penguin Books, and *The Babylonian Gilgamesh Epic: Critical and Cuneiform Texts*, 2003, Oxford: Oxford University Press.

Challenging theological questions

Jean's dying raises challenging theological questions which need addressing; foremost are those of suffering and unanswered prayer. The first concept is complex, frequently clouded by failure to distinguish different types of suffering. Some suffering is the result of injustice – a guilty verdict on an innocent man; some the result of oppression – a country subject to a political dictatorship; and some the exploitation of the powerful over the weak – rape, poor pay given to economic migrants. This is not part of God's intention for creation, it is the result of human choice. We are called as Christians to participate in God's saving work and challenge such suffering, bringing God's justice. A second type of suffering is persecution for the faith, the result of human torture in various parts of the world today. This can be a witness to God (1 Peter 2.20–23), but needs challenging. A third type of suffering is natural suffering, expressed by Iris Murdoch in her novel *The Unicorn*: 'Suffering is no scandal. It is natural ... All creation suffers. It suffers from having been created, if from nothing else. It suffers from being divided from God.' It includes mortality, loss and grief, pain, disability and natural disasters. Some of this suffering might be explained: for example, there is a medical, causal link between a mother's contact with German measles at a certain stage in her pregnancy resulting in serious damage to her unborn child. Is natural suffering because this world is contrary to God's will or because God made it this way but intended it to be otherwise? If God is all-loving and omnipotent, why does God not control suffering? At theological college, preparing for hospital visiting, we discussed the patient's question, 'Why me?' Our tutor said: 'The answer is "Why not?"' I found 'why not?' a hard answer faced with an individual. Some Christians believe suffering is God's way of testing our faith. For me this raises questions about the nature of the God revealed in Jesus: it seems to suggest an immoral God. Others understand suffering as a punishment for sin, yet suffering is indiscriminate of people, 'saint' and 'sinner'.

The dominant model of a theology of creation existing from the fourth to the eighteenth century was that God created *ex nihilo* signifying that matter is good; creation is finite and closed – everything has its God-given place, a closed system of cause and effect, a stable home for humans to prepare for eternity. Creation and hierarchy mean social and personal relationships can give clear patterns of authority and stability. Creation has a purpose. Humans are free agents who can choose or reject a relationship with God; at the end suffering is justified in the overall plan of God.

Irenaeus, the second-century Bishop of Lyons, questioned this in his day. He taught that creation was emergent and purposeful, moving from innocence and immaturity to knowledge and complexity towards an end, the *eschaton*, when suffering was transformed in a new creation (Rev. 21.1–4). Anthropologists state that the first humans struggled with a hostile environment, necessitating selfishness and violence to survive, but gradually became capable of the moral awareness of love and sacrifice, putting the need of the tribe before personal needs. When God is not self-evident, there is a distance between humans and God, so that humans have freedom in relation to God. God is the world's foundation, not intervening but able to influence it through God's presence within human hearts.

If God loves, then this must include God's ability to suffer, for it is when I love that I can suffer for the loved one. When the mode of God's power is vulnerability, God is willing to be pushed to the margins, becoming good news to the marginalized, poor and suffering. In the cross the Son suffers God-forsakenness, the Father suffers the absence and loss through the Son's death, the Spirit is the bond of love that unites God at the moment of separation; it is the relationship of the Trinity.

Hauerwas considers that 'historically speaking, Christians have not had a "solution" to the problem of evil. Rather they have had a community of care that made it possible for them to absorb the destructive terror of evil that constantly threatens to destroy all human relations.'[3]

Much suffering has no sense, but some sufferers use it creatively to grow, to develop fortitude, perseverance and to bless others – Jean's courage inspired patients and staff. For others, their suffering challenges their faith in God, which may be lost. Unexplained suffering raises in us the need for 'religious protest' or a 'sacred discontent', as we continue reflecting on experience and searching for answers.

Intercession – changing God's mind?

Intercessions for the sick can be understood as an attempt to change God's mind, arising from belief in an interventionist God. If nothing happens, or the person dies, questions are raised, illustrated by Jean's friends. God is not impervious to suffering, and there are incidents in the Scriptures where we are told God 'changes his mind' (Gen. 18.23f.; Ex. 32.7f.). Jesus healed a daughter whose mother challenged him for his lack of care (Mark 7.24–30). Jesus called his disciples to pray and taught them to persist in prayer (Luke 11.1–13). In prayer we can offer the person and ourselves to God, seeking God's will and purpose.

---

3 Stanley Hauerwas, 1990, *Naming the Silences: Medicine and the Problem of Suffering*, New York and London: T & T Clark, p. 53.

Questions for reflection and response

- Bring to mind your first experience of death; the feelings that it evoked and how it affected you. Record it in your diary of reflection.
- Explore the persons in the dying of Jean. If there is a group, let half of the group each choose a major character – Jean, family member, friend, vicar, medical professional. Sit together in a circle – a 'goldfish bowl': let this group, in role, then discuss feelings about Jean's dying. Let others sit outside the circle, watch and listen. After ten minutes, the 'watchers' are invited to comment.
- Prayer is a source of comfort and strength to Christians. What might be the content of prayer for Jean? James 5.13–15 may help.
- Draw your life line, or a significant decade of it, showing the positive and negative times in your life: for example it may be like a temperature chart! Look at the result. Where and why was God at work?

Reflection on the cultural context

To minister today it is important that as lay and ordained Christians we have an understanding of our rapidly changing cultural context, the world in which we, and those to whom we minister, 'live and move and have our being'. This section addresses that need. I begin by a definition of death and a brief historical background.

Definitions and perceptions of death

In his *Historia Naturalis*, the Roman author Pliny the Elder wrote, 'so uncertain is men's judgment that they cannot determine even death itself' (77–79 CE). In the first edition of the *Encyclopaedia Britannica* in 1768 the definition was brief, 'the separation of the soul and the body', reflecting the context of a religious society. In the fifteenth edition of 1974, the definition was thirty times longer and solely from a biological standpoint. Medical advances make it more difficult to determine if a person is dead. The nearest definition is: 'the final cessation of activity in the central nervous system noted especially by a flat electroencephalogram for a predetermined length of time'. However, death can be 'reversed' with an electric shock, cardiopulmonary resuscitation (CPR); breathing and heartbeat can sometimes be restarted; without a functioning heart or lungs, life can be sustained with a combination of life-support devices, organ transplants and artificial pacemakers.

Perceptions of and preparation for death have changed through the centuries, noted in the writings of the social historian Philippe Ariès. He begins with 'tamed death', anticipated through natural signs and a dying person's premonition: an honoured tradition of the Knights of the Round Table and typical of the Early Middle Ages. It needed preparation by the dying: being at peace within one's self, making peace with others and God, so that the dying could rest, knowing their immortality was assured. The Middle Ages emphasized humanity's collective judgement at the end of time, but by the fifteenth century the focus was on individual judgement immediately after death, which called for preparation during life.[4] The need was met by the emergence of a manual, *Ars Moriendi* (Art of Dying), to educate priests and lay people in ministry to the dying (see Chapter 2).

Death today

Today attitudes are very different: Ariès states that society denies death. It has become 'excluded, invisible, wild, untamed by ritual or community'.[5] This Ariès believes is related to the dominant model of Western health care, the medical model, a sociological term to indicate that, from the mid-twentieth century, the understanding of death and dying is dominated by medicine. The medical model states illnesses of body and mind have an underlying cause, which can usually be diagnosed, removed, reversed or replaced in treatment. The patient is cured and can return to the status quo existing before the illness. If the illness persists and the doctor fails, it is he or she rather than the priest who presides at the death.

Historical changes – the medicalization of death

Ariès traces the medicalization of death to the end of the Second World War. Prior to this, health was a lottery dependent on class and occupation; medical care for the working class was poor, if it existed; life expectancy was short. In the United Kingdom, the Beveridge Report (1942) stated a hope for welfare assistance from 'the cradle to the grave'. National Insurance was created in 1946 and the National Health Service in 1947. Public health improved with slum clearance and new housing. Primary causes of death, infections, such as tuberculosis, cholera, smallpox, scarlet fever

---

4 Philippe Ariès, 1974–75, *Western Attitudes toward Death: From the Middle Ages to the Present*, Baltimore and London: Johns Hopkins University Press, p. 28.

5 Philippe Ariès, 1981, *The Hour of Our Death*, trans. Helen Weaver, New York: Knopf, p. 585.

and measles, were largely eradicated. Sulphonamide drugs and penicillin revolutionized medicine, increasing the power of the medical profession to cure previously life-threatening diseases, manage accidents and increase the lifespan. In 2010 there were 461,016 recorded deaths in England. Infant mortality was the lowest ever recorded, 4.3 deaths per 1,000 live births. Death was pushed out of sight, many living well into retirement.

Life expectancy in the UK		
Year	Males	Females
1900	44 years	47 years
1999	75 years	80 years
2010	78.2 years	82.3 years
		UK Government Office of National Statistics

Significance of the medical profession

Robert Lambourne noted society's innate belief in the power of medicine to bring positive outcomes, leading to doctors being held in awe.[6] Langdon Gilkey called doctors 'priests in white coats'.[7] Doctors are seen as 'playing God', sustaining life and postponing and changing the process of dying, so that death is drifting into a peaceful sleep. Sheila Cassidy, a former medical director of a hospice, states: 'As doctors we are trained from the cradle to fight disease and to save life. It is instinctive. Disease is the enemy and death the ultimate disaster.'[8] The *British Medical Journal* stated: 'Modern medicine may even have had the hubris to suggest implicitly, if not explicitly, that it could defeat death … Death has become medicalized, reaching its apotheosis perhaps with … prolonged death.'[9] An example is that of Ariel Sharon, former Prime Minister of Israel, who had a stroke and fell into a coma in January 2006. He died in January 2014, never having regained consciousness.

The power of doctors changes how patients are perceived: as in the 'sick role', when they are in the 'dying role'. Patients are encouraged to be

6 R. A. Lambourne, 'Towards an understanding of medical theological dialogue', in Michael Wilson (ed.), 1983, *Explorations in Health and Salvation*, Birmingham: Institute for the Study of Worship and Religious Architecture.

7 Langdon Gilkey, 1970, *Religion and the Scientific Future*, London: SCM Press.

8 Sheila Cassidy, 1988, *Sharing the Darkness: The Spirituality of Caring*, London: Darton, Longman and Todd, p. 15.

9 *British Medical Journal*, 15:320 (January 2000), pp. 129–30.

passive rather than active. In a hospice where I worked this was known as 'pyjama-induced paralysis'. Have we pushed medical staff into this position of seeing death as failure by the awe in which we hold them?

Significance of the place of death

A key characteristic of the medical model is the place of death. Increasing numbers die in institutions, either hospices, hospitals or residential care.

Place of death

5% hospices (NHS and non-NHS)

18% residential homes (Local Authority and private)

21% home

53% hospital

Office of National Statistics, 2011

Previously patients died at home, surrounded by family; increased geographical mobility and the numbers of women working decreases this possibility. Hospitalization means medical care is in the hands of experts, not the family. Ariès notes that dying in an institution, particularly a hospital, is 'hidden'. There is 'anonymity' of patients, attended by strangers, doctors and nurses. Patients may be attached to life-support systems, which may depersonalize the relationship between doctor and patient and create dependency. The person becomes 'the bowel cancer'. His or her body is displaced by the physicians' diagnostic and therapeutic relationship to the patient's pathology. It becomes a familiar complaint that medicine treats 'me' like an 'it'.[10] Death ceases to be public, family and friends may not be present, yet within the hospital everything continues as if nobody dies; when relatives are present, they may become more aware of their own mortality.

Life-sustaining services characterize hospital buildings, available to aid the medical profession in diagnosis and treatment: medical photography, scans, X-rays, radiography, radiotherapy, chemotherapy, diagnostic testing, pharmacies and research. The research laboratories of pharmaceutical organizations increase the variety of drugs, extending life for the terminally ill. There are advances in medical techniques: organ transplants, the first heart transplant by Christian Barnard on 3 December 1967. The

---

10 Allen Verhey, 2011, *The Christian Art of Dying: Learning from Jesus*, Grand Rapids, MI and Cambridge, UK: Eerdmans, p. 34.

Human Genome Project completed the annotating of the hereditary code on 26 June 2000 with the possibility of preventing hereditary conditions. Gene therapy clinical trials were held in the spring of 2013 in the UK to give quality of life to heart-failure patients.

Significance of the undertaker's profession

In a hospital, when death happens, the deceased's body is quickly prepared and removed lest other patients and relatives are upset. Jane insisted on 'laying out' her mother, much to the dismay of the nursing staff. Later she said it enabled her emotionally to realize her loss and begin grieving. With the professionalization of undertakers, families are seldom involved in the preparation of their deceased for cremation or burial; undertakers are in charge, with the mourners becoming clients. To reduce stress, either the body is not seen again or is viewed in the chapel of rest in a coffin, transformed to look as lifelike as possible. Today many do not experience seeing death until adult life, though the presence of children was normal in Victorian times. An understanding of death is part of our 'primary socialization'. It is crucial for our childhood basic grasp and interpretation of reality. Neither do children learn how to grieve through observation of older family members.

In summary, the medical model of death is impersonal, professionalized by medical staff and funeral directors. It can be surrounded by machines and strangers, privatized, passive, solely physical rather than holistic. The medical profession alone cannot be blamed for this model, the public are involved in a conspiracy to ignore mortality. Do the doctors over-react, believing they can defeat death? The profession are only doing what society demands; we, the public, have to take our responsibility. There are devoted nurses and doctors who care, listen and are guided by their patients. Advances in medicine are a blessing: the good use of pain-easing drugs, enabling patients to be cared for at home; pacemakers giving quality of life to those with heart disease. I have given examples to argue that in the twenty-first century our attitudes to death have been dominated by the advances of medical science. Death has been silenced and distanced. Verhey, an American ethicist, indicates three challenges to this argument: the Hospice Movement, the Death Awareness Movement and bio-ethics (see p. 43).

Changes affecting faith commitment

Parallel to medical advances were changes in society. The 1960s was an age of professionalization, experts, particularly in medical science, defining death and seeking to postpone it. Psychologists and trained counsellors gradually became the experts in the grieving process, taking over the pastoral work of church ministers. These changes affected society's attitudes and behaviour in regard to death. Medical science, as all science, is considered factually verifiable; Christianity is an act of faith, yet traditionally it gave meaning to death and the hope of a life after death.

Christianity began to be abandoned, not for atheism but as individuals sought their own authentic spirituality in, for example, the New Age Movement (NAM). Steve Bruce states that 'the holistic spirituality milieu (NAM) is intrinsically interesting, the numbers involved ... too small to make any difference to the overall religiosity of the UK'. Philip Sheldrake suggests that religious institutions in preaching, creeds and liturgies largely focus on the question, 'What or Who is God?', yet behind the spiritual quest is a different question, 'Who am I?' Religions are exploring an answer to the first question, which increasingly is not being asked.[11] There is a mismatch. The question 'Who am I?', however, is about meaning in life and might lead to issues of finitude and mortality.

Individualism was a characteristic of society; many made their own decisions regardless of institutional authorities, figures and texts and were willing to live with the consequence. Individualism and a search for meaning were particularly expressed in the youth culture illustrated by the Beatles' quest to explore Eastern meditation. In the 1960s there was a growing materialism: happiness was dependent on buying certain products and a hedonism of 'eat, drink and be merry for tomorrow we die' (Isa. 22.13; 1 Cor. 15.32). Conversation about mortality and death was silenced. But this utopian state did not last, life became more uncertain.

The twentieth and twenty-first centuries

The bombings in New York in 2001 and in London in 2005 were incidents of global terrorism, arising from deeply distorted religious ideologies and political, often racial, differences. Voices expressing concerns on climate change became more strident, with the fifth Intergovernmental Panel on Climate Change – The Physical Science Basis (27 October 2013) stating

---

11 Philip F. Sheldrake, 'The Crisis of Postmodernity', *Christian Spirituality Bulletin* (Summer 1996), pp. 6–9. Sheldrake noted that within the mystical tradition the two questions are related.

the threat to the existence of the cosmos. There was the fear of nuclear proliferation. There was concern about the world's sustainability for fresh water and food, with a rise in world population projected from 6.5 billion to 9 billion by 2050. The global community, through increased communications, became aware of the injustices and inequalities of the planet. The economic crisis of the developed countries resulted in the UK privatizing sections of the NHS and freezing wages for many, leaving a socially divided, aimless and fragmented society. Yet institutional religion continued to be in the spotlight, its leaders making statements about political policy and its economic effects, particularly on the poorest, raising media comments, 'keep religion out of politics'.

The demise of Christianity is evident in the statistics of the 2011 Census of the population of England and Wales. In a population of 56.1 million, Christianity is the largest religious group (33.2 million), a decline of more than 4 million since the Census of 2001, contrasting with a rise of 1.2 million in Islam. Around one in four stated that they had no faith. Encounters with the practices of Islam, Hinduism and Sikhism raised questions of the uniqueness of Christianity. The British Humanist Association said that the statistics on Christianity showed a significant cultural shift in a society where 'religious practice, identity, belonging and belief are all in decline ... and non-religious identities are on the rise'.[12] The Annual Statistics of the Church of England for 2011 show that the average Anglican weekly attendance fell by 0.3 per cent to 1,092,484; however, 20 of 44 dioceses showed increases in 2011.

The UK is multicultural and its values diverse. It is also considered secular, that is, religious thinking, practice and institutions have lost their social significance. In Britain, Steve Bruce's research on secularism states that religion, Christianity in particular, has continued to decline.[13] He quotes Peter Brierley on church membership from 1900 to 2010, declining from 34 per cent to 11 per cent of the population.[14] There were three areas of growth: charismatic/evangelical congregations; Pentecostalism – largely due to the migration of West Africans; and experimental worship such as Fresh Expressions. These, however, 'do not come close to off-setting the decline in the major churches'. Religious legitimation of rites of passage has declined. There is a reliance on inheritance, that is, childhood experience

---

12 *I* newspaper, 12 December 2012, p. 4.

13 Steve Bruce, 'Post-Secularity and Religion in Britain: An Empirical Assessment', *Journal of Contemporary Religion* 28:3 (2013), pp. 369–84, http://dx.doi.org /10.1080/13537903.2013.831642.

14 Peter Brierley, 2011, *UK Church Statistics 4, 2005–2015*, Tonbridge: ABCD Publishers.

of faith and socialization. In 2010, under 15s made up 18 per cent of the population but only 11 per cent of churchgoers; those aged 15–29 were 20 per cent of the population but only 10 per cent of church-goers. Testing whether religion was gaining or losing public salience is difficult; gaining is the popularity of faith schools between 1998 and 2008. But Bruce notes there was 'a slight hardening of attitudes to religion ... [which] has become more contentious'.

The British sociologist Grace Davie stated that, in Europe, Christianity was replaced by people turning to alternative forms of spirituality, yet the institutional church still had a role. She notes Europeans' gratitude that 'churches perform, vicariously, a number of tasks on behalf of the population as a whole'. Europeans may not practise religion on a daily basis but recognize its worth at critical times in the life of the community and, personally and regularly, at baptisms, weddings and funerals.[15]

Questions asked

Faith questions were raised in response to the loss of 3,000 lives in the destruction of the World Trade Center, New York (11 September 2001). In response, Sam Harris, in the USA, blamed Islam, while directly criticizing Christianity and Judaism. In the UK it was Richard Dawkins's book *The God Delusion* (2006) that had an impact. These writers are the new atheists, reductive materialists, who frequently criticize religion without understanding it, quoting biblical texts without contexts, and confusing 'folk religion with reflective theology'. In the context of the twenty-first century, a medicalized approach to death dominates; there is less conventional religious certainty, which results in doubts relating to a life after death, while there is a growth in spirituality.

Questions for reflection and response

- How often, in the last 24 hours, have you heard the word 'death' (media, conversations with neighbours, reading/watching the news)? Record and comment on these incidents.
- Assess the evidence for 'medicalized death'. What resonances does it have in your experience? How might death be different?

---

15 Grace Davie, 2000, *Religion in Modern Europe: A Memory Mutates*, Oxford: Oxford University Press, p. 59.

- 'For centuries a priest "presided" over death, now it is the medical profession; traditional religion has lost its place in society.' Comment.
- What part does the media play in our understanding of death? Illustrate your answer from TV soaps, hospital dramas, detective series, news.

Insights from Scripture and the tradition

Our gratitude for medicine reflects the Hebrew Scriptures. (I use the phrase 'Hebrew Scriptures' of the Old Testament, since these are a living faith for Jewish friends.) The psalmist cries out, 'Bless the Lord, O my soul ... who heals all your diseases' (Ps. 103.4); in Ecclesiasticus, 'Honour physicians for their services, for the Lord created them, for their gift of healing comes from the Most High' (38.1–2).[16] The physician learns the skills of making and giving medicines, for 'the Lord created medicines out of the earth ... By them the physician heals and takes away pain.' Later we read 'and from [God] health (*shalom*) spreads over all the earth' (Ecclus. 38.4, 7–8).[17]

Creation stories – being human

Hebrew faith is down to earth: Genesis reflects life through stories, rather than abstract ideas. The Jews did not begin by worshipping the one God, the Creator. God in the exodus delivered them from slavery and brought them into existence from nothing, establishing a covenant relationship. This led them to believe that this must be the God who created the world.

Genesis 1—11 is an ancient and composite text, forming the introduction to the story of salvation, dealing with the universals of our human experience, setting out why we need to be saved, from what and for what, and why God is doing it the way God is. There are four different pictures of creation (Gen. 1.1—2.4; 2.4b—3.24; Ps. 74.12–17 and 89.5–18; Prov. 8.22–31), each emerging from a different experience, raising questions about life, faith and the world. Humanity is a paradox, created in the image and likeness of God (Gen. 1.26), 'a little lower than God' (Ps.

---

16 Ecclesiasticus (Sirach) is part of the Wisdom literature, written in Jerusalem in Hebrew about 180 BCE, translated into Greek, in the Septuagint (LXX), so read in the early Church.

17 I am grateful to Allen Verhey, 2011, *The Christian Art of Dying: Learning from Jesus*, Grand Rapids, MI and Cambridge, UK: Eerdmans, for bringing these verses to my attention.

8.5–8), given dominion over the works of God's hands (Gen. 1.26),[18] yet self-centred, living in broken relationships with others and with God (Gen. 3). The stories of the creation are considered by scholars to be influenced by other stories in the Ancient Near East and brought back from the Jewish exile in Babylon.[19] Genesis 1.1—2.4 is a poem in which order is created from chaos, separating light from dark, ending with the creation of humans and the Sabbath. The climax is not humanity but the Sabbath, a day for God's blessing and worship of the Creator; it is possibly a hymn explaining the significance of the Sabbath. Underlying the story are theological insights:

1 God is a loving Creator and Sustainer.
2 There is delight in the material world. The personification of 'Wisdom', present at creation, rejoices in the world and delights in the human race (Prov. 8.27–31; Ps. 104). Christian history has often not taken the material world seriously, seeing it as either infected by sin or despised because inferior to the spiritual, but our bodies are 'material'. The alienation of body/spirit is not Hebraic but comes from the influence of Greek philosophy, Gnostics in the early Church, and Augustine, formative for the Western Church.
3 The story witnesses to the interdependence of life, plant and animal.
4 'God created humankind in his image and likeness': humans are unique in their relationship with the Creator.

In the Ancient Near East kings were held to be in 'the image of God', that is, they were God's representatives. In Genesis humans represent God in caring for creation (1.26). But what of likeness? Origen (184–253) distinguished between 'man', 'receiving the honour of God's image in his first creation, whereas the perfection of God's likeness was reserved for him at the consummation' (cf. 1 John 3.2).[20] Irenaeus explained this as Adam and Eve being like innocent children who needed to grow in self-consciousness to become morally aware adults.

The second creation story (Gen. 2.4b—3.24) is from a human perspec-

---

18 N. Lohfink, 1982, *Great Themes from the Old Testament*, Edinburgh: T & T Clark, pp. 178–9, argues that the Hebrew word translated 'dominion' has the basic sense of 'to wander around', 'accompany', 'pasture', 'rule', understood in the context of shepherding.

19 Myth in its original meaning, that of a story using symbol to convey a deep truth.

20 Origen, 1973, *On First Principles* 3.6.1, trans. G. W. Butterworth, Gloucester, MA: Peter Smith, p. 245.

tive. Here the 'LORD God formed man from the dust of the ground, and breathed into his nostrils the breath of life and the man became a living being' (Gen. 2.7). The Hebrew word *ruach* means 'breath' and is physical and spiritual. Spirit is embodied in the world; if God withdraws *ruach* everything disintegrates into dust (Ps. 104.29). The breath of God's life fills the world and holds together all things (Wisd. 1.7). When the breath of a man leaves him, he expires and dies. The word *nephesh* is translated as life/soul/spirit/self/flesh. Humanity is both physical and spiritual, holistic. We use the expression 'embodied'. The idea is reinforced by a wordplay on the word *Adam* (human/earthling) and the Hebrew word *adamah*, meaning ground/earth. Central to the creation stories is the uniqueness of humans as created to reflect, and be in communion with their Creator: humans may be, as the cosmologists today tell us, 'the debris of exploding stars', but within us is 'the breath of God'.

Death and sin

Genesis 3 is a story illustrating the difference between the goodness of God's creation and humanity's disobedience and death. It begins in a paradise of harmony between man and woman, humanity and God. The garden is to be enjoyed, there is one condition, God commands the humans not to eat the fruit of a particular tree. A serpent questions Eve, casting doubt on God's intentions. Eve saw the fruit, ate and gave it to her husband. There followed their shame at nakedness, the covering of their genitals and hiding from God (3.7–8), The sense of shame brings distrust between God and humans. Questioned by God, each blamed the other, then the serpent. Each was punished (3.16–19), yet God protects by providing clothing. God expels both from the garden since humanity had become like God, knowing good and evil; they might, 'Take from the Tree of Life and live for ever.' Cherubim guard the gate (Gen. 3.22–24). The story suggests the entry of death into the world as punishment for disobedience; immortality is lost and humans become mortal. This is also suggested in the Wisdom literature (538 BCE), 'for God created us for incorruption, and made us in the image of his own eternity, but through the devil's envy death entered into the world' (Wisd. 2.23–24). The serpent becomes the devil. This is an anachronism of later Persian influence; in the Ancient Near East the snake was often associated with wisdom and the human potential for discernment. Also in Wisdom, we have 'from a woman sin had its beginning and because of her we all die' (Ecclus. 25.24). Yet both eat, hide from God and are punished. In the rabbinic tradition, the Torah is identified with Wisdom and is the Tree of

Life through which God 'planted eternal life within us' (Prov. 3.13–18; 11.30; also 13.12; 15.4).

The significance of Genesis 3

A repeated theme throughout the Scriptures is the nature of God as Creator, who sees sin, which spoils creation; as Judge, then Saviour, God offers humanity a new start.[21] Judaism believes sin is an ever-present human reality. However, there is a choice to turn from sin (Gen. 4.7). There is a graciousness in God, who does not will the death of the sinner but their repentance (Jer. 18.1–10; Ezek. 18.21–23), which involves recognizing wrong, seeking God's gracious mercy, asking forgiveness and changing. Repentance is possible because God gives a new heart of flesh (Ezek. 36.26).

Paul and Augustine on Genesis 3

Romans 5 is the source of some of Christianity's most challenging, controversial and distinctive doctrine. Paul says that sin entered the world through one man, Adam, and because of sin there was death. Paul suggests that Adam's sin and guilt were inherited by later generations: 'just as sin came into the world through one man, and death came through sin, and so death spread to all because all have sinned'. He explores the idea of Christ as a second Adam, righting Adam's sin/death and bringing eternal life (Rom. 5.21). Paul's theology is very compact and has challenged scholars.[22] Much hinges on the word translated 'because' (v. 12). C. K. Barrett suggests the translation, 'because of whom all have sinned'. He comments: 'That is, all men sin and all men die because they sin; but Paul does not add ... they sin, or ... die because they are physically descended from Adam.'[23] The idea of inherited sin is not present in Genesis 3 and is denied by the prophets (Jer. 31.29–31; Ezek. 18.2–4).[24]

---

21 David Wenham, 2003, 'Genesis', *Eerdmans Commentary on the Bible*, Grand Rapids, MI and Cambridge: Eerdmans, p. 37. The idea of God as judge of sin appears possibly as early as the tenth century BCE (Gen. 18.25) and later (2 Sam. 8.15; Ps. 96.10–13; 98).

22 It seems that Paul's writing derives from Greek ideas. Tarsus, his birthplace/home, rivalled Athens as a centre for Greek philosophy, a Hebraic view of the world (Gal. 1.14) and his own idiosyncratic thinking.

23 C. K. Barrett, 1957, *The Epistle to the Romans*, London: A & C Black, p. 111.

24 However, in David's confession – 'I was born guilty, a sinner when my mother conceived me' (Ps. 51.5) – is this a metaphor of the severity of David's sin?

The doctrine of *original sin*, is developed by Augustine (354–430 CE), influential in the Western Church's theology and interpretation of Genesis 3. He taught that Adam and Eve's act of disobedience led to feelings of shame, evidenced in an uncontrollable stirring of the genitals, so that they covered themselves. He used the word *concupiscence* (desire) for the act of procreation through which sin was transferred to successive generations. Our conscious rational mind is separate from sex, the one great force that escapes its control.[25]

Today's interpretations

In Judaism, Genesis is a parable of the human condition, not history. Adam's responsibility for the sins of humanity and the doctrine of inherited sin is not found in mainstream Judaism, which teaches that humans are born sin-free and untainted, and later choose to sin and bring suffering on themselves.[26] Genesis 1—3 is life-affirming; though aware of sin, blessing dictates the agenda. This is in sharp contrast to the interpretation of Augustine.

The Greek Fathers, such as Irenaeus, and the Orthodox Church emphasize the cosmic dimension of the Fall; because of Adam, humans are born into a fallen world but, though fallen, are not deprived of free will nor totally depraved. It is not a 'fall' but a 'failure to develop into the fullness of being human'. Sin originates with the devil (cf. 1 John 3.8). The Roman Catholic Church teaches that humans are made in the image of God; within are powerful urges for good and evil. Because of the effects of original sin, humans inherit a fallen nature that is weakened and inclined to evil; humans do not bear 'original guilt' from Adam and Eve's disobedience, though 'the devil' has acquired a certain domination.[27]

---

25 An emphasis on 'original righteousness', the image of God in creation, in contrast to original sin, is developed in creation theology by Rupert Sheldrake in the UK and Matthew Fox and Thomas Berry in the USA. Fox wrote of four paths: Via Positiva, Via Negativa, Via Creativa, Via Transformativa. Both Fox and Berry are priests.

26 'Inherited sin' is considered a Greek, Pauline Christian interpretation and not a Hebrew concept by James Barr, 1992, *The Garden of Eden and the Hope of Immortality*, London: SCM Press, pp. 1–20; Jonathan Sacks, 2011, *The Great Partnership: God, Science and the Search for Meaning*, London: Hodder and Stoughton; D. Berger and M. Wyschogrod, in Helen P. Fry (ed.), 1996, *Christian–Jewish Dialogue: A Reader*, Exeter: University of Exeter Press, p. 199; Jonathan Magonet, 2004, *A Rabbi Reads the Bible*, London: SCM Press.

27 A useful though challenging piece on this subject is found in Rowan Williams, 'Redeeming Sorrows: Marilyn McCord Adams and the Defeat of Evil', in M. Higton (ed.), 2007, *Wrestling with Angels*, London: SCM Press, pp. 255–74.

Anglicanism follows Luther in teaching that humans inherit Adam's guilt and are in a state of sin from their conception (Article IX of the 39 Articles). In a 1938 Anglican report there appears a greater range of understanding:

> Man is by nature capable of communion with God, and only through such communion can he become what he was created to be. 'Original sin' stands for the fact that ... man ... if left to his own resources and to the influence of his natural environment cannot attain to his destiny as a child of God.[28]

Douglas Davies notes that Christianity may be defined as both positive and negative in attitudes to death. The positive is that death, the outcome of sin, is overcome through the love of Christ, the comfort of the Spirit and God's ultimate faithfulness; this is good news. The negative is that death is 'the central moral pivot around which God works with the cross as its symbol'. It is death conquered by life, but 'there remains a certain Christian romantic commitment to death as evil that can be adjudged as less than valuable'. Western Christianity has tended to emphasize guilt and sin, prominent in the Roman Catholic theology of the Mass, in the Protestant theology of Christ's cross and in literalist interpretations of Genesis 3.[29] This negative emphasis was evident in my hospice work with Peter. After Sunday school and being an active choir boy, in the army he decided to join the confirmation class. The day before confirmation he found a note from the padre, saying that he could not be confirmed because he was divorced. There was no attempt at a pastoral conversation, he was simply refused. Later, in asking for baptism for his first child, a cleric refused on the grounds of his divorce. Sixty years later all this came bubbling out. As Peter had been rejected by the church as not worthy, sinful, he cried out, 'What am I to do? I am dying. Will I go to hell?' No one had told Peter that he was created a child of God, a God who seeks us out, and is more ready to forgive than we are to seek.

Development of the idea of Sheol

Gradually in Judaism there developed hints of a shadowy life after death, joining the departed, being gathered to one's fathers, in the underworld. (*Sheol*, Hebrew: the land of forgetfulness, or *Hades*, Greek of the Septua-

28 1938, *Doctrine in the Church of England*, London: SPCK, p. 64.
29 Douglas Davies, 2008, *The Theology of Death*, London and New York: T & T Clark, pp. 8–9.

gint, or the *Pit*.)[30] There are 65 biblical references to the descent to Sheol. The dead were a shade or shadow of their former selves. There are prayers to be delivered from Sheol (Ps. 88), considered meaningless, even horrific (Ps. 55.4f.), since it prevented a person from praising God (Ps. 88.10), having relationships within his community (Gen. 2.18; Isa. 38.18–19), or knowledge of God's presence. Seeking advice of a shade is recorded once (1 Sam. 28.3); however, the fact that the practice is condemned by the law (Lev. 19.31; Deut. 18.10–12) and the prophets (Isa. 8.19; 65.2–4) suggests it existed more widely.[31] Sacrifices and feasts for the dead were condemned (Ps. 106.19–22). Little is known about Sheol. In some of the psalms there is questioning and protest at the finality of Sheol: 'Are your wonders known in the darkness, or your saving help in the land of forgetfulness?' (Ps. 88.4, 10–12). How could this absence of God be reconciled with knowledge of God's presence on earth? Later, with a growing stress on the individual's relationship with God and an understanding of God's omnipotence, death was thought of as undercutting the relationship and challenging the nature of God's concern (Eccles. 9.1–10; Job 10.8–13). This led some of the psalmists to deny the finality of death; if Sheol was part of God's universe, then God's presence must extend beyond death (Ps. 16.9–10; 23.4; 73.28; 139.8). The emphasis in these psalms of lament is the praise of God; there is no mention of an afterlife, rather hope in God's faithful promises on this earth for a future of blessing: the basics – food (Hos. 2.21–22), water (Isa. 35), peace among the nations and with the animal kingdom (Isa. 2.4; 11.6–8).

The coming of a judgement day

The 'Day of the Lord' is a theme in the prophets. Amos denounced Israel, in the name of God: 'You only have I known of all the families of the earth; therefore I will punish you for all your iniquities' (Amos 3.2). The destruction was punishment for idolatry, the attempt to buy God's favour through sacrifices while neglecting the poor (Amos 5.11–12, 21–22), yet within is the glimmer of hope. 'Seek good and not evil, that you may live … establish justice in the gate; it may be that the LORD, the God of hosts,

---

30 However, Jon Levenson suggests since the ancestors were not gods, but mortal and fallible, the focus was elsewhere: 'it lies in this life and the ever-present possibility of obedience to God's known will'. Jon D. Levenson, 2006, *Resurrection and the Restoration of Israel: The Ultimate Victory of the God of Life*, New Haven and London: Yale University Press, p. 66.

31 These practices were common among surrounding nations and considered pagan.

will be gracious to the remnant of Joseph' (Amos 5.14–15). In Hosea (4 and 5) there is condemnation of people and priests, and a plea, 'to return to the LORD' and 'he will bind us up. After two days he will revive us; on the third day he will raise us up. That we may live before him' (Hos. 6.2). Revive is a reference to 'restoring to health' after wounds brought death close; two to three days refers to a short time, since death was thought of as separation from God (cf. Ps. 6.6). It is unlikely to be a reference to resurrection.[32] The idea of a descendant of David who will usher in redemption is found in later prophetic writings. During the exile the idea of a messiah-deliverer emerges, with the return of Elijah as herald (Mal. 4.5). The word 'messiah' had been used of Saul, David, Zedekiah, Cyrus, King of Persia (Isa. 45.1) and a Suffering Servant, sometimes the faithful remnant of Israel, at other times an individual (Isa. 52.13—53.12), anointed with oil as a sign of God's choice.

The exile of God's people in Babylon is compared with death: Jerusalem and the Temple had been destroyed, and with it, some thought, God. Ezekiel, prophet of the exile, spoke words of hope – God is about to act. 'Not for your sake, O house of Israel', but 'for the sake of my holy name' (Ezek. 36.22). 'Then the nations ... shall know ... that I am the LORD' (36.26–38). Israel had rebelled against God, committed idolatry, behaved immorally, God's name had been profaned, crops had failed, towns laid waste. Yet God will recreate, 'will remove from your body the heart of stone and give you a heart of flesh' (36.26). The waste places will be rebuilt, the land become as the Garden of Eden, not because of Israel's repentance, but because of the gracious nature of God. Ezekiel tells of a vision of a valley of dry bones and the gradual restoration of the corpses' sinews, flesh, skin (Ezek. 37.1–14). The Talmud tradition classifies this event as 'a parable'. The Lord God says, 'These bones are the whole house of Israel ... I will put my breath into you and you shall live again, and I will set you upon your own soil. Then you shall know that I the LORD have spoken and have acted' (37.11–14). Here we have a metaphor of resurrection, given at an improbable historical time of exile. It is a prophetic sign, God recreates, 'God will bring his chosen people out of the depths of exile and restore them to their land.' Jon Levenson comments that there is no reason to think Ezekiel saw the individuals resurrected in the valley as immortal: 'What does not die is the people Israel, because God has, despite their grievous failings, honoured his indefeasible pledge to their ancestors.'[33] There is no other statement of a future hope except

---

32 The choice of 'on the third day' may allude to the Babylonian cult of the dying and rising of the fertility gods, the rising beginning on the third day.

33 Levenson, *Resurrection*, pp. 158–63.

possibly Isaiah. 26.19, 'Your dead shall live, their corpses shall rise.' In the context of persecution, it is a hope rather than a belief in the continuation of the nation.

For the Jew, the idea of existence after death without a body was unthinkable: a human is embodied. Resurrection would involve a body, in a world that was recreated and renewed. It is likely that this belief was due to Jewish apocalyptic thinking, arising from the experience of the Maccabean Revolt (168/7–164 BCE) against the Greek overlord Antiochus Epiphanes. Justice was demanded. God was just and must reward the faithful violated martyrs of the Maccabean family. This crisis of faith led to the answer of a double, this-worldly, resurrection: to life for those loyal to God under persecution, and condemnation for the disloyal (Dan. 12.1–4). Levenson states:

> it is not primarily an answer to the challenge to God's justice ... the resurrection of the dead is best seen ... as another statement of the continuing Jewish need to uphold both the fact of death and the promise of life, while expecting and celebrating the victory of the God who promises life.[34]

The idea of an immortal soul

Scholars suggest various reasons for the rise of thinking of a soul: the influence of Zoroastrianism, the religion of the Medes and Persians conquerors of the Jews (539–333 BCE), or the Greek conquest and Greek philosophy experienced by Jews of the Dispersion (333–160 BCE; cf. Wisd. 3 and 5; 4 Macc.). From the second century BCE, the rise of mystery religions helped ideas of a soul and its afterlife. In the Gospels there is a clear difference between the Sadducees who did not accept resurrection and the Pharisees who did. The classical expression of the soul's immortality is Plato (424–347 BCE) in *Phaedrus*, where the body is the soul's tomb. The soul both pre- and post-exists the body. The body prevents the soul exercising its knowing; in the *Timaeus* Plato is more positive about bodies having a role in the exercise of rationality. Plato's early view had an impact on popular views and Paul's interpretation. As a result, for Paul, the material world, including the body, is often seen as negative, in contrast to the soul which is positive. Philo (20 BCE–50 CE) influenced Christianity, seeing the soul as the way of communication with God.

---

34 Levenson, *Resurrection*, p. 180.

Conclusion of the Hebrew Scriptures

God's promises for life, blessing and hope to achieve a Golden Age seemed to end in failure. Disillusioned, the writers concluded that if their belief in a God who intervened in history was not fulfilled by human activity, it would be in a final judgement led by a Messiah. In the apocalyptic literature there was a hope that God would defeat the powers of sin and death and establish sovereignty in this world. It is likely that this thinking emerged in the first century CE, when Jews were persecuted. Questions arose about the injustices in life. There must be a time when God righted these. For some this would be a new world, a Garden of Eden. The central belief was that 'at the end of history, God will resurrect the dead and restore them to full bodily existence'.[35]

The New Testament

E. P. Sanders notes that in the time of Jesus, 'We are left knowing that Jews ... probably most, believed in an afterlife and in individual reward and punishment ... at some times some people indulged in detailed fantasies about the other world.'[36] Some Jews found a belief in God's goodness no longer possible; the only immortality was living on in the mind of God. A Jewish prayer says: 'We remember those who have departed. They have not died into the grave but into the love and eternity of God.' God had the first word and will have the last. How, the writer does not know. Christianity rooted in Judaism has a great deal to say about eternal life, a gift of God, evidenced in a quality of life lived now and not interrupted by death (John 3.16, 36; 4.14). We are embodied and need a body to be human, yet we know that at death the physical body disintegrates. Paul in 1 Corinthians uses the metaphor of the seed sown which must die to be transformed into new life.

Insights from other faiths

The Abrahamic faiths

Jonathan Sacks, who retired in 2013 as the Chief Rabbi in the UK, states: 'to a quite remarkable degree the Hebrew Bible is reticent about life after death and never uses it to reconcile people with their condition on earth

---

35 Levenson, *Resurrection*, p. ix.

36 E. P. Sanders, 1992, *Judaism: Practice and Belief 63 BCE–66 CE*, London: SCM Press.

... this world, this life, is where we meet God and either do or fail to do his will'. In Judaism there is little development of a theology of an afterlife since it is unknown; what Jews know is the present, which they live to the full, in just lives, worshipping and honouring God.

Islam has roots in both Judaism and Christianity. For Muhammad this world was transitory, though Muslims give credence to it because it is what they experience. The true life is after earthly life and is an act of faith: 'Who will give life to bones while they are disintegrating? ... He will give them life who produced them the first time; and He is, of all creation, Knowing' (Qur'an 36.78–80). The Muslim is accountable for the way he or she lives, because behaviour shapes future character. Life after death is necessary – a response to God's attributes. God's justice and mercy have no meaning if there is no life after death. It is characterized by a day of judgement, the fires of hell or the garden paradise of heaven. In Islam the word *Jahannam* derives from Gehenna; the Qur'an contains 77 references to it.

The Eastern faiths

Within Hinduism and Buddhism this life is the first of many lives. The way of life now, particularly concern for the marginalized, affects life beyond this one. This belief is expressed in the law of karma, the essence of which is that our past determines who we are and will be. This doctrine was a reincarnation of a life until the final goal of being one with the ultimate is reached, *moksha*, or entering the deathless state of nirvana. In Indian Hinduism the law of karma has a more subtle and complex character. John Hick comments that it is not the present conscious self that is reborn. Rather, 'In each incarnation there is a new empirical self, which comes into existence at conception and ceases at death.' Underlying the series of selves is an eternal spiritual reality, the *jiva*. This is manifest in various expressions, including the physical body which perishes at death and the 'subtle body', *linga sharira*, which lives beyond death and 'is later re-embodied by attaching itself to a developing embryo'. The subtle body bears the individual karma, and selects the appropriate kind of birth. Memories of previous lives exist only in the *jiva*. In the last earthly life, the individual has transcended self-centredness, and is 'consciously one with the universal atman, or self, which is ultimately identical with Brahman, the eternal absolute Reality'.

The Buddhist understanding is similar, 'except that which is successively reborn is not a continuing entity, the karma-bearing "subtle body", but the stream of karma itself'.[37] The Advaita Hindu and the Theravada Buddhist practise meditation and mindfulness and consciously avoid the domination of human desires and passions in their spiritual quest of identification with the divine.

Questions for reflection and response

- How often have you heard a sermon on death in a Sunday service? Why is this? Prepare a sermon or talk on death using a verse from Genesis 3.1–24.
- Philip Larkin wrote a poem entitled 'This be the verse', a reflection on original sin. Look it up and comment.
- Reflect on the concept that the doctrines of creation and salvation must be brought together. Note down your thinking.
- In Genesis 3, sin and death are associated. How does this relate to the experience of Jean? How do you understand Genesis 3 in relation to death?

Cultural context in dialogue with Scripture and the tradition

As people of God our understanding of God, our theology, will emerge as we bring the insights of our cultural context and those of Scripture and tradition into dialogue. This is why theology is so exciting, since it is always provisional and in process. It is our theological reflection that guides and informs our ethics and our pastoral practice.

The cultural context of Jesus as an observant Jew in first-century Palestine, was the Hebrew Scriptures. In the twenty-first century our context is very different. We live in the developed world. Popular opinion appears dominated by the advances of science, understood as rational and factual, which have, within medicine, extended life expectancy and distanced ideas of mortality, a concept known as 'medicalized death'. In the UK Stephen Hawking, Brian Cox and Richard Dawkins are household names, though their books may not have been read. Public interest in the sciences can be judged by the number of published 'popular' books, from the 1980s, that raise questions previously addressed in philosophy and theology.[38]

---

37 John Hick, 1989, 'Reincarnation', in Alan Richardson and John Bowden (eds), *A New Dictionary of Christian Theology*, 5th edn, London: SCM Press, p. 491.

38 A useful resource is John Weaver's book, 2010, *SCM Core Text Christianity and Science*, London: SCM Press.

Institutional religions, particularly the Abrahamic faiths of Judaism, Christianity and Islam, have been criticized for fundamentalism, and in some cases acts of terrorism, yet there has been a search for meaning in life expressed in turning to more individualistic spiritualities.

Is it possible to bring together insights from the twenty-first century dominated by medical sciences with those of beliefs rooted in a Judaeo-Christian text more than 4,000 years old? Some Christians answer by keeping the science of today in a separate compartment from their faith. However, both science and religion seek to understand the way the world is, its workings and meaning for human life.

The scientist, through hypothesis, seeks to interpret what he or she observes, but this is not straightforward. There is no clear link between theory and experiment. John Polkinghorne, a former professor of mathematical physics and now a priest, states: 'Scientists do not look at the world with a blank gaze; they view it from a chosen perspective and bring principles of interpretation and prior expectations of meaning to bear upon what they observe.'[39] Effects such as friction, temperature fluctuations, purity of the sample and universality can influence an experiment. Michael Polanyi's central thesis is that, though science is concerned with the impersonal physical world, its pursuit is an activity of persons. Discoveries involve creativity and imagination.[40] Radical revisions of existing hypotheses may need to be made, necessitating a paradigm shift. Science is a process, continually evolving. This is seen in the varying scientific disciplines. Quantum physics and cosmology describe the nature of the universe; evolutionary biology, the world around; genetics and psychology, the study of the brain and the nature of being human; the social, political and economic sciences describe the significance of history.

The Christian religion is about belief in God, which is an act of faith. There are no arguments in the Bible for the existence of God; God simply 'is'. Christianity is about the relationship of God and the world, particularly humanity and God's longing for fellowship with creation. Theology is created from the triad of Scripture, tradition and reason, to which was added, at the Lambeth Conference of 1988, the experience of God's people. Scripture is an interpretation of events in the life of an individual author inspired by God within the faith community. Christian orthodoxy is not fixed, but a conversation between past and present, Scripture and reason, tradition and experience. Theology is a process. Jonathan Sacks

---

39 John Polkinghorne, 1998, *Science and Theology: An Introduction*, London: SPCK, pp. 9–10.

40 Polkinghorne, *Science and Theology*, pp. 15–16.

states: 'Faith is not certainty ... it is the courage to live with uncertainty.'[41] There are parallels between science and religion – both are in process.

In the twenty-first century belief in a creator has become more compatible with developments in natural sciences. The fine-tuning which enabled creation can be used here. Roger Penrose and Stephen Hawking suggested a 'physical singularity' point from which the universe expanded following a Big Bang. The uniformity of the expansion of the universe, its size and age, the presence of chemicals and existent laws of gravity allowed complex life to evolve. Carbon, essential for the development of life, was manufactured from helium in large stars, released by supernovae explosions. There is a growing sense of the openness of the natural world associated with quantum indeterminacy. In the evolution of life, animals and plants mutate; some survive, others do not. There is unpredictability in some systems, 'chaos', within an overall framework of dependable physical laws. Some cosmologists see a fine-tuning in the initial conditions of existence. Only this can account for the intricacies making life possible, the 'anthropic principle', which is suggestive of purpose and for some the possibility of a designer. The Judaeo-Christian tradition praises God as Creator.

Within the biological and human sciences, human beings are considered nothing but survival machines for their genes. Reductionism is much more prominent here than in the physical sciences. The mind is likened to a sophisticated computer. There is no place for differences in personality and creativity. Different cells, liver, heart wear out at different rates. Viruses kill defective cells. The passing on of genetic codes to cells comes with sexual maturity; then evolution loses interest and there is a self-destruction in cells. Without death there could be no evolution, the latter being the sole purpose of life. Death is thought of as natural. Richard Dawkins, in *The Selfish Gene*, claims that our hereditary material is basically selfish. This selfish gene leads to competitive advantage through fitness. Born selfish, humans have to learn to be altruistic believes Dawkins, but he gives no account of how to become altruistic, nor why it is needed; this is not surprising since nature is amoral.[42] Science does not deal with questions of morality, yet scientific discoveries raise moral and religious issues. The story in Genesis 3 addresses the question of evil in the world. Moral decision-making is needed in science.

Douglas Davies, a theologian, states that for twentieth-century genetics,

41 Jonathan Sacks, 2011, *The Great Partnership: God, Science and the Search for Meaning*, London: Hodder and Stoughton, p. 97.

42 Richard Dawkins, 1976, *The Selfish Gene*, London: Flamingo.

a new narrative of the way things are has emerged and death occupies a different place within it ... death has yet to play the important role awaiting it as one key symbolic force of this debate. Death for Genesis Adam is not the same as death for Genetic Adam.[43]

Science must be addressed. Genesis is story, Adam is everyone. We are all egocentric, wanting our own way, leading to the death of relationships. We need salvation. The Scriptures recognize, though crying against mortality, it is part of creation. For Genetic Adam, death is part of the evolutionary process and is natural, a given part of the cycle of life not a moral concept.[44] For Davies this would mean a 'repositioning of the sin–death link established in Genesis and ... dominant for much of Christian theological history'. Seeing death as natural does not avoid human loss and the pain of grief, 'but ... to approach death as natural to life and not as alien ... in this sense death is part of creation and salvation'.[45] We are self-aware and so know that we sin, suggesting that the image of God, though defaced is not obliterated in us. The Latin tradition of the Western Church tends to emphasize sin and guilt, original sin. The Orthodox tradition of the Eastern Church emphasizes original righteousness, the grace of God, glory and resurrection. Creation and sin/salvation need to complement one another.

For scientists such as Paul Davies, Francis Collins and John Polkinghorne religious faith is compatible with their work in science.[46] Science and religion are parallel narratives. This leads to action; for the scientist this is seen in technology as an outcome. I have noted the influence in medicine, which has increased the lifespan of many in the developed world. Religion leads to action in lives following the example of Jesus, for some working in medicine to support patients and challenge disease, for others protesting against inhuman policies in politics.

Scientists and Christians talk of process, of beginnings and a final ending, giving death a place. Each recognizes the interdependence of all life. Scientists note the abuse of the planet causing changes in climate and

---

43 Davies, *Theology of Death*, pp. 6–7.

44 Sacks, *Great Partnership*.

45 Davies, *Theology of Death*, p. 9.

46 Paul Davies, 2007, *The Goldilocks Enigma: Why is the Universe Just Right for Life?* London: Allen Lane; Paul Davies (ed.), 2010, *Information and the Nature of Reality: From Physics to Metaphysics*, Cambridge: Cambridge University Press; Francis Collins, 2006, *The Language of God: A Scientist Presents Evidence for Belief*, London: Free Press; John Polkinghorne, 2007, *Exploring Reality: The Intertwining of Science and Religion*, London: SPCK; and *Quantum Physics and Theology: An Unexpected Kinship*, Yale: Yale University Press.

global warming; in the Scriptures creation praises God, and humanity is given responsibility for the care of the earth.

A rapprochement between science and faith allows the development of a theology that recognizes the mystery in life at the beginning, the First Cause, God – a theology of creation. It recognizes that human life is unique, to be honoured and respected, created in God's image – a theology of humanity. It recognizes that death is a natural culmination of life – a theology of death. It recognizes that humans search for meaning to make sense of experience, that we need one another for this to be possible, we need relationality and interdependence – in a theology of the Trinity.

Questions for reflection and response

• What might a theology of the material world look like?
• How do you understand the relationship between science and religion?
• Why is death not the same for Genesis Adam and Genetic Adam?
• What is the distinctiveness that the Judaeo-Christian faiths give to our understanding of what it means to be human?

Pastoral practice

How does the theology, teased out above, affect our practice? Those who are caring for the dying and the bereaved, and conducting funeral rituals, need to be aware of the context of life in the twenty-first century; the different understandings of death brought by the advances in medical science; the changing attitudes to Christianity, coupled with the search for meaning in life and for alternative spiritualities.

A theology of creation leads us to recognize that the material world reflects the Creator, that humanity is created in the image and likeness of God. This means that we will see in all we meet that image, whoever they are. This leads us to recognize our interdependence on each other, and God, our relationality expressed in a theology of the Trinity. The creation is to be respected and guarded. Our physical bodies are a 'temple of the Holy Spirit'. There is a wrestling with the possibility of an afterlife God-given. A theology of death will enable us to see death as common to all living things, not simply inevitable but natural; not something to be feared but to be accepted, allowing us to live in the present, as Moltmann states: 'Death acts as a catalyst to plunge us into more authentic life modes and it enhances out pleasure in the living of life.'[47] To be able to

---

47 Moltmann, *Coming of God*, p. 50.

stand alongside the dying and bereaved to minister to the reality of their experience, we need as ministers of the gospel willingly to face our own mortality. A theology of death as natural will challenge the biblical understanding of the connection of death as the result of sin, evident when those with a terminal illness believe that their death is a punishment for sin. We all sin, we are self-centred at the expense of others. However, we know that there is repentance and forgiveness; we can be received back by a God who waits patiently to receive us. This understanding will inform our ministerial care and our preaching: the emphasis is on God's love, mercy and grace rather than our sinfulness.

Society in the twenty-first century is witness to the demise of institutionalized religions, yet it seems that people still turn to the Church in times of the death of a loved one – Davie's 'vicarious religion'. It seems as if the need for ritual and symbol, to convey those experiences in life that are too deep for words, are innate in humans: Christian churches have historical resources and can provide these in ministering to the dying, to the bereaved and in funeral liturgies.

Questions for reflection and response

- What might be included in a theology of death?
- Why is theology important? Think about this with reference to one of the theologies mentioned in this section.
- How will a theology of humanity influence our care for the dying and bereaved?
- Think about how any part of this chapter could be used in some way in your church.

Further reading

Philippe Ariès, 1974/75, *Western Attitudes toward Death: From the Middle Ages to the Present*, Baltimore and London: Johns Hopkins University Press.

Douglas Davies, 2008, *The Theology of Death*, London and New York: T & T Clark.

Jonathan Sacks, 2011, *The Great Partnership: God, Science and the Search for Meaning*, London: Hodder and Stoughton.

John Weaver, 2010, *SCM Core Text Christianity and Science*, London: SCM Press.

2

Care of the Dying and of Their Carers

The last stages of life should not be seen as defeat, but rather as life's fulfilment.
Cicely Saunders[1]

This chapter begins with an experience of the fears of a dying man, followed by theological reflection on fear, forgiveness and an afterlife. It considers the context of care today and the changes from the past, using insights from the disciplines of sociology and psychology, government reports and autobiography. The chapter examines the Hebrew Scriptures on dying, and the New Testament, including the implications of the dying and resurrection of Jesus on understandings of the afterlife. Context and Scriptures and tradition are brought together in critical theological dialogue, understanding care as presence, reflecting a theology of incarnation, presence and hope informing and undergirding our practice of ministry with the dying.

Pastoral circle

Pastoral practice:
rites of pastoral ministry
to elderly and dying.
Presence and hope

Experience –
theological reflection:
a dying man needing
forgiveness; rites of
confession

Cultural context:
government reports;
'a good death';
spirituality emphasis

Scripture/tradition
and context:
theology of incarnation,
presence and hope

Scripture and
tradition:
insights on dying;
dying of Jesus;
afterlife

---

1 Cicely Saunders 'The Last Stages of Life', *American Journal of Nursing*, 65 (March 1965), p. 70.

Experience

> Alf, aged 92, had been in a specialized ward in a care home for years, suffering from dementia. He had suffered a stroke following surgery for bowel cancer. His daughter Judy was visiting him. Alf was getting weaker and spending more time in bed.
>
> One Sunday Alf asked his daughter if he was dying. She talked to him about life and death. He was fearful at the thought of meeting his Maker; he felt guilty and inadequate. His daughter reminded him of his good qualities: he had followed his conscience at personal cost as a conscientious objector in the Second World War; he was a faithful husband and had worked hard all his life to bring up a family of five children; he had been the Sunday school superintendent and a deacon of a Baptist church.
>
> Judy said that making mistakes was part of being human, all 'sin and fall short of the glory of God'. Yet God knew him and loved him as he was, 'warts and all'. The priest of his church could be asked to visit him and assure him of God's forgiveness. This happened a few days later and Alf was able to die in peace.

Reflection on experience

Marie knew that her cancer was terminal. She was a Christian whose faith was dear to her and she thought deeply about it. One day she said to me, the hospice chaplain, 'We prepare ourselves as Christians for the important occasions in our lives – confirmation, marriage – but how do we prepare for dying?' Marie's question was challenging. Other patients have asked about dying. It was a question that I had responded to experientially with patients and staff, now it needed theological reflection, the subject of this chapter.

For the patient, dying is a process of isolation and detachment from all that holds a person to life – possessions, attachments and relationships. We have forgotten how to let go. Have we, as the community of faith, neglected our responsibility to minister to and be alongside people who are dying?

Alf was frightened of dying, feeling guilty and unworthy. Fear of dying and guilt about sin and judgement are experiences particularly for older Christians, at the end of life. Origins may lie in their upbringing and later formation in the faith, reflecting a judgemental God, threats of hell and a lack of mercy and grace. If the dying person has someone to hear and to receive their fear, speaking it aloud is a form of confession.

Sin and guilt are an admittance of the shadow side of life; in Shakespeare's words, 'This thing of darkness, I acknowledge mine.' Francis of Assisi expressed the shadow side as 'love the leper inside'. Paul confessed, 'I do not understand my own actions. For I do not do what I want, but I do the very things I hate' (Rom. 7.15f.). We need forgiveness before death for intended and unintended wrong to others, who are like us, created in the divine image (Gen. 1.26), known and loved by God (Ps.139.13–18).

In the past, the ministry of reconciliation, sometimes called sacramental confession, was associated with the Roman Catholic Church and High Anglicans. For others it was considered unnecessary since we ask forgiveness publicly when we pray the Lord's Prayer. It was also thought that it gave the priest inappropriate power, as if the priest controlled giving or withholding God's forgiveness; difficult was the Catholic wording *ego te absolvo*, 'I absolve you'. In recent years Protestants have begun to recognize benefits to the individual of private confession, being spoken, heard, acknowledged, and words of forgiveness received. It was the words in John 20.23 – 'Receive the Holy Spirit. If you forgive the sins of any, they are forgiven them; if you retain the sins of any, they are retained' – which led Luther to keep penance as a sacrament, together with baptism and Eucharist.

Alf said: 'If I'm dying what can I do? I'm frightened.'

His daughter Judy said: 'Dad, when you die, you will leave that body of yours that doesn't work well any more. You will be free – like a bird. I have been present when people die, most people of your age drift into a peaceful sleep.'

Alf said: 'But meeting God?'

Judy said: 'You believe in God. You always have. God believes in you even more than you believe in him. God understands you and at your end is waiting to welcome you.'

His care assistant said: 'We are not a nursing home, but we want Alf to stay with us until he dies. We love him, and one of us will be with him to hold his hand when he gets frightened.'

Judy arranged for the priest, who was known to Alf, to visit his room in the home and hear his fears, sense of guilt, help him to make his confession and die in peace. We need to know that if we confess our sins, there is forgiveness and absolution, which we cannot earn, rather it is the gift of God's grace and mercy. The need is to accept forgiveness from God, to seek forgiveness from those we have wronged, and above all to forgive ourselves (Luke 11.4). In the Church of England's *Common Worship* (CW) service book is a section called 'Penitential Material'.[2] Mark Earey suggests a toolkit, the framework of this rite of passage:

- *Separation* – acknowledging what has happened.
- *Liminality* – confession and absolution.
- *Incorporation* – dismissal as a forgiven person who has responsibility to pray for others.[3]

He also suggests a fourfold shape to the service: Gathering, Word, Response and Sending.

Gathering is setting the scene. In the *Methodist Worship Book* this is through the Lord's Prayer giving the context for forgiveness. A word of Scripture can be, 'Jesus said: Before you offer your gift, go and be reconciled. As brothers and sisters in God's family, we come to ask our Father for forgiveness.'[4] The Response was when Alf was able to say sorry and ask for forgiveness. His priest, who was kneeling beside his bed, stood and made the sign of the cross in oil on his head and said, 'Alf you are forgiven by God.' He ended by saying, 'Be at peace, pray for me, a sinner, and remember the love and mercy of God.' This pastoral act, through his priest and following Jesus' command, gave Alf assurance of God's presence. A few days later Alf died in peace.

Questions for reflection and response

- Make a list of why a Christian and a non-Christian person might be fearful of dying. Comment on the theological appropriateness of fear.
- How can we prepare people for dying?
- What part does forgiveness play for the dying?
- Why is it important for forgiveness to be mediated in word and action?

2 *Common Worship: Pastoral Services and Prayers for the Church of England*, 2000, London: Church House Publishing, pp. 268f.

3 Mark Earey, 2012, *Worship that Cares: An Introduction to Pastoral Liturgy*, London: SCM Press, p. 161.

4 *Common Worship*, 2000, p. 275.

Reflection on the cultural context

A brief history of preparation for death

Humanity in previous centuries was aware of death as ever present. Life was short because of disease, war, starvation and accident (cf. Rev. 6.1–8). There were reminders of dying, for example a genre of artworks, *The Memento Mori*, 'remember your mortality … you will die', painted on a cemetery wall in Paris in 1424, the *danse macabre*, with its depiction of Death the Grim Reaper dancing and carrying away rich and poor alike. The dance showed 'each character dancing with his or her own death throughout life'.[5] The genre is thought to have had a moralizing purpose, emphasizing the fleeting nature of earthly pleasures, luxuries and achievements, together with an invitation to think of the afterlife. At the same time, in the fifteenth century, the focus was individual judgement immediately after death, thus it became urgent to prepare in life.[6] The need was met by a manual, *Ars Moriendi* (Art of Dying), to educate priests and lay people in dying ministry.

Death was simple and public; rituals and community gave meaning to death, common to all, the effect of sin, a hope in the resurrection of the body and knowledge that the community would continue to remember the deceased after death. The English version was one of Caxton's first printed books, *The Book of the Craft of Dying* (1450). Chapter 1 of the book focuses on dying and assumes that deathbed repentance can yield salvation. Chapter 2 confronts the dying with five temptations and their corresponding remedies. Chapter 3 gives questions that lead the dying person to reaffirm faith, repent sins and commit fully to Christ's passion and death. Chapter 4 asks the dying to imitate Christ's action on the cross and provides prayers for 'everlasting bliss that is the reward of holy dying'.[7] Chapter 5 is for the family and friends of the dying, to give the dying a crucifix and images of the saints, encourage them to repent, receive the sacraments and draw up a testament disposing of their possessions, while family consider preparation for their own deaths. Chapter 6 describes when the dying can no longer speak, those with them speak for them, reciting prayers as they 'commend the spirit' into God's hands.

---

5 Ivan Illich, 1976, *Limits to Medicine: Medical Nemesis: The Expropriation of Health*, London: Marion Boyars. This includes a tracing of the history of death.

6 Philippe Ariès, 1974, *Western Attitudes toward Death: From the Middle Ages to the Present*, Baltimore and London: Johns Hopkins University Press, p. 28.

7 Frances M. M. Comper, 1977, *The Book of the Craft of Dying and Other Early English Tracts concerning Death*, New York: Arno Press, p. 31.

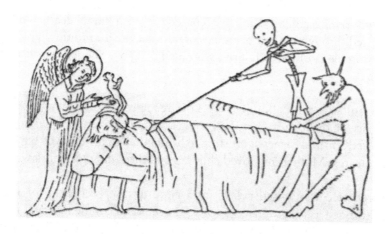

The versions of the *Ars Moriendi* began a tradition of Christian manuals which became widespread through the networks of the Dominicans and Franciscans. The tradition grew within Roman Catholicism and was later adopted and modified by the Renaissance Christian humanist Erasmus and Protestant Reformers, placing the art of dying within the broader art of living, which necessitated a consistent *memento mori*, an awareness and preparation for one's own death.

The illustration, from a fourteenth-century English manuscript, shows the dying person's struggle with temptations before attaining a good death. The devil has a hooking staff and Death a soldier's pike, both tempting to snare the soul of the dying man. The threatened soul, pictured as a tiny person, prays for help. An angel offers protection.

The first Anglican guidance on dying was found in Jeremy Taylor's *Holy Living, Holy Dying* (1650/51) to be used by those in good health to prepare for an appropriate death by living a virtuous life.[8] He also wrote *The rule and exercises of Holy Dying with prayers and acts of virtue to be used by Dying Persons*. There were three precepts to prepare for a holy death.

1 He that would die well must always look for death, everyday knocking at the gates of the grave.
2 He that would die well, must all the days of his life lay up against the Day of death by a pious life.
3 He that desires to die well and happily, above all things must be careful that he does not live a soft, a delicate and a voluptuous life.

---

8 Nancy Lee Beaty, 1979, *The Craft of Dying: A Study in the Literary Tradition of the* Ars Moriendi *in England*, New Haven, CT: Yale University Press.

Ariès referred to a good death, a prepared one, as a 'tame' death. This rite has lasted through the centuries, despite the decline in traditional religion. One example is Queen Victoria, who died in 1901. She left a will which stated:

> I die in peace with all, fully aware of my many faults, relying with confidence on the love, mercy and goodness of my Heavenly Father and His Blessed Son and earnestly trusting to be reunited to my beloved husband, my dearest Mother, my loved children and three dear sons-in-law.[9]

This reflected traditional beliefs in 'a good death': preparing for judgement through asking forgiveness of sins, depending on the love and mercy of God and a belief in personal resurrection. At her death Victoria was surrounded by her family, her nurse and her priest to hear her confession and ease her journey into the next life.

Changes in understanding dying

The successes of medical research resulted in changes in the nature of dying, from the acute infections of the past followed by a quick death, to the chronic, protracted and uncertain conditions of terminal illness and decreasing abilities in old age today. In the late twentieth and early twenty-first centuries, other than by accident, it is degenerative diseases such as cancer and heart disease that now cause death. Diagnostic testing and genetic coding have enabled earlier treatment. Treatment methods have increased, including surgical techniques of transplants, chemotherapy and radiotherapy and an extensive range of drugs. These treatments, which vary according to the individual, take their toll on the energy levels and the well-being of both patient and carer.

Today – emphasis on quality of life for the dying

Traditional religious beliefs and rites are declining but there is an increased interest and emphasis on spirituality and a concern for the quality of life of the dying in government reports. In July 2008 the UK Department of Health published the *End of Life Care Strategy: Promoting High Quality Care for All Adults at the End of Life*. The report's implementation meant

---

9 T. Rennell, 2001, *Last Days of Glory: The Death of Queen Victoria*, London: Viking, p. 144.

access to: opportunities for patients to discuss personal needs and preferences; recorded care plans; co-ordinated care and support irrespective
of who delivered the service; 24/7 advice and clinical assessment; high-
quality care during the last days of life on the model of the Liverpool Care
Pathway (LCP); and services treating patients with dignity and respect.
The services would be monitored and high quality assured, and a national
End of Life Care Research Initiative set up. However, the media have been
full of anecdotes of bad deaths, particularly in respect of the LCP.[10]

The LCP was designed as a checklist to help medical staff assist patients
to a humane, dignified and pain-free end, without the paraphernalia of
tubes and machines that can increase distress. Some doctors, religious
leaders and pro-life groups have alleged that patients are put on the LCP
without their consent, or that of their families. Families claim that their
relatives were denied food and drink, leaving them to 'linger in misery for
weeks'.[11] There is also a debate concerning prolonging life when there is
nothing further that medically can be done and the patient is tired of living
(see dyingtolive.org.uk). A friend, whose husband was dying, continued
to feed him. 'You know it won't help him,' a nurse said. Another said: 'I
hope others will do as you are doing; it is of so much comfort, psychologically and emotionally, to the patient.' Approximately 170,000 persons
a year receive palliative care, of whom 130,000 are placed on the LCP.
The Care Minister, Norman Lamb, announced an independent review
chaired by Rabbi Julia Neuberger (15 July 2013).

The National Care of the Dying Audit for Hospitals, led by the Royal
College of Physicians (RCP), collaborating with the Marie Curie Palliative
Care Institute Liverpool (MCPCIL), reported on assessing the quality of
care received by 64,580 people who died in 149 hospital trusts in England
during May 2013, through reviewing case notes and issuing a questionnaire to 858 relatives.[12] These are the findings on the quality of care:

- Professionals recognized 87 per cent of patients were in the last days
  of life but only told 46 per cent of those patients capable of discussing
  this.

---

10 Lcp liv.ac.uk/mcpcil/Liverpool-care-pathway includes: before, at, after death.

11 There are more local schemes: South London Health Service AMBER care, run
by Guy's and St Thomas' NHS Foundation Trust; Royal Marsden London Coordin-
ate My Care trains professionals specialist nurses and GPs to interview and record
the wishes of patients as a personalized care plan and notify the local ambulance
service and NHS 111.

12 Royal College of Physicians, *Significant variation in standards of care for
people dying in hospital*, 14 May 2014.

- Communication with family/friends occurred in 93 per cent of cases, on average 31 hours before a death.
- Most patients (63–81 per cent) had medication prescribed as required for the five key symptoms often experienced near the end of life – pain, agitation, noisy breathing, difficulty in breathing and nausea/vomiting. In the last 24 hours of life only 44 per cent needed pain relief and 17 per cent medication for shortness of breath.
- 59 per cent were clinically assessed to see if they needed artificial hydration; only 17 per cent of conversations were with patients capable of conversation; 36 per cent were with relatives. Artificial hydration was in place for 29 per cent of patients at the time of death.
- 45 per cent of patients were clinically assessed for artificial nutrition, but only 17 per cent is recorded as a discussion with patients capable of discussion; it was discussed with 29 per cent of relatives. Artificial nutrition was in place for 7 per cent at time of death.
- Only 21 per cent of patients were asked about their spiritual needs.
- 87 per cent of patients were assessed five times or more in the final 24 hours of life, in line with national guidance.

Findings from bereaved relatives:

- 76 per cent of those completing the questionnaire reported being very or fairly involved in decisions about care of their relative; 24 per cent did not.
- 63 per cent thought that the level of emotional support given to them by the health care team was good or excellent; 37 per cent thought it only fair or poor.

Findings on the organization of care showed:

- Only 21 per cent of sites had access to face-to-face palliative care services seven days a week; 73 per cent provided care on weekdays only.
- Mandatory training in care of the dying was only required for doctors in 19 per cent of trusts, and for nurses in 28 per cent. In the previous year, 82 per cent of trusts provided some form of training; 18 per cent had not provided any.
- Only 56 per cent of trusts conducted a formal audit of care for the dying in the previous year, despite previous recommendation that this should be done at least annually.

- 53 per cent of the hospital trusts had a named board member with responsibility for care of the dying; 47 per cent did not. 42 per cent of trusts had not discussed care of the dying in the previous year.

Care of the dying is still not good enough. Ten recommendations were made, including:

- mandatory training in communication skills
- regular audits
- decisions in the last hours of life made by a multidisciplinary team
- decisions about artificial hydration and nutrition made by a senior experienced clinician
- pain control assessed at least every four hours
- the availability of a pastoral care team.

The definition of 'a good death'

The End of Life Care Strategy included the patient's definition of a good death:

- being treated as an individual, with dignity and respect
- being without pain and other symptoms
- being in familiar surroundings
- being in the company of close family and/or friends.

Being treated as an individual, with dignity and respect

Every person is unique and care must reflect and respect individuality and lifestyles. Cicely Saunders (1918–2005), founder of the modern hospice movement, stated: 'You matter because you are you and you matter until the last moment of your life, we will do all we can not only to help you die peacefully but to live until you die.'[13] People at the end of life should be able to participate in valued activities and relationships, for example have access to suitable transport and the internet/Skype to communicate with family.

---

13 *Cicely Saunders: Selected Writings 1958–2004*, 2006, Introduction by David Clark, Oxford: Oxford University Press, p. xxiii.

How often (in percentages) the patient was treated with dignity and respect in the last three months, by setting or service provider.				
Service provider	Always	Most of the time	Some of the time	Never
Community nurses	78.6	15.2	4.1	2.1
GPs	72.8	16.8	8.3	2.2
Care home	62.1	27.6	8.9	1.4
Hospital doctors	58.8	26.0	13.4	1.9
Hospital nurses	51.8	27.1	18.8	2.4
Hospice doctors	83.5	7.6	6.1	2.8
Hospice nurses	82.1	10.2	5.4	2.3

Office for National Statistics[14]

Hospices score well. Perhaps this is not surprising in that they are specialist units in terminal care that have been honed to the needs of patients since their foundation. A range of professionals: medical specialists, psychologist, speech/physio/music/art therapists and complementary therapists offering different types of massage are supplemented by volunteers bringing their life skills to patients. The range of terminal illnesses treated has been extended from cancer to include motor neurone disease (amyotrophic lateral sclerosis in the USA); MS and chronic obstructive pulmonary disease (COPD).

Diagnosis of a life-threatening disease may itself be emotionally painful, coming out of the blue, affecting patient and relatives. I remember that at my sister's final diagnosis the hospital consultant said, 'I am sorry there is nothing else I can do.' Later her husband asked me what the consultant meant. The patient begins a new journey at this point: outwardly, through clinics, hospital appointments, day care, home care, hospice and, as the disease progresses, the psychological and emotional reactions to hair loss, that of physical functioning, indignity of incontinence, dependence, and the inner journey of feelings and reactions to information, new symptoms, fears and anxieties, which can become isolating. From uncertainties come questions, often a desire to make sense of what has happened and the strength to live while dying.

14 The National Bereavement Survey (VOICES) of deaths registered between 1 January 2012 and 30 April 2012. Of 144,000 deaths, they took a stratified sample of 49,207 informants, contacted between 4 and 11 months following the death.

Loss involves the loss of what has been and what could have been ... losing what has been enjoyed up until now ... paid employment ... a role in the home, or in a local club or church. What could have been refers to losing one's future [with] many plans unfulfilled.[15]

Hospice care is holistic, addressing 'total pain': physical, mental, emotional, social and spiritual. It has become a benchmark for palliative care. Sheila Cassidy comments as a hospice doctor, 'the hospice movement, with its philosophy of openness, is producing a marvellous healing of the medical and nursing profession's wounded attitude towards death and dying, a recapturing of the ancient acceptance of death as part of life'.[16]

Being without pain and other symptoms

Hospice professionals are experts at pain control. Cicely Saunders in the 1960s discovered that, with few exceptions, medical and surgical textbooks disregarded the problems of pain, treating it too late by injection. Saunders showed how, using the drugs she had in anticipation of, rather than in response to pain, patients could be kept comfortable. The hospice movement has professionalized 'palliative care' (palliative means 'to cover') as a medical speciality, integrating it into hospital medicine as a specialized unit, the hospice itself, an 'at home' service working with families, and in an advisory capacity in residential and nursing homes. Advances have been made in pain management using cocktails of drugs and the development of new drugs. However, for a dying patient drugs may simply mask the real cause of the distress, which is emotional, social and spiritual suffering.

Michael Kearney, a hospice medical director, works to enable a good death for those with a terminal disease, using the ancient Greek model of Hippocrates and Asclepius (see pp. 195–99). He suggests that pain is 'the experience that results from damage to tissue that is part of a person'.[17] Doctors can assess, treat and mainly bring pain under control. In contrast, 'suffering' is the experience that results from damage to the whole person,

---

15 Sioned Evans and Andrew Davison, 2014, *Care for the Dying: A Practical and Pastoral Guide*, Norwich: Canterbury Press, in association with Westcott Foundation, pp. 51–2.

16 Sheila Cassidy, 2002, *Sharing the Darkness: The Spirituality of Caring*, London, Darton, Longman and Todd, p. 59.

17 Michael Kearney, 2000, *A Place of Healing*, Oxford: Oxford University Press, p. 4.

such as a patient's recognition that their illness is terminal and the inner anguish it may cause. Kearney recognizes the importance of medical pain relief but also suffering, which is psychological and spiritual. He notes that healing is about becoming whole, and that death is the final healing. He creates an environment for the patient, 'where what is fundamental, natural and indigenous to the human psyche can most easily do its own work of bringing about integration, balance and wholeness'.[18]

Kearney uses visualizations and dreams to create 'the environment that best facilitates this process of inner healing ... in practice ... a combination of effective care and human companionship helps to establish a secure, inner space for that person to be in'.[19] Following conversations about physical health, the patient is invited to close her eyes and imagine herself in a scene, which begins a story. The story uses archetypal symbols such as a journey, a river, travelling in a boat, meeting a stranger and accepting a gift. Later Kearney asks about the experience.[20] We each have a story of the incidents and experiences of our lives. Kearney is able through the visualization to enable patients to discover the strands of their lives that are troubling them. This takes time. Finding meaning and purpose affirms living and allows peaceful dying.

Many terminally ill patients are pained by spiritual questions, such as 'What have I done to be punished like this?', 'What next?', 'Will I see my loved ones again?' and 'Will I be remembered when I am gone?' These are deeply existential/spiritual questions for which there are no easy answers. Spirituality is about the 'essence of a person', 'what makes a person tick'. It has become something of a buzz word in medical contexts, with imaginative work done, for example, within nursing groups.[21] It may be defined as the search for 'Ultimate meaning within life with reference to a power, often transcendent, that is other than self', a secular concept that is person-centred and makes no assumptions about belief. Religion has a spiritual dimension: 'The outward expression of a spiritual understanding and a framework for a system of beliefs, values, and rituals based on an ultimate source of being, usually described as God.' A number of models are used to assess spirituality, for example questions such as, 'When life is hard, how have you kept going? Is there anyone or anything that has

---

18 Kearney, *A Place of Healing*, p. xxii.

19 Kearney, *A Place of Healing*, p. 5.

20 See e.g. in Kearney, *A Place of Healing*, and 1996, *Mortally Wounded: Stories of Soul, Pain, Death and Healing*, Dublin: Marino Books.

21 W. McSherry and L. Ross (eds), 2010, *Spiritual Assessment in Health Care Practice*, Keswick: M&K Publishing. In 2011 Royal College of Nursing produced '*Spirituality in Nursing Care: A Pocket Guide.*'

helped you keep going?' A NICE document (National Institute for Health Care Excellence 7.23) stated: 'Spiritual care is a responsibility of the whole team, even if a specific individual holds the role for ensuring its provision.' Much UK practice in the area of spirituality is ad hoc, reticent about not offending against or contravening religious practice. Sensitivity and training is still necessary. There is concern about spiritual needs. Those people who say spirituality matters to them express it as the need:

- for support in dealing with loss
- to transcend circumstances
- to be forgiven and to forgive
- to find meaning, purpose and hope
- to feel that God is on their side
- to prepare for death and dying
- to express anger and doubt.[22]

There is little research on the health benefits of spiritual care.[23] My experience as a hospice chaplain is that as patients came to trust me, many of these needs were raised: this was not dependent on the patient being religious but my being 'open' to listen to their stories and respond appropriately.

Being in familiar surroundings

The hospice at-home team supports the patient to die at home if that is their wish. Most people with a terminal illness, however, finally die in hospital, since home may not be possible or appropriate for a variety of reasons: because of a crisis at home; the main home carer cannot cope; the lack of community facilities; no empty beds in the hospice; a belief that the hospital has more expertise. Some of the family cannot bear the thought of the loved one dying in the home in which they will continue living after the death. If at home, the patient is certainly likely to be surrounded by friends and family.

---

22 H. G. Koenig, David McCullough and B. Larson, 2001, *Handbook of Religion and Health*, Oxford: Oxford University Press.

23 M. Holloway, S. Adamson, W. McSherry, J. Swinton, 2010, *Spiritual Care at the End of Life: A Systematic Review of the Literature*, London: National End of Life Care Programme/Department of Health.

Place of residence and death

Statistics (see p. 39) suggest an estimated 350,000 patients need palliative care each year; fewer than half, 170,000, receive it. Hospices tend to be urban, often with a rural threshold; they are small, so that care can be kept intimate, but this means that they have to prioritize needs. In Chapter 1 I noted that in hospitals particularly, death is seen as a failure. An article in the *British Medical Journal* states that 'if death is seen as a failure rather than as an important part of life, then individuals are diverted from preparing for it and medicine does not give the attention it should to helping people die a good death'.[24] The article further states that 'for the minority who die under the care of Palliative Care teams care is probably good but there is a suspicion that for the majority who die in acute hospitals or nursing homes the experience is bad'. Hospitals tend to be concerned with fighting death rather than care for the dying, and fulfilling their duty of care.

A research study of what community nurses considered to be a good death includes eight themes: symptom control; patient choice; honesty; spiritual care; inter-professional relationships; effective preparation and organization; and the provision of seamless care.[25] There is much in common with the patient's definition. Nurses state: 'A good death is where the patient has come to terms with the fact that they are dying, they are at peace with themselves.' Research suggests that there is a need for education, training and reflection among professionals working with people at the end of life – we are still not good at death.

The list above assumes that the patient wants to know the process of dying and to take control. Jean in Chapter 1 did. Some patients do not even consider the possibility that they are dying, others are kept in a conspiracy of silence by their medical carers and/or families, some of whom think that if they talk to the patient about dying, it becomes a self-fulfilling prophecy. Other patients and their relatives each know when the dying stage is reached but do not talk about it. This could be a 'coping' mechanism. The *BMJ* report states that dying must be brought back into life: 'We believe it is time to break the taboo and to take back control of an area (death) which has been medicalized, professionalized, and sanitized to such an extent that it is now alien to most people's daily lives.'

24 *British Medical Journal* 15:320 (2000), pp. 129–30.

25 C. Griggs, 2010, 'Community nurses' perceptions of a good death: a qualitative exploratory study', *International Journal of Palliative Nursing* 16:3, pp. 139–48.

Being in the company of close family and/or friends

When caring for a patient at home, much depends on the carer. The NICE guidance defines a carer as 'lay people in a close and supportive role who share in the illness experience of the patient and who undertake vital care work and emotional management'. This may be a spouse, partner, child, other relative, friend or supporter who cares about the person.[26] It is estimated that currently 500,000 people support those with a terminal illness, providing £71 billion to the health and social care economy in 2007.

The carer has needs, for example their own emotional support which is subsidiary to their main focus. This is difficult if the illness is lengthy, though it is helped if there is a big family to share the care. The needs of carers are also practical:

- Information to help provide palliative care.
- Day-to-day palliative care involves incontinence care, diet, hydration, feeding and swallowing, access to specialist services and equipment, patient positioning and lifting for comfort, medication and symptom management. Carers need to know how to do these tasks safely.
- Carers say health professionals seem reluctant to provide information and guidance.
- Carers wanted education and training before a patient has a hospital discharge.
- Phone access to help in everyday caring and in the event of an emergency.[27]
- Knowing what to expect in the dying process itself.[28]
- Honesty from professionals about the patient's condition (providers use 'patient confidentiality' and 'data protection' as reasons against this).

Little is done to support the real and genuine needs of carers in a work which is significant, in being able to note the day-to-day changes in the health of the patient. My own family discovered the emotional cost of caring for my sister in her last months of life.

26 Social Care Institute for Excellence (SCIE) of the NHS, 2013, *Dying Well at Home: Research Evidence*, p. 14.

27 P. Bee, P. Barnes, K. A. Luker, 2009, 'A systematic review of informal caregivers' needs in providing home-based end-of-life care to people with cancer', *Journal of Clinical Nursing* 18:10, pp. 1379–93.

28 The Marie Curie Cancer Care publication, *Being Cared for at Home Towards the End of Life* is excellent.

Advance care planning

Advance care planning is recommended for everyone expected to die within 12 months. It needs to be done in good time when the person is able to make decisions and communicate these. If a patient is willing, dying can be a time to rearrange life's priorities, bringing a sense of freedom and being able to choose. It can include:

- practical arrangements, such as preferences for the type and place of care at the end, whether and in what circumstance the patient might wish to go into hospital; any advanced decisions to refuse treatment and/or a lasting power of attorney for health and welfare decisions, which may include a decision not to undergo resuscitation; setting affairs in order – legal and financial matters such as making a will; writing requests for the funeral.
- leaving a memorial/legacy; organ donation.
- personal issues, which may include making peace, healing rifts, with nearest and dearest, saying goodbyes, the provision for care of children; arranging for pet care; who is to be present to care at the end; making peace with God, asking for a religious person to be present at the end.

An advanced care plan is a living document, so may change. It is helpful if this is written and signed, witnessed and dated.

Service professionals find it difficult to initiate conversations with patients over advanced planning, because: it changes when symptoms change; it affects their relationship with the patient; other professionals are assumed to have done it; patients are in denial. It is sensible to make these plans alone or with the support of a nurse, chaplain, volunteer or members of the family. One patient asked me to help her prepare her funeral. She gave this to her family who were then able to enjoy her life until her death. Another wanted to know if it was suitable to write to her grandchildren about her death. She left a letter for them saying that death was like a playground slide – 'it was great letting go'. Others made memory boxes for children.

The process of dying

Understanding dying was informed by Elizabeth Kübler-Ross (1926–2004) who wrote *On Death and Dying* in 1969, recording her work with the terminally ill. She listed stages of dying (denial, anger, bargaining, despair/depression and acceptance), which are used in training workshops. A key issue was to undermine the silence around dying and insist that in the mid-twentieth century it was 'natural'.

Denial is a characteristic of hearing a diagnosis of a terminal illness, expressed as 'it cannot be true'. It is the shock and numbness of a disclosure of imminent death.

Anger follows: 'Why me? It's not fair! What have I done?' 'Who is to blame?'

Bargaining then follows, sometimes with God: 'If you cure me, I will live life differently.' This can be understood as an attempt to alter the terror of reality.

Despair/depression is expressed with words such as, 'There is no point in living.' A profound sense of grief and hopelessness at the impending death, yet beginning to accept the certainty of death, allows the person to disconnect from life and relationships.

Finally, a state of *acceptance* surfaces, a coming to terms with mortality, a period of peace and quiescence and, for the Christian, hope. There is no compulsory timetable or order of grief; sadly this has sometimes been forgotten. As time passes, the dying withdraw into an internal world, illness becomes the centre of their world.

Challenging the taboo on talking about dying

The Dying Matters Coalition was set up by the National Council for Palliative Care, to support the 2008 Strategy (www.dyingmatters.org). Their mission is to support changing knowledge, attitudes and behaviours towards death, dying and bereavement, and through this to make 'living and dying well' the norm. It has members from the NHS, voluntary and independent health care sectors. Dying Matters Awareness Week, began in May 2009 and is annual, extending in 2014 to Wales, Scotland and Northern Ireland, while influencing enterprises in Europe, New Zealand and Australia. It produces excellent resources.

The first official death cafe in Britain took place in September 2011, organized by Jon Underwood, 'to create an environment where talking about death is natural and comfortable'. Underwood stated:

> In my experience, when people talk about death and dying, all their pretences disappear. You see people's authenticity and honesty among strangers. Although it might sound really weird and wonderful to say you attend a death café, it just feels very normal.[29]

29 Matilda Battersby, 'Tea and Mortality – death cafes', *I* newspaper, 28 August 2012.

In recognizing the significance of mortality he pointed out, 'death is a catalyst to think about important things in life'. Underwood mentions that we 'out-source' death to hospitals, behind closed doors, but gradually death is being brought out of the shadows.

Funeral festivals advertised in national newspapers are organized by funeral directors concerned that people should know the choices that are open to them: prepayment funeral plans, wills, advanced directives or the disposal of their bodies, a choice of who presides and where the funeral service takes place and what that service might include.

A task for trainee journalists, 'training and life coaching classes', encourages people to write their obituaries and plan funerals. This is a reality check to ask the questions, 'Why am I here?' and 'What do I want to be able to say about my life at the end?' In the USA, Legacy.com publish self-written obituaries each month; the UK equivalent is ObitKit.com.

Guides to dying well were published, for example, by Rabbi Julia Neuberger.[30] There have been popular films such as *The Bucket List – Time to Start Living*, which explored using the time remaining to two dying men, *Shadowlands*, *Dying Young*, *I didn't want that,* on end-of-life wishes, *Life Before Death* and *The Fault in Our Stars*. In the UK the Wellcome Institute had a display from autumn 2012 to spring 2013, 'Death: A Self-Portrait, the Richard Harris Collection'. A newspaper stated:

> Death in a secular and medicalized world has been made into something to be put off. All credit to the Wellcome foundation for holding a show that reminds us that death has been an intrinsic part of life through most of human history.[31]

A sign of change in public attitudes to dying

Published accounts of dying have become popular. Albom Mitch's book *Tuesdays with Morrie* is the story of Morrie Schwartz (1916–95), a professor, and Albom, a former student, and their conversations over Morrie's final months with motor neurone disease.[32] Schwartz comments, 'To know

---

30 Stephen Levine, 1986, *Who Dies? An Investigation of Conscious Living and Conscious Dying*, Dublin: Gateway; R. Reoch, 1997, *Dying Well: A Holistic Guide for the Dying and their Carers*, Stroud: Gaia; Julia Neuberger, 1999, *Dying Well: A Guide to Enabling a Good Death*, Hale: Hochland and Hochland.

31 *I* newspaper, 19 November 2012.

32 Albom Mitch, 1997, *Tuesdays with Morrie: An Old Man, a Young Man, and Life's Greatest Lesson*, New York: Doubleday, p. 81; and Morrie Schwartz, 1998, *Letting Go: Reflections on Living while Dying*, London: Pan Macmillan.

you're going to die and be prepared for it at any time ... that way you can actually be more involved in your life while you're living.' John Diamond (1953–2001) wrote about his fight with cancer in his weekly column in the *Guardian*, an illness which made him mute but did not destroy his facility with words. Dying at 47, he was not courageous in the face of death, but had courage to write about his struggle openly.[33] Kate Law, spokeswoman for the Cancer Research Campaign, said of Diamond:

> Stories like his ... have helped bring cancer out of the closet in Britain ... By describing ... how he continued to attend dinner parties even though he could no longer swallow – he helped show others that they too must try and continue life as normally as possible.

Philip Gould (1950–2011), a former New Labour spin doctor, wrote a book on his experiences of, living with and fighting cancer. He commented, 'if you accept death, fear disappears'.[34] Christopher Hitchens (1949–2011), a British-born journalist and writer who worked in the USA, wrote a reflection on living with oesophageal cancer.[35] François Mitterrand, the former President of France, wrote of healing in suffering:

> At the moment of utter solitude, when the body breaks down on the edge of infinity, a separate time begins to run that cannot be measured in any normal way. In the course of several days, sometimes with the help of another presence that allows despair and pain to declare themselves, the dying take hold of their lives ... It is as if, at the very culmination, everything managed to come free of the jumble of inner pains and illusions that prevent us from belonging to ourselves.[36]

Etty Hillesum, a Dutchwoman, who died in Auschwitz, wrote:

> The reality of death has become a definite part of my life. My life has, so to speak, been extended by death ... by accepting destruction as part of life and no longer wasting my energies on fear of death or the refusal to

33 John Diamond, 1998, *Because Cowards Get Cancer Too: A Hypochrondriac Confronts His Nemesis*, London: Times Books.

34 Philip Gould, 2012, *When I Die: Lessons from the Death Zone*, London: Little Brown.

35 Christopher Hitchens, 2012, *Mortality*, London: Atlantic Books.

36 Marie De Hennezel, 1997, *The Intimate Death: How the Dying Teach Us to Live*, London: Little Brown, Foreword, p. ix.

acknowledge its inevitability. It sounds paradoxical; by excluding death from our life we cannot live a full life, and admitting death into our life we enlarge and enrich it.[37]

I have quoted these experiences since they illustrate how dying can be experienced with many differing emotions, yet when accepted and faced may be seen to give greater meaning and significance to life.

The terminally ill sometimes have a degree of control of death and often wait until they're alone, the visitors have gone, and then they relax, let go and die. We each die our own death. To talk about the end and caring for the dying is about the meaning and value of our lives in the present, as well as what, if anything, follows. As the baby in the womb knows nothing about the future life outside the womb, neither do we know about the possibility of a next life.

Modern medicine and philosophy have redefined death as 'brain dead'. Our identity as persons emerges from birth. Modern genetics, evolutionary psychology and neurophysiology state that our thoughts, feelings, character, memory, our unique history and identity are shaped, influenced and dependent on our physical brain and body. Can I be reduced to electrical impulses in the brain? 'To live as a human being is to be self-conscious and self-consciousness is a function of the brain. When the brain dies the person dies.'[38] Yet for many there is a 'confident expectation'. For Moltmann, 'Christianity is completely and entirely and utterly hope.'[39]

Questions for reflection and response

- Look at Edvard Munch's picture *The Scream*. What might it tell you of the anguish of hearing a terminal diagnosis?
- Comment on the reason for those, like John Diamond, who write of their experience of terminal disease.
- Thoughts on death and dying – fill in this form quietly and on your own; notice your emotions as you do it, and put in your journal:
  ○ At what age would you like to die?
  ○ Where would you like to be (include the sounds/sights/smells around)?
  ○ Who would you like to be with you?

---

37 Patrick Woodhouse, 2009, *Etty Hillesum: A Life Transformed*, London and New York: Bloomsbury, p. 82.

38 Alan Billings, 2002, *Dying and Grieving: A Guide to Pastoral Ministry*, London: SPCK, p. 28.

39 Jürgen Moltmann, 1980, *Theology of Hope*, London: SCM Press, p. 11.

- ○ What are they saying to you?
- ○ What would you want to say to them?
- ○ What concerns you most about dying?
- Extend by research ideas of the self/soul and its life.

Reflection on insights from Scripture and the tradition

The Hebrew Scriptures

Basic to the Hebrew Scriptures is the fact that dying is part of the natural order. Humanity is finite and limited, 'like the beasts that perish' (Ps. 49.12; Isa. 14.11). Yet against this is the idea that dying is a curse and affliction, suffering a punishment for sin, though challenged by Job. Elijah too faced a challenge with the widow of Zarepath's remarks relating sin and death (1 Kings 17.17).

God gives life. Those who respond and obey God's commandments receive a long life, when dying is a fulfilment. Abraham is promised, 'You shall go to your ancestors in peace; you shall be buried in a good old age' (Gen. 15.15). Seminal is that a Jew's immortality is in his descendants, a promise made to Abraham when he was childless and old (Gen. 12.2; 13.16; 15.5; 17.4–8). Those blessed by God die 'full of years' (Gen. 35.29; Judg. 8.32; Job 42.17), 'in ripe old age, as a shock of grain comes up to the threshing-floor in its season' (Job 5.26). In contrast, a bad death was premature, violent and without an heir, such as Absalom's (2 Sam. 18). Death was universal, it could not be avoided, nor minimized. It was lamented: we 'flourish like a flower of the field; for the wind passes over it, and it is gone' (Ps. 103.15); 'we must all die; we are like water spilled on the ground, which cannot be gathered up' (2 Sam. 14.14). There was no hint of an afterlife at this time in history. The spirit was thought to linger round the body prior to its departure; physical decay allowed ultimately the clean bones of the deceased to be gathered to the ancestors, placed in an ossuary. There were no explicit references to an afterlife. There is Sheol's 'shadows', but usually this presupposes and is identified with the grave. The prophets had spoken of a future judgement 'Day of the Lord'. Later there was mention of a future leader, God's Messiah (Isa. 11.1–9). During the Babylonian exile (sixth century BCE), ideas of a life beyond death began to take shape (Ps. 139.8). These ideas were expanded at the time of the Maccabean revolt, together with the concept of a soul (see p. 23).

The New Testament

Jesus' ministry was exercised within an atmosphere heightened by apocalyptic expectation, an age when there were diverse eschatologies: personal extinction (Sadducees, Mark 12.18–27); literal physical /bodily resurrection and judgement at the Last Day (Pharisees, e.g. Paul, Acts 23.6; Phil. 3.5); immortality of the soul (Essenes); a mode of existence like angels in heaven (Qumran community); or the coming of a Messiah and judgement. Paul showed hostility to death, seeing it as the consequence of Adam's sin (Rom. 5.12–14) and the last enemy (1 Cor. 15.26).

Jesus went to help the dying daughter of Jairus (Mark 5.21), making himself ritually unclean by touching the girl. He healed the dying centurion's servant/son; was moved in the face of sickness and impending death. Jesus inherited the thinking that suffering was related to sin, though challenging it (John 9.1–3). He showed compassion in attending to the needs of those caring for the dying, bringing comfort, speaking of death as 'sleeping'. Jesus showed care to Martha and Mary at the sickness of their brother, Lazarus, though he waited before attending to their plea for help. He wept at Lazarus' death while speaking of resurrection now and at the Last Day (John 11). His ministry challenged attitudes to dying, identifying with the loved ones of the dying.

Jesus' teaching was concerned with the Kingdom of God (Matthew: Kingdom of Heaven) – life as God intended it. He preached that the Kingdom was already dawning. In the synagogue, he read the Isaiah scroll which recorded signs of God at work, and said, 'Today, this Scripture has been fulfilled in your hearing' (Luke 4.21). He sent out 70 friends to extend his ministry, instructed them to say 'The kingdom of God has come near to you' (Luke 10.9) and, in answering John the Baptist's question 'Are you the one who is to come, or do we look for another?', he directed the disciples of John to see the signs of the Kingdom in his ministry (Matt. 11.2–11). There was also a 'not yet', the Kingdom was not fully present (Luke 11.2). Many of the parables were about judgement and keeping awake for the end time (Mark 13.26). Sometimes Jesus suggested that this would happen in the lifetime of his listeners. Both Paul and Jesus said that the Day of the Lord/coming of the Son of Man/the Second Coming was unknown – there would be signs, but the importance was the present. It did not happen as expected, although some theologians today believe that the Second Coming was the gift of the Holy Spirit (John 14.18–27) or the resurrection.

Jesus' passion is central to the Gospels, between a third and a quarter of each Gospel is devoted to it. Only humans are self-consciously aware that death awaits us all: we may anticipate, plan, fear, dread and seek to avoid death. Jesus spoke openly about his death as his departure (Luke 9.31). He was anxious about death (Luke 12.50). He did not expect his followers to welcome death: 'Are you able to drink the cup that I am about to drink?' John 14—17 is a meditation on Jesus' words in the upper room, during a meal. There are words of comfort, care and reassurance in preparation of his followers for his death. In Gethsemane he asked his disciples to watch, 'I am deeply grieved, even to death' (Mark 14.33–34), and his sweat was 'like blood' (Luke 22.44) as he prayed to God, asking to avoid death, and finally committing himself to God's will. In his dying he showed concern for his mother (John 19.25–27) and asked forgiveness for those who crucified him (Luke 23.34). In Gethsemane and on the cross, Jesus' desolation shows his full humanity (Matt. 27.46; Mark 15.34) and God-forsakenness. Finally, in an act of trust and completion, he said, 'Father into thy hands I commend my spirit' (Luke 23.46).

In Jesus' own dying we have a representative death, words of forgiveness, comfort and provision for loved ones, fear, dread and acceptance at the last. There are parallels today in the words and actions of some of the dying to whom we minister. Jesus died as we all die.

Christian history

Good news of immortality is central to the creeds and liturgy. 'We look for the resurrection of the dead and the life of the world to come' are words from the Nicene Creed. In the sacrament of baptism the baptized is 'an inheritor of the kingdom of God'. In the sacrament of Eucharist, the Orthodox receive the bread of 'immortality', Anglicans and Roman Catholics, the bread of 'eternal' or 'everlasting life', connecting words at the Last Supper with Jesus' future coming (1 Cor. 11.23–26; Matt. 26.29; Mark 14.25; Luke 22.18). In marriage are found the words 'till death do us part'; funerals and ethics both refer to a life beyond this one. Resurrection is fundamental for understanding the salvation of humanity from sin, giving a hope for a life beyond. The doctrines of salvation and atonement revolve round the good news of an eternal hope.[40] 'Blessed be the God and Father of our Lord Jesus. By his great mercy he has given us a new birth into a living hope through the resurrection of Jesus Christ from the dead' (1 Peter 1.3).

---

40 There are varieties of salvation – it is not the same for everyone: freedom from fear, obsession with possession, the ego. What are we saved from? For?

Heaven, hell and purgatory

In Hebrew there is no word for heaven or hell. In ancient writings heaven is identified with the sky, the place where God dwells. Heaven is being in the presence of God, recreated as the person God intended us to be; it is a place of ultimate justice, when judgement is passed on evil and life's wrongs righted. Is it paradise? Paradise means 'garden'. Today popular belief points to somewhere nice, a continuing of the happy families here, for reunions, with family and pets, unlike the gospel understandings!

Hell is the biblical Gehenna/Hades. This was understood as the Valley of Ben-hinnom, the rubbish dump outside Jerusalem, a place of horror, infamous for the worship of Moloch, who required the sacrifice of children (2 Kings 23.10; 28.3; Jer. 7.31–32; 19.2, 6). In the New Testament hell is associated with unquenchable fire (Mark 9.13), eternal fire (Matt. 18.8; cf. 25.41), a furnace of fire for the wicked (Matt. 13.42, 50). Hell can be our own creation here. The seventh-century mystic Isaac of Nineveh comments:

> A handful of sand, thrown into the sea, is what sinning is, when compared to God's providence and mercy. Just as an abundant source of water is not impeded by a handful of dust, so is the Creator's mercy not defeated by the sins of His creation.

For Isaac, hell was to know God's love but not accept it. This is likely to be symbolism, to awaken a sense of responsibility before God, understood as the Judge of all. Choices made in this life leave a mark on the character and will have to be accounted for.

Purgatory (Latin: *purgare*, to make clean, to purify); the definition is 'those who die in God's friendship, assured of their eternal salvation, but still have need of purification to enter the happiness of heaven'. At death humans have seldom reached holiness; purgatory hints at the possibility of development, growth and purification. Praying for the dead is found in 2 Maccabees 12.42–46.

What of a life beyond death?

What we do know is that this life is an opportunity to reflect God's love, particularly for the marginalized. For the rest, it is in the hands of the mercy and love of the God we experience in Jesus, crucified and risen. Paul writes, 'Now hope that is seen is not hope. For who hopes for what is seen? But if we hope for what we do not see, we wait for it with patience' (Rom. 8.24–25).

Insights from other faiths

The Abrahamic faiths

Judaism is a practical religion, focused on the spirituality of everyday life. Death is taken seriously as an inevitable part of life. When a Jew is dying, traditional prayers are said, including the key declaration of Judaism, the Shema: 'Hear, O Israel: The LORD is our God, the LORD alone. You shall love the LORD your God with all your heart and with all your soul, and with all your might' (Deut. 6.4–5). Pious Jews hope to die with these words on their lips. The words can bring comfort to the dying and the relatives present, and bring them into a larger community of faith and history. Sometimes a formal confession of sins is included. The task is to create an emotionally supportive environment, even if the dying person is unconscious. Traditionally, it is a religious duty to stay with the dying so that she or he does not die alone. At death, the words 'Blessed is the truthful Judge' are uttered. When the undertakers are informed they arrange to bury the dead as soon as possible in a Jewish cemetery. The body is washed, usually by a person of the same sex, and wrapped in a white linen shroud. The body is not left alone until burial.

Muslim customs in regard to dying are almost universally practised. Ideally Muslims would wish to die at home. The hospital or hospice setting is not in keeping with tradition – but sometimes needed by the patient for medical reasons. In our hospice a Muslim patient arrived in an anxious state. His concern was that his bed should be facing Mecca, so a compass was found, together with a timetable of the regular prayer times. He was in a single room, necessary for the number of family and friends visiting, who were concerned to pray for the patient's welfare in the world to come. There is time to seek forgiveness for sins inadvertently committed. Members of the immediate family stay at the bedside and recite from the Qur'an as a person dies, reminding him or her of God's mercy and forgiveness. Daily prayers play a significant role in the day-to-day life of a Muslim; they assume a greater role in times of suffering. Ablutions happen before prayer; at this point it is important for the relatives to help a sick patient.

The Eastern faiths

For Hindus death is a natural process in the existence of a soul that makes reincarnations in response to karma. Prolonging life is considered as interfering with karma and is not encouraged. Hindus prefer dying at home, where family members can sing, pray and read the Scriptures to help the dying individual to focus on Brahman. Hindus and Sikhs seek cremation as soon as possible after death. Buddhist traditions vary. Death is regarded as of major significance; for the dying, it marks the moment when the transmigration begins to a new mode of existence dependent on the karmic forces accumulated during a lifetime. For the living, death is a powerful reminder of the Buddha's teaching on the impermanence of life. It also provides an opportunity to assist the dying as she or he fares on the journey to the new existence, within the round of rebirths.

Questions for reflection and response

- 'The demise of Christianity has meant that belief in an afterlife has no meaning for many people, it is replaced by an emphasis on the quality of dying.' How can this be used by a pastoral visitor?
- Comment on the statement by Douglas Davies that Jesus' 'death is representative death; it is the obvious example to us that we will all die'.
- Christians today are roughly equally divided between believing in a life after death, and the belief that life ends with death. Comment on this.
- How significant is hope as a Christian concept?

Cultural context in dialogue with Scripture and the tradition

I noted that, in the twenty-first century, death, at one time the task of the Church's representatives, is now in the hands of the medical profession. The Christian faith today has lost much of its credibility, for example the biblical assumption that our planet is the centre of the universe and the centre of God's concern is questioned. Cosmologists show us that we are part of a galaxy, one of billions. Humanity as the crown of God's creation was called into question by Darwin's theory of evolution and the survival of the fittest. Critical biblical scholarship from the 1870s onwards has challenged faith for many. Freud stated that humans were not rational creatures; the human mind was nothing more than a complex organism reacting according to discoverable laws.

The Theos think tank interviewed online 2,036 adults from Great Britain in September 2013: 39 per cent believed in the existence of a soul, 32 per cent in life after death, 26 per cent in heaven, 16 per cent in reincarnation, 13 per cent in hell, 13 per cent in the power of the deceased ancestors. In total, over half, 54 per cent, held at least one of these spiritual beliefs.[41]

---

41 Theos, 2013, *The Spirit of the Things Unseen: belief in post-religious Britain,*

Emphasis has moved from the hope of an afterlife to that of the quality of the dying process as 'a good death'. In a Christian society a good death meant preparation for death: repentance, confession, absolution, a peaceful death with the hope of resurrection. This strand of dying has continued, as seen in Alf's death, but for those for whom Christian insights are dubious it is the quality of the end of this life that is the priority. Quality includes the end-of-life strategy, pain relief, advanced planning, dying with loved ones near, each significant. There is, for some, a recognition of a difference between pain that is physical and suffering understood as spiritual, and also for many a 'secular' spirituality that needs to make sense and meaning of life, suffering and dying.

In popular culture there is a belief that 'we carry on' but 'somewhere nice', away from the horrors of life today, but there is no mention of God. There is a yearning for justice, the righting of this world's wrongs and an expectation that this is only possible in an afterlife of some sort. Recently, the mother of a woman with Down's syndrome, now aged 50, bedbound and totally dependent, said to me, 'Susie has never reached the potential of being fully human, there must be more, where she is completed.' I wondered if she would then be the Susie I have known as a caring, loving person? If we are present at a death, we are aware of the silence and stillness, and speak of something changing; the atmosphere is different. Is it simply the life force, as in Hebrew thought? Is this the soul? This raises questions. If the soul is immaterial, could it support personal identity? The soul set free from the body survives; however, this seems inadequate since it is through our bodies that we express ourselves and are recognized. If there is to be an afterlife it needs the reconstitution of the physical, yet we know that our physical body turns to dust. It is not a transforming but a remaking of the person; this may be thought of as Paul's spiritual body. This is in another world. The physical sciences know of other worlds. Life beyond death is a hope, based on God's grace.

Modern existentialist philosophy is compatible with an afterlife, stating that an awareness of our finitude is crucial to authentic living. In accepting mortality, existentialist philosophy urges that 'this is achieved only as we strive for personal integrity of authentic existence ... [involving] living responsibly, accepting our limitations, and striving to achieve what we can, while avoiding retreating into impersonal conformity'.[42]

---

available at www.theosthinktank.co.uk. Important also is the Immortality Research Project, funded by the Templeton Foundation, and available on a number of US websites.

42 Jeff Astley, 2010, *SCM Studyguide: Christian Doctrine*, London: SCM Press, p. 214.

Near-death experiences (NDEs) suggest possible survival after death and research is reinforcing this. My late sister had what can only be described as a NDE. Following the removal of a drain after surgery for a brain tumour, in a trance, Angie said to her sister Rosie, 'It is lovely here, Mum and Dad are with me, the sun is shining. It is beautiful.' Her sister said, 'Angie, come back, come back. We need you. Your daughter needs you, we all love you.' Angie 'returned'. Telepathy is also a phenomenon, suggesting that there is more to a mind–body relationship than we had previously understood.

Does this dialogue of cultural context and Scripture lead to any theology informing to pastoral practice? Here are my tentative thoughts. In his ministry Jesus cared for the dying. He came alongside those who were suffering and brought life and healing. He experienced anguish with death, fear and horror in the Garden of Gethsemane. He cried out to God on the cross, 'Why have you forsaken me?' (Matt. 27.46). He prayed for forgiveness, offering it to another (Luke 23.34, 42–43). He died accepting and offering himself to God, 'Father into your hands I commend my spirit' (Luke 23.46). Incarnation speaks of Jesus' identifying with the human condition. The true humanity of the theology of incarnation and presence is seen here, as is the encouragement in government reports on 'a good death' for all. Sadly, this does not happen. There is also a theology of hope, though not always in God, but a hope for a peaceful death.

Questions for reflection and response

- Do you consider that scientific discovery has made Christian faith impossible? Give reasons.
- In the twenty-first century, dying and death is marginalized in everyday conversation and regular Christian teaching. Yet we all die, experience the death of loved ones and see death on the media. How can Christians respond?
- Why are there 'folk' beliefs in a life after death?
- What theology emerges for you from this section of the chapter?

Pastoral practice

In this and following chapters I am using the term 'minister' of those lay or ordained who work with the elderly and dying. The minister and members of a church's pastoral team may visit congregational members in a hospice, hospital, at home or in a residential home, and take services in these places. The person visited may have an illness, which could be terminal or simply be housebound because of age and infirmity.

Our faith must derive and make sense of our lived experience – the distinctive dimension of our care. If we are to help others in their dying as ministers, we must have worked through the issues of our own mortality in the light of our faith. The minister needs to know what can credibly be said in the light of recent scientific findings and where silence is more important than words – the dying do not want glib answers.

As ministers concerned with the care of the dying we need to be people who are non-discriminatory in approach and strive to allow the dying to be cared for in a manner consistent with that person's own beliefs and religious and cultural traditions. This is a ministry of presence, an incarnational theology: Jesus accepted people as they were. Patients and the elderly are not 'pew fodder'. To be alongside a patient and relatives it is crucial to acquire skills of listening, acceptance, summarizing, being silent and establishing a rapport. We need empathy and genuineness, remembering that with each person we meet we are standing on holy ground.

Responses to Kübler-Ross's stages of dying

Initially, when a person hears their diagnosis, emotions are volatile. The world of everything that gave meaning to life collapses. Mental and emotional distress causes idiopathic pain. Anger includes strong feelings. Why me? There is anger with God, with medical staff, family, friends, themselves. If you as the minister are the object of anger, deal with it gently. Paul wrote of death as the wages of sin and this is interpreted by some as suffering as a punishment. The person may not want to ask family or burden them. The minister may bear the dying person's anger and respond, 'Cancer strikes randomly. God may not intervene. But you are valuable for you are a child of God. And what you have achieved in your life is of abiding significance.' Anger is short, because it requires energy and there is not a lot of this. It takes time to accept; the patient may be overcome with fear, panic or sadness, thinking of the implications of death. The minister needs to reassure. There is a stage of unreality. This is when the brain tends to protect the concept of non-existence. Sometimes there is denial – perhaps the doctors have made a mistake – searching for another opinion, a refusal to talk about the diagnosis, in which the family colludes. The minister may be co-opted into praying for a miracle. Don't collude, a prayer for strength is more appropriate. The minister should check with the patient, and staff/relatives if possible, the seriousness of the news; to give hope, not of miraculous recovery but of support – physical, mental and spiritual. The minister could help to use the present time in positive ways, for example writing a letter to a grandchild to be given after the death. We are sustained in life by hope. What hope is there for the terminally ill? The minister has a different hope: recovery is not possible but dying well and preparing yourself and those around you is. It is a hope in Christ, who shared our humanity and is present with us in our suffering, and conquers death in resurrection. A theology of hope is significant.

There may be fear: of what death is, a wall, a gateway, a snuffing out, a ceasing to be; fear of the process of dying; or fear of judgement and the afterlife. Patients ask what is going to happen when they die? An answer is, 'I don't know'. There is a difference between 'knowing' and 'faith'. The answer 'I don't know' from a minister can help, since a patient will realize ministers haven't got it all sorted! The answer may create laughter and open the situation up to discovery and theologizing. The New Testament tells us little about the afterlife. Alan Billings comments:

> the question for Christians today is not whether some absolute proof of life after death can be offered – such proof is simply not available – but whether speaking about life after death can be done in ways that are credible in the light of contemporary knowledge about the world and human life.[43]

There may be anxieties about dependency, losing control of the body, interminable pain and being able to cope in the last stages of illness. As ministers, we listen and help to find peace of mind, which may mean hearing confession, seeing life from a different perspective, how the patient will form part of the lives of loved ones after death.

The dying need time to explore, to help them make meaning of a life. A characteristic of human life is that we are meaning-makers. These meanings may be religious or not, simply lived but not thought out. This is a putting together of the incidents that make up a life. It can become a stretching, a growing, not a narcissism. If that for which I have lived – family, church, faith, God, political party – continues, then death is not so threatening. This meaning uncovers slowly. The minister helps the person to make sense of life; to see life has abiding value that death cannot destroy. There may be unresolved issues of meaning. We need to be sensitive to these existential anxieties. The doctors in particular often have little time to deal with this, we do as ministers – this is incarnational presence.

---

43 Billings, *Dying and Grieving*, p. 30.

In a hospice or other institution, where we do not know the patient, we are not there to proselytize and cannot know the patient's experience. We can build a relationship of trust. There are likely to be moments of despair when the minister can reassure. Some treatment leaves patients physically down, less able to pick themselves up mentally. Christians worried about their faith may be helped by thinking about Jesus in Gethsemane. Humans experience the mechanism of fight or flight in times of danger. Is there a third way? That of holding it? Of acceptance? If we know where in our body our tenderness to ourselves is, we can go to that pain within ourselves.

Those we work with need to be taken seriously – particularly the hidden curriculum 'the base clef', the underlying story, to be given time. We need to affirm the patient's individual personhood and humanity and to protect their dignity, self-worth and identity. Self-worth is based on the value others have for the dying: the wider community, in voluntary or paid work, in relationships and friendships. When dying, these roles are threatened. It is hard for the person to believe that he or she is valued. In life we are sustained by loving relationships. Sometimes the dying are protected so that visitors do not see the changes in appearance. Then a patient may ask, 'Have they written me off?' The sympathy of caring diminishes over time. The minister brings the love of the congregation and stands for God.

Dying in old age

Ministers can be disconcerted, seeing dying as loss, whereas older people may have a different perspective, believing in death as a sleep of transition from this world to the nearer presence of God, or simply to oblivion. An elderly person may be tired and find daily living an increasing burden; at this time the thought of not waking again is a matter of relief and not a cause of anxiety. Family and doctors do not necessarily agree and keep up a pretence of life. Few Christian ministers now have the opportunities of using bedside rituals – hearing confession, anointing with oil, reading Scripture, or a final communion, which help to give death a shape. The rites are still helpful for some in our Christian community, as they were for Alf; other Christians are too fatigued. Some elderly people approach death with relative serenity of mind – they may not want to talk of Christian hope, other than in prayer. Others may experience anxieties in the face of death and want emotional and intellectual reassurance. The minister needs to be clear about the nature of the anxiety, simply asking, 'Is, there something you would like to talk about?' There may be mood swings at the end – simple prayers, offering a cross to hold, anointing, or the sacrament may be appropriate. Visiting my 92-year-old father just before he died, I mentioned that it was Candlemas, when we remember the words of old Simeon as he greets the child Jesus and his parents (Luke 2.28–32). I began the words of the prayer – the Nunc Dimittis – and to my amazement my father joined in. Something deep in his psyche remembered the words from his childhood and young adulthood. If the person's condition is controlled by drugs, or the person is in and out of consciousness, the minister may simply be present, watch and pray for the carers, touch (though great sensitivity is needed here), or leave a small cross for the dying person to hold.

Illustrations of ministry to the dying and their family

On one occasion when I was called in to a family whose relative was dying, I simply stood with the family, and eventually they asked me to pray for their loved one; on another occasion the patient had dipped in and out of consciousness for several days, and the family were trying to hold on saying, 'Don't go'. I suggested that they might like to tell the mum how much they loved her, thank her and then tell her that she could be at peace. They did this and she died later in peace.

One day I was berated by an older male cleric for not bringing someone to faith before he died; this man's soul would be held against me at Judgement Day, he said. I did not know the patient well and responded that I was not to be this man's judge. I did not know his faith; that was in the hands of God. Christians can lose their faith in their suffering; conversely it can grow. I heard of a Christian man with dementia, who had fought in the Malaysian jungle years before. A week before he died he was fearful, crying out believing that demons were attacking him. His wife asked him if she could pray. Her words, in the name of Jesus, told the demons to come out and angels to come. He died a week later smiling at the angels.

The emotional effects of ministry to the dying

This ministry is a privilege, it confronts us with our own mortality; detachment is difficult. We need to show our human emotion. Pain and dying happen to us all. To the extent that we can live with this and be ourselves, then we can be with others in constant pain and dying. Ministers to the dying and their relatives must have a quality of presence in their lives which is dependent on their assurance of God's presence with them.

Questions for reflection and response

- Think about a recent loss (personal not professional). Remember your emotions. Think of it in terms of shape (round, jagged?); colour (passionate red, life-giving green, sad black?). Use crayons or paints to convey your emotions. Later, share it with someone, asking what the painting conveys to them. Add to your journal.
- Explore how you might give pastoral care to a member of your congregation who has lost their faith at the end of life.
- How can you minister to someone whom you are asked to visit and is dying but you do not know?
- In ministering to the dying:
  - What is challenging about being with those in pain/dying?
  - What is God's gift to them?
  - How do you think of God in these situations?
  - Where is God? What is God doing?

Further reading

Alan Billings, 2002, *Dying and Grieving: A Guide to Pastoral Ministry*, London: SPCK.

David Clark et al., 2005, *A Bit of Heaven for the Few: An Oral history of the Modern Hospice Movement in the UK*, London: Observatory Publications.

Sioned Evans and Andrew Davison, 2014, *Care for the Dying: A Practical and Pastoral Guide*, Norwich: Canterbury Press, in association with the Westcott Foundation.

Derek Murray, 2002, *Faith in Hospices: Spiritual Care and the End of Life*, London: SPCK.

This chapter is likely to be influenced by UK parliamentary legislation on assisted suicide. My interactive domain is dyingtolive.org.uk.

3

Ministry to the Bereaved

A woman went to the Buddha carrying in her arms her dead son. She asked for his healing. The Buddha asked her to find a few grains of mustard seed, but they must only come from a house where no one was touched by death. After a year's search the woman returned, having found there was no such house.
Traditional – source unknown

This chapter begins with the experience of a distressed widow, on which I reflect theologically. Throughout life there is loss. Death is noted as the ultimate loss for ourselves and for those we love. The context of the twenty-first century is examined, stating the historical background, illustrating the immense changes in attitudes to bereavement. I look at the process of bereavement from research in the human science of psychology, of Colin Murray Parkes and Elizabeth Kübler-Ross. The factors affecting bereavement are examined. I consider the Scriptures' approach to mourning. Context and Scriptures lead to theologies of vulnerable presence, incarnation and hope, which guide our pastoral responses.

Pastoral circle

Pastoral practice:
ministry of vulnerable
incarnation and presence

Experience –
theological reflection:
concern of a Christian at
the death of her atheist
husband

Cultural context:
dramatic changes in
grieving

Scripture/tradition
and context:
theology of presence/
incarnation

Scripture and
tradition:
mourning in
Hebrew and
NT; afterlife,
resurrection

Experience

> Linda and I met to think about the funeral service for her late husband Maurice. He had suffered a stroke in his mid-fifties and recovered almost completely due to the care he had received. Maurice was so thankful that he wanted to show his gratitude in some practical way and help other, less fortunate, stroke victims, so he established a swimming club. The club was a lifesaver to many of the clients, who found people in similar situations and experienced practical hints that can only come from a fellow sufferer. Friendships were made, which resourced people outside the club meetings. Maurice was the friend of everyone who came, an inspiration and encourager of many through the years. Sadly, he contracted cancer and died in the hospice.
>
> The crematorium was full to overflowing for Maurice's funeral. People were standing at the back, many from the club who wanted to honour him and recognize his friendship and devotion to them.
>
> A few days after the funeral a distraught Linda rang me. She was a faithful Christian; her husband had no faith. Would she ever see him again? I arranged to visit her.

Reflection on experience

Belief in a life after death was central to Christianity from the beginning (1 Cor. 15.3f.; Rom. 10.9), dependent on the resurrection of Jesus. The early Christians believed that they would be the 'first-born from the dead' (Col. 1.18). Jesus would return; those alive, together with those who had died in the faith, would be caught up with him, the natural body replaced by 'a spiritual body' continuous and discontinuous with it, as Jesus' resurrection body had been. Humanity would be transformed to be as God intended. In the second century, resurrection was controversial, chiefly because of the idea of the reassembling of the physical body. The later creeds declared, 'the third day he rose again from the dead … He shall come to judge the quick and the dead. I believe in the … resurrection of the body, and the life everlasting' (Apostles' Creed). 'We look for the resurrection of the dead, and the life of the world to come' (Nicene Creed). The centrality of resurrection faith is that there is a new beginning of life with God; the challenge is the holding of this belief when divorced from its eschatological origin. Until the late twentieth century the over-arching Christian story, from creation through to salvation, influenced the beliefs and values of those living in the West. The story was familiar in its language, symbols, metaphors and stories, but in a post-Christian era this is no longer the case. The discoveries in the sciences call into question traditional views of an afterlife. This thinking was the backdrop for the conversation with Linda.

Linda, crying, said: 'I have a firm faith and know that I will be with God when I die, but what about Maurice?'

I said: 'Please tell me about him.'

Linda said: 'He did not believe, so I will never see him again.'

I said: 'Hmm ... you will never see him again?'

Linda: 'Well, I will be with God, my Father in heaven, but Maurice won't be in heaven. You see, he didn't believe. He wouldn't come with me to church. He just didn't understand God stuff.'

I said: 'Perhaps God understood Maurice? You did say that God was like a father and most fathers know and love their children.'

Linda said: 'Yes, Maurice loved our children and helped me to bring them up right. They both do voluntary work in the community, and are now great parents themselves.'

I said: 'Well, fathers are concerned about their children. They love them. I wonder, does God love us like the best of fathers? A father who wants the best for us?'

Linda said: 'I'd never thought of it like that.'

I said: 'We believe that we are children of God; whether we go to church or not, God still loves us. God loves each of his creation and longs to enter a relationship with us. Do you remember the story Jesus told of the sheep and the goats in Matthew's Gospel? Jesus talked about those who visited the sick, fed the hungry and helped those in need. Then he said, 'as you did it to the least of my brothers and sisters, you did it to me ...''

Linda said: 'Yes, I know that story. Are you saying that God knows this?'

I said: 'Yes. I believe that it's living for others that counts, rather than what we believe.'

Linda said: 'Oh.'

I said: 'Those who attended Maurice's funeral were witnesses to his friendship and kindness to them in their time of need. This was living a Christlike life. God in his loving mercy knows and loves Maurice and you will meet him again – how, we do not know – it is the mystery and hope of faith.'

We talked together, thinking about the line of the hymn 'There's a wideness in God's mercy, like the wideness in the sea' (Frederick Faber, 1814–63), and of J. B. Phillips' book *Your God is Too Small* (1961), which challenged thinking about the nature of God. Theology reflects and is reflected by the thinking of the time in which it is set. The 1960s were a period of challenge in which Christianity and Christian doctrines were rethought, in Linda's situation doctrines about the nature of God and God's relationship with each of God's people.

Linda's bereavement following the death of her husband was devastating. We are each interconnected, a person known and loved by us is part of our lives. Bereavement entails changes in a wide network of relationships and sometimes changes to our world-view, perhaps challenging our faith, through thinking that God is absent. However, through facing loss and accepting the mystery of suffering, our spirituality and faith may be strengthened, but if we cannot face loss we may get stuck in grief.

Life is a series of losses: the shelter of the womb from the moment of birth is a traumatic deprivation of our security. We are born into a society, initially a family whom we did not choose. At birth we lose control of temperature, noise, sights and even food intake. Throughout life we experience a range of losses, mini deaths and bereavements: the loss of milk teeth, mobility, a sense, a limb, health. We lose things – a credit card, purse, key. In human relationships we may lose a friendship, an ambition, a marriage. In old age and retirement we lose a wage, social status and role. Death is the ultimate loss – a final separation from all that we know. Loss involves emotions – fear, loneliness, denial, anger, despair and depression. It could be said that our reactions to these little 'mini deaths', whether we are able to expand our understanding and grow through loss, or shrink and recoil, can be a significant development in our humanity. How we 'cope' with our daily losses may help us in our final, ultimate loss.

Questions for reflection and response

- If you had taken Maurice's funeral, how would you have reacted to Linda's subsequent distress?
- List and reflect on some of your own losses. Record them in your diary of reflection.
- How can we think theologically about loss?
- Loss through bereavement may feel like the absence of God – a dark night of the soul. How do we help someone who is experiencing this?

Reflection on cultural context

Grieving and mourning are not the same. Alan Billings defines grieving as 'our personal, emotional response to the death of our loved ones', whereas mourning is 'the behaviour which particular social groups deem appropriate in the face of death'. It is assumed that grieving is natural, universal and purely psychological, but mourning is determined by culture. Billings maintains that both are influenced by culture.[1] Tony Walter adds a definition of bereavement as 'the objective state of having lost someone or something'. He argues, 'Culture affects grief as well as mourning, and indeed grief underlies the very constitution of society.'[2]

Changes in facing grief

In the twenty-first century we have been distanced from dying by medical advances and so denied it; denial of death is accompanied by denial of mourning. Changes in regard to grief have been dramatic in the last 150 years, 'shaped powerfully by the decline of religion, the two world wars, demographic change and the medical revolution'.[3]

Death was commonplace in the Victorian age. Three of every twenty babies died before their first birthday due to disease and maltreatment. Industrial accidents took their toll on the lives of child labourers. This was higher among families in the northern industrial cities and working class. Life expectancy was 42 years. Rituals helped women in the often-repeated death of their infants and children. The public path of rituals arising from a strong faith and family support gave a structure for coping with infant deaths. Religion played a significant role. Most middle- and upper-class people and half the working class attended church in 1851. The Evangelical Revival led by Moody, Sankey and Spurgeon in the Keswick Convention, and Booth of the Salvation Army, reached the peak of influence in the 1860s with an emphasis on family prayers and Bible study. These Evangelical expressions of Christianity encouraged men as well as women to show their emotions, weeping together at the death of loved ones.

---

1 Alan Billings, 2002, *Dying and Grieving: A Guide to Pastoral Ministry*, London: SPCK, p. 74.

2 Tony Walter, 1999, *On Bereavement the Culture of Grief*, Buckingham and Philadelphia: Open University Press, p. xv.

3 Pat Jalland, 2013, 'Changing cultures of grief, 1850–1970; from Archbishop Tait to C. S. Lewis', in Stephen Oliver (ed.), *Inside Grief*, London: SPCK, p. 52.

Rituals at a death were in the home: windows were closed, clocks stopped and mirrors covered. Usually bodies were kept in the house in an open coffin until the funeral, which meant that the bereaved were faced with the reality of death and began grieving. There were three stages of mourning, lasting, for a spouse, a minimum of two years. The woman was dressed in black and veiled; black was a colour of respect, considered the absence of light and life. Men wore a black armband and hat. The bereaved were not seen outside the home in any other clothing. Cost prevented distinctive clothes for the working class, who dyed their clothes for the period of mourning and bleached them afterwards. The deceased were remembered through mementos – lockets, brooches and rings containing locks of hair, death masks, portraits and pictures of the loved one. A future consolation was the belief in the resurrection of the body.

Funerals were elaborate and expensive public occasions but helped the psychological needs for grief. The elaborateness of a funeral indicated the importance of the deceased, even if it meant hardship for surviving families. Graves were important places to visit, remember and mourn. Rituals varied according to age, gender, region and social class, particularly in the north of England and the Celtic fringe.

Ritual traditions owed much to Queen Victoria. This was the Romantic period in art and literature. Marriage became one for love rather than money or property; therefore the demise of a partner was devastating. Victoria's husband Albert died at 42 after 21 years of marriage. She was a widow for 40 years. The funeral was attended by thousands lining the streets. Victoria wore black for the rest of her life. This set the tone of an obsessive celebration of grief for her subjects.

The agnostic was omitted from this picture, isolated in an age when faith was traditional and dominant. However, from about 1880, the Church's influence began to decline through the challenges of biblical criticism, geological findings and Darwin's theory of evolution. Mortality and death receded, 'perceived as the monopoly of the elderly',[4] through public health reforms such as public sewers, a clean water system and the medical understanding of communicable diseases.

The Great War 1914–18

The Great War dramatically changed responses of grieving. It was estimated that one in four soldiers were seriously wounded and one in eight killed, over 700,000 in all. The horror of trench warfare, with bodies

---

4 Jalland, 'Changing cultures of grief', p. 57.

shattered by shells, led to overwhelming communal grief among soldiers. Survivors were required by the authorities to silence their emotions. In 1915 the War Office issued a command that bodies were to be buried where the dead fell and not returned home for burial. Without bodies, there could be no funerals, places to grieve, or public recognition of a loss. The result was that aspects of mourning were suppressed. Families at home would often not be told of a death. If there was no body, a soldier might be reported as simply 'missing', women were instructed to be brave and show courage for their men, who, paying the ultimate sacrifice for their country, would be rewarded in the next life. Grieving, the psychological process of accepting a death, was ignored, particularly affecting those who had last seen their loved ones alive and well and who were now presumed dead.

The soldiers, who had faith, could not reconcile their Sunday school God of love with the horror they were experiencing. The Church suffered, for example in the demise of the doctrine of hell, since chaplains dare not mention this in the light of the young they buried. A Church of England enquiry, *The Army and Religion* (1919), found that the Anglican Church lacked the sacramental rituals to cope with death and grief, unlike the Roman Catholic Church, whose chaplains ministered through confession and absolution before the battle and, subsequently, extreme unction to the dying. The Established Church had lost its way, felt its own grief, sorrow and loss of competence. Spiritualism grew, many turning to it, in the hope of accessing their departed loved ones through a medium.

Alienation

Many ordinary people felt alienated from those in authority who had not been able to reunite them with their dead. The Cenotaph in Whitehall was established as a temporary memorial, replaced in 1920 by a stone monument designed by Edwin Lutyens to gather the nation's tribute on an annual Armistice ceremony. The memorial was to be duplicated across the country, with the names of the fallen inscribed. The Imperial War Graves Commission set up foreign graves. The first tour to these graves was in 1919. By 1931, 140,000 were visiting every year, enabling some release of emotion, an aid to the grieving process and an end to guilt felt by survivors who had not been able to say goodbye to loved ones. For some, the inter-war years (1918–39) were obsessed by thoughts of death. For others, death was not mentioned, presumably a natural wish to forget the horrors experienced. In addition, others were challenged by the effects of economic depression.

The Second World War

Pat Jalland notes that the Second World War 'marked a deeper break with the past than the Great War and the process was cumulative. A pervasive model of silence about death and of suppressed grieving became entrenched in the English psyche.' Churchill called for courage and stoicism during the blitz of British cities: 'The dark side of the blitz story was sanitized to sustain morale.'[5]

Women imitated men in suppressing their grief. News of the Holocaust shook people's faith in humanity; it seemed a prostitution of medical science, bringing disbelief. Nuclear proliferation became a fear. After the war, public grief was discouraged: grief was privatized and despised, the idea being to keep busy and pretend to be cheerful, grieve in private, in silence. Thoughts about death were pushed further to the margins with the Welfare State provision of pension rights and sick leave, relieving some of the financial distress of bereavement; medical advances resulted in longer life, and death becoming more remote.

Changes after the war

In the 1960s the funeral followed by burial was replaced by an increase in cremation, a shorter ceremony, decreasing the time for family to grieve. This was particularly hard for couples who had been married 50 or 60 years and now were separated by death. The disappearance of the coffin at a crematorium was distressing. The ashes were often scattered with no witnesses, so there was no place to mourn. When my mother died and was cremated, our vicar suggested that her ashes were buried in the churchyard, marked by a memorial stone and a service. This became important to my father, who had a place to tend and mourn, which he visited daily in the first months of bereavement. My youngest sister, cremated 17 years later, asked that her ashes be scattered on a favourite woodland walk. There is no publicly marked place, and though her husband and daughter visit on the anniversary of her death, her best friend is sad not to have a spot to grieve – for her, it is as if Angie never was.

The 1960s were called 'the expressive revolution', characterized by a greater freedom of emotions, especially for women. The work of churches offering pastoral care to the bereaved was gradually taken over by professionals, psychiatrists and social workers, through counselling. Theological questions were raised by Bishop John Robinson in *Honest to God* (1963), which reassessed major Christian doctrines including the

---

5 Jalland, 'Changing cultures of grief', p. 63.

afterlife and resurrection.[6] Influential for the bereaved was an anonymous book written by a Christian on the death of his wife in 1960. He describes his grief as 'a state of psychological paralysis', his grief unpredictable, a challenge to his faith: 'it was like a long ... winding valley where any bend may reveal a totally new landscape'.[7] The book, *A Grief Observed*, became a guide to grief at a time when the bereaved received little to help. C. S. Lewis died in 1963 and subsequently the book was published under his name, contributing to a changing cultural climate in attitudes to grief.

Bereavement is no longer communal

No longer communal, bereavement is of the immediate family. This is evidenced by notices in the paper, 'family flowers only', 'donations in lieu', limiting something friends could do, ignoring their part in the life of the deceased and their grief. At the same time church attendance, giving hope in a life to come, continued to decline. Billings noted:

> 1960–80 reversed the pattern of the traditional society in four crucial respects: the dead were made to disappear; grief was privatized; the bereaved were socially more isolated ... and the traditional (Christian) understanding of death began to lose its hold on people's minds without anything else particular taking its place.[8]

The re-emergence of the significance of grief

The Hospice movement, 'born' in 1967, with its teams of professionals and volunteers helped patients and their relatives prepare for bereavement, 'anticipatory grief'. Relatives might play down or deny grief, stating to nurses, 'The patient is the one you must care for, not me.' Parkes' research suggested the denial or avoidance of distressing thoughts might enable people to get through the periods of crisis, but

> denial is an unstable defence which cannot be maintained ... given ... proper support most people who choose to express their anticipatory grief do come through it, tears die down. This may enable them to communicate more effectively with the patient than they would if they felt it necessary to avoid potentially distressing topics about which the patient

6 John A. T. Robinson, 1963, *Honest to God*, London: SCM Press.
7 C. S. Lewis, 1961, *A Grief Observed*, London: Faber and Faber.
8 Billings, *Dying and Grieving*, p. 82.

is ready to talk ... accurate information and emotional support given before a death will reduce the risk of such problems afterwards.[9]

The process of grief – Colin Murray Parkes

Colin Murray Parkes gave a much needed empirical base to grieving. His research was published in 1972 under the title *Bereavement: Studies of Grief in Adult Life*. Grief is not a pathology: most people cope with sensitive support. Bereavement is a process, and there are several models for it. Parkes notes three major components present from the onset and obvious at different times after the loss:

1 The urge to cry and search for the lost person – humans share with other social animals a tendency to pine, coupled with an impulse to cry aloud. This tends to recur in episodes, 'pangs of grief', triggered by any reminders of the lost person or of the events associated with the loss.
2 An urge to avoid or repress crying or searching – we are aware that it is illogical to search and cry for someone who is dead, but from childhood, in the West, we are urged not to cry. This is particularly true for boys and men. There are social pressures to limit the overt expression of negative emotions. Funerals and the subsequent public social gatherings are 'often an ordeal rather than a support to the bereaved'.
3 The urge to review and revise internal models since the death of a loved one invalidates assumptions about the world, for example behaviours that formerly involved or relied upon the existence of that person. A widow may have relied on her husband to change light bulbs or pay bills. She must now do it. 'Widow' status is very different from that of a married woman, so that a widow seeing couples happily shopping can find it very distressing.

Models of grieving are useful, but tend to ignore the variation between people and the fact that people move back and forth between the phases. Parkes thought of the characteristic phases of grief as:

1 Numbness and blunting of senses; anxiety, restlessness and physiological accompaniments of fear.
2 Pining and yearning to find the dead person in some form, maybe so real that the bereaved catches glimpses of the deceased and thinks that

---

9 C. Murray Parkes, [1972], 1986, *Bereavement: Studies of Grief in Adult Life*, London: Penguin, p. 995.

they are going mad. (This often surfaces in bereavement groups at the hospice. Reports have been so numerous that it is now accepted that as many as 50 per cent of widows have a sense of 'presence' of the loved one, but a person can get stuck in seeking this comfort.)

3 Disorganization and despair, feelings of internal loss of self, even of mutilation of the self, and the adoption of traits, mannerisms or symptoms of the deceased.

4 Reorganization and recovery.[10]

These are normal features of the process of grieving and may last two years or longer. It is helpful if church communities offer periodic services of comfort and remembrance, where the dead are remembered and valued (see p. 162). Funeral companies often train their staff and offer a caring service before and after the funeral. For those with a religious faith, bereavement counselling by a pastor has a dimension which other counsellors may lack. When the bereaved have little or no faith, a minister who is not determined to proselytize may have a pastoral role.

The process of grief – Elizabeth Kübler-Ross

Elizabeth Kübler-Ross saw the emotional stages that terminally ill patients experience in their approach to death to be broadly relevant to other losses.[11] Stages were denial, anger, bargaining, depression and acceptance. These may be cyclical, some may be skipped, bereavement may progress upwards as a spiral or zigzag unpredictably. It is uncertain how applicable the stages are in different cultures, therefore it is important in caring for the bereaved that the stages are seen as guides only.[12] Self-help groups were formed to support particular specialist groups of bereaved people.

Differences in bereavement

It must be remembered that each loss and process of grief is different since the relationship with the deceased was unique. There is a difference between men and women in bereavement, particularly if the couple were older. In British culture there is a taboo on men's expression of emotion. Women are allowed to cry. Attitudes to mortality vary. Tony Walter main-

10 Parkes, Bereavement, p. 202.

11 Elizabeth Kübler-Ross, 2005, On Grief and Grieving: Finding the Meaning of Grief through the Five Stages of Loss, New York: Simon and Schuster Ltd.

12 Elizabeth Kübler-Ross, 1979, On Death and Dying, London: Routledge.

tains: 'women have got used to a life being limited by biology ... it is men who can live with illusions about omnipotence over nature'.[13] Women tend to be the couple's initiator in terms of their social relationships, and are more likely to have social networks to which they can turn for support. Widowers can withdraw into isolation, whereas women may turn to the church. Stroebe and Stroebe show that in the first six months after a bereavement there is, especially for men, nearly a 40 per cent increased chance of death, either through illness or accident.[14] Bereavement is very physical, and the body can become exhausted and prone to disease. The bereaved with a close family network are less likely to be affected.

Factors affecting grief

The relationship between the deceased and the bereaved – ambivalent or close – is a factor affecting grief. For example, parents don't expect to bury their child. Mike had tears in his eyes when talking about his son Dan, killed 30 years ago on a motorbike. The nature of the attachment to the deceased affects grief. John Bowlby's work on attachment theory, with child evacuees and parents in the 1940s, is now being related to adults; if there was a security of attachment rather than ambivalence or dependency then bereavement will be harder to bear. The nature of the death is a factor in grief: death may come after a prolonged terminal illness, which may result in relatives' relief that suffering is over. Then guilt may set in or grief may be mitigated in part by feelings that the loved one no longer suffers. An unexpected death through accident can revive emotions connected with previous unresolved losses. With a violent death, such as war or murder, there may be no body, so there is likely to be an absence of any sort of closure and an ongoing ache until the body is found. A further factor is the historical antecedents of the bereaved. There are variables within a personality, such as how earlier losses were dealt with, or how a person is reared, for example having positive life-coping skills to deal with loss. The primary loss is that of a relationship. There may be a secondary loss, such as a widow having to move house through living on a reduced income.

In the 1980s, talk of a process of grief ending with a resolution, a letting go of the deceased, was questioned. There was a growing suspicion of

13 Tony Walter, 1990, *Funerals and How to Improve Them*, London: Hodder and Stoughton, p. 53.

14 M. Stroebe and W. Stroebe, 1993, 'The mortality of bereavement: A Review', in M. Stroebe, W. Stroebe and Robert O. Hansson (eds), *Handbook of Bereavement: Theory, Research and Intervention*, Cambridge: Cambridge University Press.

professionals and those who said that emotional ties between the bereaved and their loved ones should be broken. Walter suggested an integration: the bereaved carrying with them the deceased, since the latter was part of the present life story. Carl Rogers had encouraged the counsellor to be 'non-directive' and 'non-judgemental', which meant not being prescriptive about what was and was not 'good grief'. Some professionals had found this hard to follow. In earlier years religion had given comfort and the promise of an afterlife, but as the influence of faith waned, by the twenty-first century 'the focus was on the emotions felt by the bereaved: the dead after all, were dead'.[15]

Recent changes – new rituals of grief

Gradually at the end of the twentieth century new rituals of grief emerged. For example, in Bradford's Centenary Square hundreds gathered to observe a minute's silence and a service marking the twenty-ninth anniversary of 11 May 1985, when 56 fans died in a football stadium fire. Wreaths were laid at a memorial in the city. At Hillsborough football stadium 96 died in a crush on the football terraces in 1989. Scarves were hung on the railings. Flowers and toys were left at the gates of the ground and on the pitch. Relatives have formed a group and have in 2014 a new public enquiry into responsibility for the disaster. The full facts of what happened at Hillsborough are not yet known and life is on hold until there are answers. Following the Dunblane school massacre on 13 March 1996, flowers were laid outside the school. Impromptu wayside shrines, particularly at the side of roads, have become a significant part of the landscape, indicating a death yet demonstrating people taking control and their need for symbols and rituals of grief. In 1997 Diana, Princess of Wales died in a car crash in Paris. In the UK flowers were laid by the public outside Kensington Palace and Buckingham Palace as expressions of grief by those who had never met the princess. At St James's Palace a book of condolence opened. Others were opened across the country. The sociologist Grace Davie commented that expressions of grief at Diana's death gave people permission to express the suppressed grief of their own bereavements.[16]

In July 2012 the Department of Health published the first survey of bereaved relatives in England during the last three months of the life of

---

15 Billings, *Dying and Grieving*, p. 84.
16 Grace Davie, 2000, *Religion in Modern Europe: A Memory Mutates*, Oxford: Oxford University Press.

their loved one at home, in hospital, hospice or community. The report is positive, but significant were the last two days of life, when care was ranked lower than other measures; for example poor language used by nursing staff to communicate a death, such as 'We've lost Joe', or 'He's gone to a better place' or 'Jesus wanted her for an angel'. These could be offensive and harmful for the grieving process.

In the late twentieth and early twenty-first centuries the dress and rituals of grief have changed dramatically. Black clothes have mainly disappeared. I remember a funeral around 2005 conducted for a patient in the hospice, a biker. His widow came dressed in a pink jumpsuit, not to be disrespectful or indicating that there was no longer grief, but that culture required, at least in public, a happy face. A friend of a bereaved person is likely to cross the road, not knowing what to say about the death. It is best to be honest and say, 'I don't know what to say.' At work, after a few weeks, workmates expect the bereaved to have returned to their pre-mortem selves. Neither the deceased nor the feelings of the bereaved are mentioned, as if grief is something to be forgotten. Grief has to be lived. Christian groups, such as the Salvation Army, have made the funeral a time for praise and hope, but I suggest that this is too soon. Grief needs expression.

The time between the death and the funeral is significant. It is a period of uncertainty, numbness before grief can begin. Anything that delays the funeral causes great distress.

We have let the practice of mourning, which sanctioned the expression of grief, slip away. Verhey suggests that a recovery of such practices 'could nurture a recovery of an honest acknowledgment of the awful reality of death and a compassionate communal response to both the dying and the grieving'.[17] I believe that this could be in the area of an extended recognition of loss, on significant birthdays and anniversaries, on Holy Saturday and at All Souls'. It is the unexpected occurrences that reignite grief, such as when a bereaved married woman receives a form to fill in which includes the status – married, single, divorced, widow – and she realizes her new situation.

The changes in expressions of grief free people to choose the way they want to express their grief and in the support they seek and receive in bereavement. However, for others, the passing of traditional ways has diminished their possibilities for grieving. On a visit to a non-church grieving family they asked, 'What are the traditions for grief?' They

17 Allen Verhey, 2011, *The Christian Art of Dying: Learning from Jesus*, Grand Rapids, MI and Cambridge, UK: Eerdmans, p. 335.

wanted to show respect for their mother in a way that was culturally acceptable, but had no idea what this might mean.

The medicalization of dying left medical people facing death as a defeat. They are not always apt at helping the bereaved. GPs may give sedatives and sleeping pills, because they do not have time, with ever-increased workloads, or because they cannot cope with bereavement or have not been trained. In many surgeries there are now counsellors to whom the bereaved can be referred.

Questions for reflection and response

- Here is a group exercise. Each person needs four squares of paper of four different colours and a pencil. On one colour, write the names of four significant relationships, for example spouse, parent (one on each piece of paper). On another colour, write four roles you have that are important to you (e.g. volunteer, husband). On a third colour, write four possessions that sustain you (e.g. your favourite CD). On the fourth colour, list four activities that sustain you (e.g. walking, painting). Spread out your squares and look at them. Think what is important to you. Discard three squares of different colours. Look at what you have left. Discard three of the same colour. Think. A person in the group with size 7 shoes, without looking, takes four more of your squares (the person is Fate). Look at what you have left. The person sitting each side of you takes two. As a group, discuss your reactions to this exercise.
- What are the advantages and disadvantages of one of the 'stages of grief'?
- Describe a recent bereavement. Comment on it in the light of what you have read about bereavement in the twenty-first century.
- Why is the period between death and funeral so significant?

Reflection on insights from Scripture and the tradition

The Hebrew Scriptures

References to mourning are many, maybe because belief in an afterlife developed late in the history of God's people. The dead descended to Sheol: an individual's immortality was in the memory of the next generation. Sheol caused great distress, a place without God (Ps. 88.10–12). The psalmist cries out, 'Do you work wonders for the dead? Do the shades rise up to praise you? Is your steadfast love declared in the grave? ... Are your wonders known in the darkness, or your saving help in the land of forgetfulness?' (Ps. 88.10–12). The expected answer is 'no' to each question. Existence in Sheol was in a Godless place. Perhaps it is not surprising that Anthony Thiselton notes that there are 45 references using the Hebrew word *abal* (to mourn) and *abel* (mourning) and over 40 references to *saphad* (to mourn, to beat the heart, to lament).[18]

Rituals of mourning

Abraham mourned the death of Sarah, 'he went in to mourn for Sarah and to weep for her' (Gen. 23.2–11). On hearing the 'story' that Joseph had died, Jacob 'tore his garments, and put sackcloth on his loins, and mourned for his son for many days. All his sons and all his daughters sought to comfort him; but he refused to be comforted, and said, "No, I shall go down to Sheol to my son, mourning"' (Gen. 37.34–35). David 'took hold of his clothes and tore them; and all the men who were with him did the same. They mourned and wept, and fasted until evening for Saul and for his son Jonathan ... because they had fallen by the sword' (2 Sam. 1.11–12). There is an extended lament from David for Saul and Jonathan, which was to be written and passed down to the succeeding generations (2 Sam.1.17–27). David wept, 'O my son, Absalom, my son, my son Absalom! Would I had died instead of you!', a cry of utter anguish (2 Sam. 18.33). 'Their father Ephraim mourned many days, and his brothers came to comfort him' when his three sons were killed (1 Chron. 7.21–22). Mourning was not restricted to families: 'All Judah and Jerusalem mourned for Josiah ... Jeremiah also uttered a lament for Josiah, and all the singing men and singing women have spoken of Josiah to this day. They made there a custom in Israel' (2 Chron. 35.23–25). In the Hebrew Scriptures we note there were rituals for mourning and grief, laments, ashes, tearing of clothes and permanent memorials in records kept, yet there is no easy answer; suffering and death exist.

The story of Job and grief

The story of Job also illustrates customs of grief, and addresses the question of suffering. When Job lost his flocks and livelihood, and his children died, he 'tore his robe, shaved his head, and fell on the ground'. Yet he is

---

18 Anthony C. Thiselton, 2012, *The Last Things: A New Approach*, London: SPCK, p. 20.

able to praise God: 'the LORD gave, and the LORD has taken away; blessed be the name of the LORD' (Job 1.20–21). He suffers sores from head to foot and sits among the ashes; his friends do not recognize him. Seeing Job, they 'wept aloud; they tore their robes and threw dust in the air upon their heads. They sat with him on the ground for seven days and seven nights, and no one spoke a word to him, for they saw that his suffering was very great' (2.8, 12–13). Shared silence is the only answer to grief of this intensity. The silence is broken only by the anger of Job. His world had collapsed, life was meaningless, God did not seem to care. He curses the day of his birth: 'let that night be barren ... because it did not shut the door of my mother's womb ... Why did I not die at birth, come forth from the womb and expire?' (Job 3). His friends, his comforters, now speak, they know the answer: Job must have sinned to deserve such punishment. Job was having none of it, he turned outward to accuse God: 'I was at ease and [God] broke me in two; he seized me by the neck and dashed me to pieces ... He slashes open my kidneys ...' (16.12–13). Finally Job has no answers to questions of death and suffering, he continues to trust God's purposes. Today there are reactions to the death of loved ones that echo those of Job – the silence, disbelief, anger with God, and anguish.

The New Testament

In the New Testament Matthew's birth narrative concludes with Rachel and the mothers of Bethlehem grieving their massacred children, with 'wailing and loud lamentation, Rachel weeping for her children: she refused to be consoled because they are no more' (Matt. 2.18). Here again is the depth of grief. What grief did Mary experience when Simeon warned her that a sword would pierce her own soul (Luke 2.35)?

Jesus' teaching about mourning

Jesus' ministry and teaching refer to grief and mourning in the Sermon on the Mount, the Beatitudes. Jesus says to his friends, 'Blessed are those who mourn, for they will be comforted' (Matt. 5.4). 'Blessed are you who weep now, for you will laugh' (Luke 6.21). The context is significant, that of proclaiming the Kingdom of Heaven (Matt. 4.23) and particularly the future fulfilment of the Kingdom (Mark 1.15; Matt. 4.17), when the humbled will be exalted, the first will be last, the captives will go free, the blind will recover their sight and the will of God will no longer be challenged by sin and death. The statement in Matthew, 'Blessed are those who mourn', is followed by a future eschatological promise, 'they will be comforted'. But who are those who mourn and for what are they mourning? Biblical scholars refer to the just who mourn over their oppression and suffering at the hands of the wicked (Isa. 61.2). In response, God at the end turns their sorrow into joy (Isa. 60.20). Or the mourners are those who see evil reign on earth. Another scholar says it seems that the tendency is to console those who suffer with the expectation of future happiness, which only makes sense if the time is short and God's eschaton virtually present. Another states that perhaps no beatitude is more Christocentric than Jesus' commendation of those who mourn, for they are like him, prepared to live in the world, renouncing what the world calls happiness. It is, however, in keeping with Jesus' ministry that the beatitude could also refer to those who mourn their dead, shown in his concern for the widow of Nain (Luke 7.11–17), Jairus and his family (Luke 8.41–42, 49–56) and the death of Lazarus, where we are told that 'Jesus began to weep' (John 11.35).[19]

The disciples at Jesus' death

The disciples remembered what it was like to know Jesus; they were disbelieving at his death, filled with grief. They missed Jesus and longed to see him again. There was the need for comfort. The joy in reunion was short-lived (Luke 24.14; John 20.21; 16.16–24). When you lose someone you love, hope of a reunion is one of the things that may keep you going. To the griever the only happening that seems important is the return of the one who is lost. Anthony Gardiner's wife's death was

> a stark and terrible vision of death as the ultimate loss and deprivation ... deeply rooted in the Old Testament (Ps. 88); of *Sheol* as the 'the place of destruction', 'the place of darkness', 'the land of the forgotten' ... and it can also destroy our world since the physicality of an intimate relationship that gave meaning to life is gone for ever.[20]

---

19 *Eerdmans Commentary on the Bible*, 2003, A. J. Saldarini, *Matthew*, Grand Rapids, MI and Cambridge, UK: Eerdmans; *The New Jerome Biblical Commentary*, 1993, Benedict T. Viuiano, *Matthew*, London, Geoffrey Chapman; Michael H. Taylor, 1982, *The Sermon on the Mount*, Leeds: John Paul the Preacher's Press; and Stanley Hauerwas, 2006, *Commentary on Matthew*, London, SCM Press.

20 Anthony Gardiner, 1997, 'Confronting the abyss: the relationship between bereavement and faith', in Peter C. Jupp and Tony Rogers (eds), *Interpreting Death: Christian Theology and Pastoral Practice*, London and Herndon: Cassell, p. 121.

Disowning the grief would be to disown the love, and death would triumph. To comfort is simply presence, being there, listening, not attempting to console, but sharing the lament.

Paul's insights

Paul writes in Romans of the sufferings of this present time affecting the whole of creation 'subjected to futility' and of the eschatological hope, when 'the creation itself will be set free from its bondage to decay and will obtain the freedom of the glory of the children of God' (Rom. 8.21). Paul mentions hope: 'if we hope for what we do not see, we wait for it with patience' (8.25). This waiting is the silence of grieving. He also refers to the Spirit, who 'helps us in our weakness ... intercedes with sighs too deep for words' (8.26). In Gardiner's experience today, 'the pain is lessened ... not by denying the value of what we have lost, but by affirming it ... to take the path of denial, evasion, pretence, will almost certainly be deeply damaging'. He continues: 'It is only as we are able to acknowledge and accept how deeply we have been hurt, and how much we have lost, that we shall be able to come to terms with the experience, and even, perhaps, grow through it.'[21]

The nature of God

As children we may have grasped the idea of God as omnipotent, a steadfast Father in times of trouble, yet the Jesus who cries in desolation on the cross suggests a different understanding of God. Bonhoeffer wrote:

> It is not by his omnipotence that Christ helps us, but by his weakness and suffering. This is the decisive difference between Christianity and other religions. Man's religiosity makes him look in his distress to the power of God in the world; he uses God as a 'Deus ex machina.' The Bible directs man to God's powerlessness and suffering, only the suffering God can help.[22]

Where is God? Elie Wiesel, a survivor of Auschwitz, recalls the hanging of a young boy in torment, and a man in the crowd asking the question, 'For

---

21 Gardiner, 'Confronting the abyss', pp. 125–6.
22 Dietrich Bonhoeffer, 1981, *Letters and Papers from Prison*, abridged edn, ed. Eberhard Bethge, London: SCM Press, p. 130.

God's sake, where is God? And from within me, I heard a voice answer: Where is He? This is where – hanging here from this gallows.'[23]

In the crying out of Job, the psalmist's lament, Rachel and the women of Bethlehem, and Jesus there is a place where the anguish of grieving is heard. In the twentieth century it was the Holocaust when the anguished cried out.

> You may cry out to God – and against God – from the edge of hell, when meanings unravel, when relationships break, when chaos seems lord, when God seems absent. And when and if you do, may you also know the gospel that God does not neglect such a cry. May you also know that Christ weeps in your tears.[24]

In the Christian liturgy we have missed out the psalms of lament; anguish plays little part in our faith. We may often rush to get to Easter Day without the pain and silence of Good Friday, even without the absence of God on Holy Saturday.

The pain of Good Friday and Holy Saturday

Working with families one Good Friday, our exploring of the story ended with a procession, with lighted candles, to the Easter garden that the children had made. One by one we put the candles into the garden and then blew them out. We looked at the dark garden in silence, remembering what it must have felt like to be Jesus' disciples on that first Good Friday as his body was laid in the tomb and the entrance sealed. A parent later said that she had never thought of the grieving of the disciples. It reminded her of her own losses and grief, which needed to be accepted. At a later Easter I was asked to make a pastoral visit to two distraught children, whose beloved granddad had died on Holy Saturday. Without realizing, they had collapsed the years between Good Friday and today. They were sad, because Jesus was in the tomb and not there to welcome their granddad into heaven.

God in Jesus knows the dark side of life, the suffering of the cross; yet there is also hope. Bereavement is a gradual process. Paul comments, 'I am convinced that neither death, nor life ... nor powers ... nor anything in creation, will be able to separate us from the love of God in Christ Jesus' (Rom. 8.38).

---

23 Elie Wiesel, 1955, *Night*, Harmondsworth: Penguin.

24 Allen Verhey, 2003, *Reading the Bible in the Strange World of Medicine*, Grand Rapids, MI and Cambridge, UK: Eerdmans, p. 122.

Beliefs in an afterlife in the early Church

The epistles of the New Testament illustrate the tension between two components of Christian hope: the resurrection of the body and the immortality of the soul. Paul has several differing approaches: he uses a dualism, though this may suggest a process of transformation between one 'state' to another, between the old creation and the new, this world and the world to come. In Paul's view, this life is shaped and governed by law, flesh and sin; the world to come is governed by freedom, the spirit and salvation. Elsewhere Paul says that flesh and blood cannot inherit the Kingdom of God (1 Cor. 15.35–57; 2 Cor. 5.1–10; Phil. 1.19–26; 3.21). Paul was a Jew and would have held the Hebraic belief that there is no division between spirit and body. But he was a Pharisee, still grappling with Christ's freedom from the law and was influenced by views, current in his day, of the soul. Paul's metaphor of bodily resurrection is of a seed dropped into the ground and growing, about continuity and discontinuity; there is change, but the same seed. Another metaphor for the Christian community is the 'body of Christ' (1 Cor.6.15; Rom. 12.1–2). John Robinson challenges the use of the word 'metaphor': 'Paul uses the analogy of the human body to elucidate his teaching that Christians form Christ's body ... they are in literal fact the risen organism of Christ's person in all its concrete reality.' Christians, Robinson says, are not like his body: 'each of them (Christians) is the body of Christ, in that each is the physical complement and extension of the one and the same Person and Life'.[25] However, Paul's dominant theme is the resurrection of human beings into a spiritual body (1 Cor. 15.26, 35–44), which reveals his fundamental acceptance of bodies and their significance.

Some Christians expected that the dead would rise and be caught up with the living in the air, instantly transformed in greeting Christ (1 Thess. 4.15–17), a belief that can be compared with the rapture theology of twenty-first-century America, and rising to share his glory (1 Cor. 15.22–23, 35–41). In Revelation 7 the Christian dead, especially martyrs, share immediately in the life of heaven. Other Christians believed the end was imminent, expressed in the Aramaic phrase 'Maran atha – Our Lord, come', which can also be read as 'our Lord has come'; the context of worship indicates a deep yearning for the second coming. Why was this important? The times were tough. The first Christians were a persecuted, marginalized, minority group who longed for escape. The end would be a vindication of their beliefs and practices. In 1 Corinthians 15.1–5 the

---

25 John Robinson, 1952, *The Body: A Study in Pauline Theology*, London: SCM Press, p. 51.

dead sleep until the last trumpet brings general resurrection; in Revelation 20, death is followed by two judgements, one immediately after death, the second at the end of time; there is a living in the New Jerusalem in the light and presence of the Lamb (Rev. 22.35). The eschaton did not come, and today it is thought of as metaphor.

Insights from other faiths

The Abrahamic faiths

In Judaism there are a variety of beliefs concerning the afterlife. This includes secular Jews, although the faith plays little part in their lives. A rabbi comments: 'Nevertheless, the experience of death and bereavement forces Jewish people into an encounter with hallowed traditions and beliefs laid down by their ancestors.'[26] The dead live on in the genetic code, values and lives of their children and in the memory of their family. Today a gap often exists between inherited traditions and the complex emotional reality of people's everyday lives. There is an immense diversity of practice within Judaism, since 25 per cent of Jews in the UK do not belong to a synagogue. There are secular Jews, Conservative, Orthodox, Reformed and Liberal Jews. Within Judaism mourning is a ritualized process in the *shiva* house – the house of mourning of the close relative, parents, spouses, children and siblings of the deceased. A memorial candle is lit (*yahrzeit*), which symbolizes the soul of the dead, and in some homes mirrors are covered. During arrangements for the funeral, men stop shaving, leather is not worn, and in traditional families people do not wash; these are markers of loss and of the utter separation from daily life, giving a framework for the psyche to begin processing the loss.

What of the afterlife? Prominent in rabbinic teaching are three ideas: the Messiah, the Kingdom of God and the Coming Age. The term Messiah, found in the prophetic writings, referring to 'the age of redemption', continues. The 'Kingdom of God' is a term used in many ways, particularly of personal submission to the rule of God. It is this latter sense in which it is used in the prayer known as the *Kaddish*, in the synagogue service and recited by mourners: 'May he establish this kingdom in your life and days, and in the lifetime of all the house of Israel, speedily and soon, and say Amen.'[27]

26 Howard Cooper, 2013, 'Reflections on Jewish approaches to death, grief and mourning', in Stephen Oliver (ed.), *Inside Grief*, London: SPCK, p. 105.
27 Nicholas de Lange, 1987, *Judaism*, Oxford and New York: Oxford University Press, pp. 128–9.

A Muslim believes in the temporary nature of this world, which is transitory; real life begins after death. The Qur'an's three major themes are the Unity of God, the message of the prophet Muhammad, and the hereafter. Islam believes in the existence of the soul beyond death in a transformed physical existence, and in a day of judgement deciding the eternal destination of a person to paradise or to hell. Upon death there is no overt grieving; relatives are encouraged to stay calm and consider the loss as God's will, because he is the one who gives life and takes it away. In practice there are emotional cries of grief, particularly if the death is in a disaster, accident or war.

The Eastern faiths

Hindus believe in reincarnation on the basis of karma – good lives led. Hindus think of prolonging life through medical interventions as interfering with karma and do not encourage it. They prefer to die at home, with family members around them singing, praying and reading the Scriptures to help the dying focus on Brahman.

In Buddhism death marks the transition from this life to a new mode of existence within the round of rebirths. For the living, death is a powerful reminder of the Buddha's teaching on impermanence. It also provides an opportunity to assist the deceased as he or she moves on to the new existence. Tantric Buddhists believe in an intermediate *bardo* period, as much as 49 days, between death and rebirth. Tibetan monks guide the deceased's spirit through the perilous *bardo* by reading from the Book of the Dead. The *bardo* is divided into three phases. During the first it is in a swoon, constantly urged to enter the clear light of ultimate reality and recognize its own Buddha status. During the second the soul recovers and becomes aware and frightened by its own disembodied identity. It gradually becomes aware that it has died and sees the dismantling of its life. Finally it enters the 'illusory mental body' of a child, a dreamlike state. The body in a sedan chair is carried out for cremation accompanied by monks, musicians, relatives and friends. Fire is considered to burn away attachments as well as sins. Clothes and personal possessions are then auctioned. Meanwhile the soul in *bardo* is buffeted, then judged. Six weeks after death the *bardo* may still be buffeted. It may overcome its egoistic goals and egocentricity and become part of the ceaseless flow of life. It may enter a woman at intercourse and be reborn.

Questions for reflection and response

- Look at Job 2.11—3.26. Write a poem to illustrate Job's grief.
- Comment on the absence through death of a loved one expressed as an absence of God.
- Look at Romans 8. Select a few verses, meaningful to you, that might help a bereaved person. Write the verses in modern-day language and comment on their use.
- Comment on the steps of grieving within Judaism. What mourning customs could Christians recreate?

Reflection on cultural context in dialogue with Scripture and the tradition

There have been immense changes in the last century in expressions of grief and rituals and the demise of the influence of traditional Christianity with its message of comfort and hope. The medical understanding of death as 'me being extinguished', 'absence', is painful to contemplate; we shrink from it and for our loved one. Our thoughts and feelings considered by biologists as reducible to electrical activities in the brain are nevertheless dependent on those activities. We cannot exist disembodied. When the body dies, so does whatever we mean by 'me' or 'the soul'– this is what the Christian belief in the resurrection of the body, or more accurately, the reconstitution of the person, challenges; not the resuscitation of a corpse, in this world, but the remaking of persons in another realm beyond physical death. This resurrection body, Paul's spiritual body, is so constituted that we are recognizable to ourselves and to those who knew us, there is a sense of personal identity. If there is life hereafter, it must consist in God refashioning us in some bodily form – this is all we know. This is why Christianity prefers to speak of 'resurrection' rather than 'the immortality of the soul'.

The writers of Scripture had little knowledge of life after death. What they did have was their present experience of God's love, and their certainty that it was not only stronger than death but was constantly creating new life out of the nothingness of death. This conviction was eternally true and so projected on to the future. The present is the clue. Jesus' life and ministry was about the present, judgement, hell, death and new life, eternal life as a present reality. He continually summoned people out of 'death' to life. The Kingdom is about this world, and in the process of its fulfilment Jesus challenged us to live our lives before God.

A literal interpretation of the Scriptures cannot be reconciled with science; the Bible uses symbol and metaphor to express the inexpressible. The Christian tradition through the years has attempted to contextualize the mysteries of faith. However, church attendance is on the decrease. It seems that we are not meeting people's needs or speaking in a language that is understood. Alan Billings comments on this with reference to grief: 'Those to whom we minister will listen to us only in so far as we are willing to engage with them in a genuine exploration of their experiences of dying and bereavement.'[28]

Christian faith is only helpful if it illuminates our experience; it is never a substitute for our theological reflection. This is true for a theology that informs our pastoral care of those who grieve. Theologians of the twentieth century, particularly Jürgen Moltmann and Dietrich Bonhoeffer, have encouraged us in our understanding of traditional doctrines of the incarnation in the light of the suffering of the Holocaust. Both theologians explore ideas of the vulnerable God, present within incarnation; the vulnerability of the Christ child at his precarious birth, when infant and maternal mortality were high in the first century, sharing our humanity, homelessness, the murderous threat of Herod and a refugee taken to Egypt. The means of our salvation shows cruel suffering, public humiliation and utter despair; one who through his life and passion offers new life that challenges death. His life was one of sharing with the marginalized: today the bereaved feel marginalized and are offered friendship and companionship in the community of God's people. This is a theology of a vulnerable God and a theology of incarnate presence.

Today the injustice of life for many challenges thinking, and many hope for another life in which injustice is righted, evil conquered and suffering overcome; there is hope of a new and just life, the reality on which a theology of hope can be built.

Questions for reflection and response

- Explain why the importance of grieving is often ignored.
- What do rituals old and modern say about attitudes to grief?
- Why do many people hope for another life, though not in the traditional Christian expression? What form does this life take?
- Explore why grief is individual.

---

28 Billings, *Dying and Grieving*, p. 149.

Pastoral practice

Our pastoral practice in working with the grieving must reflect our faith and be true to our experience. Our contemporary context indicates a theology that is incarnational, that is alongside, not knowing all the answers; it is silent and vulnerable; it shares the grief of others, a theology of incarnational presence, a theology of a vulnerable God also listens to the cries at the absence of the deceased and at the absence of God; it may curse God; it waits in silence. It is a theology of hope that can share the hope 'that nothing can separate us from the love of God in Christ Jesus'.

'Ministers' (see p. 131) are called to help a bereaved neighbour, to support the elderly. Some may be privileged, before bereavement takes place, to know and befriend a family, who will share thoughts and feelings that they might never share with a doctor or nurse. At that time they may develop the kind of supportive relationship that makes the volunteer the best person to support after bereavement.

In preparation for ministry to the bereaved, three things are initially needed: careful selection of pastoral ministers, training and support. Sadly this is often forgotten. This is a representative ministry for the whole congregation; the minister stands for the Church and represents God.

A minister to the bereaved needs the ability to relate to people and make people feel at ease in their presence. They need practical sense, moral sensitivity, wide and varied experience of life, so they are not easily shocked or judge. They are people who can, when needed, draw on the resources of the Christian Scriptures and tradition and reflect on them in the light of the real experiences of day-to-day living. They will have worked through their own bereavements, recognizing their own needs and accepting supervision and support regularly. These qualities reflect a theology of incarnational presence. It is necessary for ministers to recognize the limits of their own skills. In particular they should know when to refer people for psychological or other medical help, perhaps a counsellor at the surgery, or Cruse. There is vulnerability for both 'client' and 'minister'.

It is helpful to meet in the home of the bereaved, since it is his or her familiar territory. When someone dies, the world of the bereaved collapses, changing beyond recognition, and may become an unfamiliar place. Daily life is changed – beliefs, thoughts, behaviour. The grief reaction is unique and individual. The person may be disoriented. Her world has collapsed. The person is grieving and doesn't necessarily know how to take the next step. Feelings of sadness, shock, anger, guilt and stress can burden. There may be 'oughts' that enter into consciousness: 'I should have visited more often'; these may be completely unrealistic. The person may be unsure what professionals are supposed to do, or how they might help. When introducing yourself, make clear that you are present to be alongside (a theology of incarnation).

Let the person talk about their deceased loved one. Do not butt in or say, 'I know how you are feeling.' It is a cliché. We never know how someone else is feeling. We cannot put ourselves in someone else's shoes. Grief is unique, because it is related to a particular relationship.

> Real listening is a kind of prayer, for as we listen, we penetrate through the human ego and hear the Spirit of God, which dwells in the heart of everyone. Real listening is a religious experience. Often, when I have listened deeply to another, I have the same sense of awe as when I have entered into a holy place and communed with the heart of being itself.[29]

I use the biblical expression, 'treading on holy ground' (Ex. 3.5).

Accept the reality of the grief by allowing the bereaved to talk. It is essential to hear the story of the relationship with the deceased, particularly when any immediate family are tired of hearing about it. It is a pastoral gift to listen. We must begin by acknowledging that death means absence, pain and despair; anything less diminishes the significance of the death. If we speak quickly or about our own bereavements, we may seem glib, as if the reality of the absence is either not being fully acknowledged or, worse, denied. This is true whether the grieving person is a Christian or not; Christianity does not free us from pain and the reality of death.

The inclination of relatives is to shield the bereaved from grief, or to be cheerful. The minister helps by listening to the pain of loss, reassuring the bereaved about the normality of many of the physical and emotional concomitants of bereavement. Remember that Job's friends were silent for seven days and nights (Job 2.13)! Pope Francis uses the image of the Emmaus walk – getting alongside and walking with people, listening to their hurts as Jesus did with Cleopas and his friend, then exploring together, seeing where the journey leads us.

The minister should provide sanction and encouragement for the expression of grief, should be able to reassure the bereaved that she or he has a right to life and the pursuit of happiness. But if at first the emphasis is on life and letting go, this may not allow time to grieve. Comments such as 'You are young enough to marry again' may be said in a kind way, but

---

29 Morton Kelsey, 1992, *Through Defeat to Victory: Seven Journeys to Faith*, London: Element Books.

they are a blow for the bereaved at this time. They cannot forget their loved one at this moment.

Change

The newly bereaved can think their dead loved ones have ceased to play a role in their lives and feel abandoned. The pastoral task is to help the bereaved see a new role. If other relatives think this is morbid, the visitor can help them see why this recollection is important – to integrate good memories in the ongoing life of the bereaved. Jesus said at the Last Supper, 'do this in memory of me'.

John Chrysostom said, 'He whom we lose is no longer where he was before; he is now wherever we are.' People live in a new relationship.

Biblical language

Biblical language uses metaphor as all our language of God. Paul talks of seeds dying and new life coming, of becoming the body of Christ. What metaphor might we use? To talk about the future is to talk about the present experience of God's love. There is no absolute proof of life after death. We need to be cautious about introducing the idea with the bereaved and do so in only the gentlest way since in our culture people may not have thought of this – it may be as disturbing as the thought of the absence of the loved one. It takes time for the possibility of a renewed presence elsewhere to help.

Starting with Christ's resurrection?

In a culture that has moved from the Christian tradition, the concept of resurrection is easily misunderstood. Jesus' human body was not resuscitated to an earthly existence – it was transformed. It was no longer subject to this world of time and space, yet for a while it was visible in it. The general resurrection on the Last Day has nothing to do with flesh and blood. Conversations with the bereaved in the language of life after death are initially likely to be more fruitful than resurrection. God is God of the living, not of the dead; God will not leave us in death; we are immortal because God chooses to bestow immortality upon us, to raise us.

The answer to 'Where is my loved one now?' is quite simply, 'He is safe with God because God made him for himself.' Beyond that there is little more that we either can, or should, add.

A *pastoral example* of *bereavement*

My niece, an only child, was 14 when her mother died. She is an intelligent young woman and had asked about her mother's condition and been truthfully answered. She was in the middle of public exams and wanted to go to school, when her mother was taken into the hospice at the end. There were disagreements in the family. The niece was doing what she knew her mother would want. One aunt thought that she should have been with her dying mother. My niece was present at her mum's death on a Saturday and wanted to go back to school on Monday. It was normality. However, she did not want it mentioned to teachers at school; being a rural area the staff knew. She wanted to be with her peer group. Grief was a long process.

Five years after her mum's death, halfway through her degree course, she was at home, though her dad was away. Early one morning her cat became paralysed. At the vet's, she was told that the cat could be operated on, but there was no guarantee it would recover. She decided to have the cat put to sleep. Later, with her boyfriend, she calmly took the body home and buried it in the garden. That evening, when the boyfriend left, she came to visit me and told me what had happened. Gradually, the grief returned and she burst into floods of tears; the cat was a last tie to her mother, they had bought it together.

There are many individuals and groups who are trained to be alongside and help the bereaved. The Macmillan service offer a self-help facility via their website. Bereaved people from across the UK can access the site via a password and comment on their day to other bereaved people. An online conversation takes place. A bereaved person known to me found this service a great strength, knowing that she is not alone and others understand what she is experiencing at the present time. Cruse provide help, as do hospice teams. As ministers of the gospel we reflect the theology of vulnerable incarnation, of presence and of hope of life in God.

Questions for reflection and response

- What qualities should we look for in choosing someone to be in the bereavement team? Give reasons.
- What is meant by a theology of presence?
- What is challenging about being with the bereaved?
- Where is God in a situation where the bereaved person being visited has no faith or has lost it in the experience of the death of the beloved?

Further reading

C. S. Lewis, 1961, *A Grief Observed*, London: Faber and Faber.

Stephen Oliver (ed.), 2013, *Inside Grief*, London: SPCK.

Tony Walter, 1990, *On Bereavement: The Culture of Grief*, Buckingham and Philadelphia: Open University Press.

4

Another Ending – the Funeral

The funeral belongs to the dead as much as the living.
Tony Walter[1]

The chapter begins with the experience of a family facing a death and the preparation for a funeral, followed by theological reflection. The cultural context of the history of funeral ministry is examined, with reflection on understandings of varying emphases and purposes and hopes for life hereafter. The Scriptures examine funerals in Jesus' ministry and his own burial. Indications are given of various church rites. Non-Christian faiths have other customs. Within the section on context and Scriptures, a theology of incarnation and hope emerges, which informs a practice of ministry that is pastoral.

Pastoral circle

Pastoral practice:
purpose of funeral

Experience –
theological reflection:
a family plans a funeral

Cultural
context:
changing funeral
patterns

Scripture/tradition
and context:
theology of incarnation
and hope

Scripture and
tradition:
funerals in Jesus'
ministry; his own
burial

---

1 Tony Walter, 1999, *Funerals and How to Improve Them*, London: Hodder and Stoughton.

Experience

> Mary was in her early nineties. She lived in sheltered accommodation in a self-contained flat. Her two sons nearby visited regularly. Her daughter, who lived away, rang her mother and visited occasionally. Mary began having medical problems and died after a short stay in hospital.
>
> Mary had lost her husband in an accident when she was in her forties. Her eldest son became the father figure. She was a practical 'hands-on' woman, seen cycling round the village into her eighties. She was a keen gardener, growing her own vegetables to make ends meet, together with fruit-picking jobs in the summer and a job as a dinner supervisor in the local primary school.
>
> Her home was in a village where she was known and loved. In her time she had been an active member of the church choir, on flower and cleaning rotas and at one time was the sacristan. Her funeral was a normal Anglican one with hymns, prayers, address, Scripture readings, committal and blessing. She wanted to be buried in the churchyard of the church where she had lived out her Christian life.

Reflection on experience

Many families today vary in their Christian allegiance, and this can be an issue when arranging the funeral service. It was so on this occasion. I knew that Mary's two sons had church commitments, one was loose, the other strong, and her daughter had little time for faith. They had invited me to take the funeral, since I knew the family. This is a shortened version of the conversation we had when I met them to talk over the funeral.

I said: 'Thank you for being prepared to talk to me today. Mary's death was not unexpected, and she had good health for most of her life. However, she will be greatly missed by many in the village and particularly you, her offspring. Please tell me about your earliest memories of your mum.'

There was a collection of stories and phrases that I was able to jot down and establish a storyline that could be used. It also brought up memories that did not agree!

I said: 'The funeral service is important for you, since it is a beginning of saying goodbye to Mum. It is important that in the service we remember her life; we remember you in your sorrow; we thank God and commit your mum to God's love and mercy. I wonder what you would like in the service that would be helpful?'

Eldest son said: 'Mum wanted the hymn "Breathe on me breath of God". I think it was used at her wedding. It is a well-known hymn so everyone will be able to sing it.'

Daughter said: 'It is traditional to have "The Lord's my shepherd", isn't it?'

I said: 'Yes, that is a very suitable hymn. Thank you.'

Younger son said: 'What about "Now the day is over"? There is a verse in that which says:

Jesus, give the weary
Calm and sweet repose
With thy tenderest blessing
May our eyelids close.

The next verse is

When the morning wakens
Then may I arise
Pure and fresh and sinless
In Thy holy eyes.' (Sabine Baring-Gould, 1834–1924)

The daughter said: 'What on earth does that mean? Mum is dead. She won't wake up again.'

I said: 'Well, some people believe that God loves them in such a way that he never wants them to be apart from him, so at death we commit the loved one to be alive with God.'

Later I asked: 'What happens to Mum after the funeral service? Where will her resting place be?'

Eldest son said: 'Well, it is a bit difficult, because we made arrangements for cremation. We are all getting older and a grave needs maintaining, and I am the only one who lives in the village. But today we found the will, and Mum wanted to be buried in the churchyard.'

I said: 'I can understand your reasons for cremation, though it is difficult to go against the wishes of your mum, but you are the living, and in some ways it is up to the three of you to decide. You could have a committal at the crematorium, and later your mum's ashes could be buried in the churchyard with a service and the laying of a simple stone. Perhaps you should think of it together and let me know.'

The family decided that Mary's body should be cremated and at a later date her ashes buried in the churchyard. This meant that the funeral had three parts: the service in church, a brief time at the crematorium, and later a time burying the ashes. Today many people do not have time for this length of funeral rite. However, it is customary in other cultures. It gives time to recognize the life and death of a believer in the context of the Christian story, for grief to begin and to progress. It is always difficult when decisions have to be made, particularly in the raw emotions of grieving. The decision here was one of burial or cremation and, if the latter, to decide whether the ashes were to be scattered or buried.

It is helpful if, as ministers, we talk to our congregations about the end of life and preparing for it. This means that they will have thought about such things and developed a theology of death.

Questions for reflection and response

• What is the challenge of meeting theological and pastoral needs in a family, when there are different beliefs about faith?
• How were the pastoral needs of the atheist daughter met?
• Why is the decision of cremation or burial of significance to a family?
• What is the theology behind a 'staged' funeral, as in Mary's case?

Reflection on cultural context

Archaeologists have read history from the mortal remains of our ancestors. A corpse was not simply abandoned. Paul Ballard comments that 'how a society deals with the reality of death embodies our deepest beliefs about the nature and worth of humanity'.[2] The method used for disposing of the dead varies. The British cremate or bury the dead. North Americans like to embalm their dead and then bury in lawn cemeteries, or cremate and send the ashes up into space. Belgians bury the dead and reuse the graves several years later. Hindus burn their dead on open pyres. Masai tribesmen leave their dead for the hyenas to eat. The Jivaros of the East Andes bury women and children under the floorboards of their huts, while placing males seated in the hut and then setting fire to it.

Our ancestors showed a sense of reverence in the face of the mystery of death which is reflected in their funeral rituals. 'Behind these perspectives

---

2 Paul Badham and Paul Ballard (eds), 1996, *Facing Death: An Interdisciplinary Approach*, Cardiff: University of Wales Press, p. 26.

lay the problem of reconciling bodily decay with some inner sense of life as consisting in more than simple bodily existence.'[3] The methods of burial were varied, from the dead who were laid in a foetal position, suggesting rebirth, to others painted with red dye or blood indicating the renewal of life, and the pyramids where the pharaoh was buried with provisions for a journey, his favourite possessions and slaves. Each ritual appears to anticipate an afterlife.

There were exceptions to the respect for death. In tribal communities honour was shown to one's own tribe but not to the bodies of an enemy in battle, which were often brutally mutilated. Another exception was child sacrifice, though this may reflect the giving of the best to propitiate a god (Judg. 11.30–40; 2 Kings 3.27; 2 Kings 16.3; 21.6).

I have noted the triumphs of science, the questioning of religious beliefs, distrust of those in authority and a growing individualism, factors that have affected attitudes and practices connected with funerals; in the Western world funerals are influenced by the Judaeo-Christian cultural tradition.

The early Church's funeral practices

From the beginning, Christians buried their dead. There was a seriousness about funeral rites because of Jesus' burial and their Jewish heritage. Neither corpse nor grave was considered polluting, as it was in many cultures, since Christians believed that Jesus had conquered death and at 'the last day' would raise the dead. Jesus' death and resurrection had consequences for the individual, a hope of life free from guilt and the fear of death, sustained by baptism into his death through immersion, and the breaking of bread, his last meal, symbolized and commanded by Jesus. The first centuries of Christianity were influenced by and incorporated local and pagan customs. Peter Jupp notes four of interest:

1   In some parts of the Church, the Sacrament was placed into the mouth of the corpse, as *viaticum* or food for the journey. This was similar to the Greeks, who placed a coin in the mouth of the corpse, to pay Charon for guiding the soul across the River Styx to the underworld. By 325 giving the Eucharist to the dying was well established.
2   Christians frowned on the drunken pagan feasts at gravesides yet began to bring *refrigerium*, refreshments, to martyrs' tombs, at an annual memorial.

3 Douglas J. Davies, 1997, *Death, Ritual and Belief: The Rhetoric of Funerary Rites*, London and Washington: Cassell, p. 111.

3 They adopted Roman commemoration days called the 'Month's Mind' and 'Year's Mind', which were celebratory Masses, a month/year after the death, rituals later forbidden by the Protestant Reformation.

4 The Church sought to replace the pagan *vestes sordidae* with white clothes. Cyprian stated Christian mourners should not wear black while their dead wore white in heaven. This did not happen, but by the third century, songs of joy and hope were known at Christian funerals. John Chrysostom stated: 'Honour for the dead does not consist in lamentations and moanings, but in singing hymns and psalms and living a noble life.'[4] There were prayers in the house while the deceased was washed, anointed and swathed in white linen.

A procession to the place of burial included the carrying of palms, lights and the burning of incense, all expressing victory over death. A short service happened around the body: praise, thanksgiving, readings and Eucharist, expressing the communion of the living and the dead, with the kiss of peace given to the corpse. Augustine commented on the bodies of martyrs not receiving a covering of earth: 'Such things as a decent funeral and a proper burial, with its procession of mourners, are a consolation to the living rather than a help to the departed.'[5] This gives us some indication of funeral rituals, and their significance at least for Augustine: funerals were for the mourners rather than the deceased.

The medieval period

During the medieval period piety was noted in deathbed and graveside rituals, obituary lists, Masses for the dead, Month's Mind and Year's Mind, relics, tomb sculpture and the observance of All Souls' Day. The funeral liturgy was the preparation of the body for burial, which was accompanied by psalms and prayers, the procession with the body from home to church and a period of prayer for the dead person, which might include the Eucharist. The final act was the procession from the church to the grave, and internment. The ancient custom of continuous psalmody for the dead person had become ritualized in the office of the dead, consisting of vespers, matins and lauds.

In the late medieval period the preparation of the body was done in private without liturgy and the Eucharist became a normal part of the

4 Peter C. Jupp (ed.), 2008, *Death our Future: Christian Theology and Funeral Practice*, London: Epworth Press, p. 69.

5 Augustine, 1984, *The City of God*, Book 1, ch. 12, trans. H. Bettenson, Harmondsworth: Penguin, p. 21.

funeral liturgy. It was followed by responsories and prayers of absolution. There was an increased stress on the need for forgiveness and fear of judgement and also the significance of the priest's absolution, an extension of his power to absolve the living. These developments are seen in the *Dies irae* (twelfth and thirteenth centuries). Earlier themes of hope and joy at funerals were drowned in a medieval emphasis on sin and death, purgatory and judgement, thinking of the soul's destiny rather than the body. The Doom paintings in English churches were used by the early medieval Church as an instrument to highlight the contrasts between the reward of heaven and the agony of hell, in order to guide Christians away from sin.

The Protestant Reformation

This was a turbulent political and religious period from Catholic to Protestant, monarchy to Commonwealth. Cranmer (1489–1556) gradually introduced his Book of Common Prayer (BCP) in 1549–50. Modified in 1552, 1559, 1604 and 1662, the final version has been widely used since, for funerals in England and across the Anglican world. It was biblical in theology. Scripture was read and expounded: the words were, in 1662, meaningful.[6] The Reformation synthesis gave the dead to the earth, in sure and certain hope of the resurrection of the body, which would be reunited with the soul for judgement, followed by heaven or hell. The doctrine of purgatory and prayers for the dead were dropped, having no scriptural authority, Requiem Masses were abolished, which simplified funeral liturgies and moved 'the centre of funeral liturgy from doing something for the departed to moral exhortation of the living'.[7]

Nineteenth and twentieth centuries

There was a Victorian crisis of faith. The doctrine of eternal punishment was an increasing dilemma for Victorians. Alternative views emerged: Anglo-Catholics prayed for the dead; different kinds of afterlife reflected a longing for continuation. However, the introduction and rise in Spiritualism weakened belief in a resurrection of the body. From 1870 a fall in the death rate began. The Great War, with its mass deaths and bereave-

6 R. T. Beckwith, 1992, 'Thomas Cranmer and the Prayer Book', in Cheslyn Jones, Geoffrey Wainwright, Edward Yarnold SJ, Paul Bradshaw (eds), *The Study of Liturgy*, rev. edn, London: SPCK, p. 104.

7 Geoffrey Rowell, 1997, 'Changing patterns: Christian beliefs about death and the future life', in Peter C. Jupp and Tony Rogers (eds), *Interpreting Death: Christian Theology and Pastoral Practice*, London: Cassell, p. 23.

ments, challenged religious beliefs: the doctrines of hell and judgement were casualties. People lost faith in the traditional concepts of an after-life. Spiritualism became increasingly popular, promising people contact with their dead through a medium. Jupp suggests four significant ways in which funeral practices have dramatically changed, all of which affect the scope of the Church's ministry: municipalization, commercialization, consumerization and personalization.[8]

Municipalization

Until 1850, Anglicans controlled the rite, site, mode and presidency of burial; the exceptions were Baptist and Quakers, who had scruples about sacraments and had their own burial grounds. The Established Church needed to reform when the rise of a public health movement, stimulated by cholera epidemics in which many died, drew attention to the squalor of urban burial grounds. In 1850/52 the Burial Laws closed 5,000 urban churchyards within eight years, transferring the responsibility for pro-viding land for burial to secular local authorities. This ended a virtual monopoly by the Anglican Church, which had lasted for a thousand years.[9] The new cemeteries provided by the local authorities were more spacious, but distant, established on the edge of towns, breaking the trad-itional geographical link between the communities of the living and dead. The practical changes affecting the Anglican funeral also challenged the theology, it being easier to develop doctrines about life after death when you are responsible for the funeral rite and the method of disposal. The control by local authorities of funerals and burial became secular and economic.

In the twenty-first century more than 70 per cent of funerals are cre-mation, and of the 30 per cent burials many happen at the crematorium. The development of cremation suggested the physical body had no post-mortem existence but the soul survived. Douglas Davies comments: 'The traditional burial service focuses on the body and its resurrection future ... the only hope that many can read into the cremation service is the hope of a surviving soul.'[10] Seven out of every eight crematoria are owned by the local authority, resulting in budgeting restraints and noted in short opening hours, length of service – varying from 20 to 40 minutes, unless

8 Jupp, *Interpreting Death*, pp. 8–14. I am using Jupp's themes, but in my own way.
9 Jupp, *Interpreting Death*, p. 3.
10 D. J. Davies, 1990, *Cremation Today and Tomorrow*, Nottingham: Grove Books, p. 33.

a double slot is booked and paid for – music facilities limiting what CDs are allowed, rotas of celebrants, and the type of gravestone or memorial permitted.

Christian ministry needs to recognize the momentous challenge to its traditional influence in leading funerals. Though the Church of England's income from funerals is large (£11 m), it is under pressure to improve its professionalism; it is called to be a 'servant church'. It has gifts to offer in the preparation, conducting and follow-up of funerals, with its historical traditions, rituals, liturgy and pastoral care.

Commercialization

Today the funeral market is worth an estimated £1 billion a year. The average funeral costs £3,284. There are more than 600,000 funerals in Britain each year. The companies have grown from part-time entrepreneurs to international chains that are part of the National Association of Funeral Directors (NAFD). In the 1930s the Co-operative Societies entered the funeral industry in an attempt to reduce costs. The US company Service Cooperation International was subject to a British buyout in 2001 and is now Dignity. As the result of criticism of standards, the Funeral Standards Council (FSC) came into being in 1993. In 1995 the Department of the Environment encouraged local authorities to sell their crematoria to private companies – a possible power base for increased commercialization, with funeral memorial masons, florists, maintenance of graves and the development of pre-paid funeral plans tying families into particular, existing, funeral firms. The Burial and Cemeteries Advisory Group of the Ministry of Justice accepted forms of reuse for old graves in 2007. This should enable people to choose burial and use Anglican churchyards again.

There are alternatives to the main funeral providers. In 1991 Nicholas Albery and Josefine Speyer developed the Natural Death Centre (NDC), whose stated aim was 'to inform, empower and inspire the public in all matters relating to death and dying, and in particular to increase awareness of funeral choices outside of the mainstream'. Dying at home for those who desired this, burial with willow and cardboard coffins, woodland burial sites and individual choice in funerals, were all encouraged and extended, diminishing the central place previously played by religion. The NDC run the Association of Natural Burial Grounds, primarily a movement for social change. Their website states: 'We have played a central part in demystifying the traditional funeral, encouraging thousands of families in having the kind of funeral they wanted, and helping create opportunity for new rituals to emerge.' However, it is debatable if vulnerable, grieving families can handle such a responsibility at a time of loss.

The NDC was followed by the charter movements of the 1990s, improving codes of practice. The *Charter for the Bereaved* (1996) and *The Dead Citizen's Charter* advanced choices and rights for individuals. The latter criticizes many modern funerals for being hypocritical, bureaucratic, dull, impersonal and hurried. Its recommendations for better funerals shows concern for the dead and bereaved, for example for a cremation, a request that clergy call to make contact with families and prepare funerals before the event. The Church has a responsibility to train its clergy in the important ministry of working with families at the time of funerals.

Personalization

It was in 1880 that funerals without religious rites were permitted.[11] Humanists have no beliefs in life after death and so celebrate the past life of the deceased and their achievements, neither are prayers part of any ceremony. With no traditional liturgies, and an individualism characteristic of postmodernism, humanists design their own ceremonies to help the need of individual families advised by the British Humanist Movement.[12]

We live in a society in flux, reflected in the rapid changes in funeral practices such as that of the funeral of Diana, Princess of Wales in 1997. There was sorrow and anger, honesty rather than orthodoxy, yet little of the Christian hope of resurrection and eternal life. It was a public, unconventional funeral, reflecting a diverse range of components: John Tavener's Eastern Orthodox 'Song for Athene', the singing of Elton John's 'Candle in the Wind', and her brother's eulogy. The 'Diana event' gave people permission to contribute more to family funerals.

Poppy Mardell runs Poppy's Funerals. She believes that people are not aware of their choices. The organization enables a funeral at any crematorium, woodland burial ground or cemetery in the Greater London area: 'Free from the formality and conventions of the traditional funeral you can create a ceremony in your own style and on your own terms. We believe families know best, so we support you every step of the way.' Barbara Chalmers launched FinalFling.com in October 2012. It concerns a person making choices about their own funeral. She was asked: 'Is it

---

11 R. Fletcher, 1974, *The Akenham Burial Case*, London: Wildwood House.

12 Jane Wynne Willson, 2006, *Funerals without God: A Practical Guide to Humanist and Non-religious Funeral Ceremonies*, London: British Humanist Association.

about putting fun into funerals?' and replied, 'No, it's putting the rich into ritual.' Chalmers has dealt with a funeral provider that does *Star Trek* and rock'n'roll themed funerals and a range of humanist funerals. These companies are suggesting choice of words, music, new rituals and funerals custom built, with coffins increasingly decorated to reflect the occupant's personality (see www.picture-coffins.co.uk).

The personalization and secularization of funerals is a trend that Christian ministers, lay and ordained, need to be aware of and is a pastoral and mission opportunity.

Anglican rites and liturgy

In the annual statistics of the Church of England for 2011, 162,526, funerals were conducted, an average of just under 2,500 a week. There are three funeral services: the Book of Common Prayer (1662), used for those who request it, mainly older church members; the rubric limits the use to those who have been baptized. The BCP rite is austere, emerging from the theological controversy of the Protestant Reformation, at the heart of which was the Requiem Mass, removed since it included prayers for the dead. However, in Westminster Abbey on All Saints' Day 1919, William Temple said in a public sermon, 'Let us pray for those who we know and love who have passed on to the other life ... But do not be content to pray for them. Let us also ask them to pray for us.' Growth continues beyond the grave and we pray for the dead not because we believe that God will otherwise neglect them, but because 'we claim the privilege of uniting our love for them with God's'.[13] Another rite is a modified version of BCP (1928), known as 'Series One', influenced by the wastage of life in the 1914–18 war and the consequent grief. The 1928 Prayer Book introduced alternative psalms and Scripture readings and new prayers, more than one expressing the belief that Christians could legitimately pray for the dead, or at least for the 'faithful departed'. Series One became authorized in 1967, carrying with it the language of the BCP. Praying for the dead has continued to be a problem. Michael Perham believes that the issue is theological and indicates a weaker view of the eschaton: does the individual come to God's judgement at the moment of death, or is there a provisionality until the end? Classic Protestant theology, within Anglicanism, believes that prayer for the dead is improper because at death destiny

---

13 Alan Wilkinson, 1978, *The Church of England and the First World War*, London: SPCK, p. 178.

is settled.[14] Bishop Ian Ramsay chaired the Doctrine Commission, which attempted an approach for all: 'May God in his infinite love and mercy bring the whole Church, living and departed in the Lord Jesus, to a joyful resurrection and the fulfilment of his eternal kingdom.' This became part of the *Alternative Service Book (1980)*. There is also a funeral rite in *Common Worship*. The Introduction to the *Pastoral Services* volume (2000) speaks of the journey through life as being accompanied by God, who may be mediated through others:

> As on a medieval pilgrimage, different people on the road have different backgrounds and a variety of family relationships ... On the funeral and bereavement journey ... these services ... put that journey in the context of the Church, the Church which prays, which celebrates which cares.

The liturgists of *Common Worship* recognized the need, for the sake of the bereaved, to 'embody a flexibility' of liturgy, 'to adjust to different pastoral situations', implied by a church on the move. Services also needed 'to reflect that dependability, consistency and stability, which is implied by the long history of the Church's worship, traditions and buildings', serving a God 'continually doing new things, drawing his new creation to himself'.[15]

The report of the Doctrine Commission of the General Synod of the Church of England, *The Mystery of Salvation: The Story of God's Gift*, defined the Christian funeral as 'a commendation of the soul into the hands of God', and in this context, 'language about the soul indicates that living centre of human personality, which is no longer present in the dead body before us'. Leaving theories behind, experience of being with someone who dies in our presence assures us that 'something has gone'. The report goes on: 'A commendation into the hands of God is a commendation into a deeper participation in the communion of God's love, which is God's being and so into the communion of saints.'[16]

---

14 Michael Perham, 1997, *New Handbook of Pastoral Liturgy*, London: SPCK, pp. 159–60.

15 *Common Worship: Pastoral Services and Prayers for the Church of England*, 2000, London: Church House Publishing, p. 3.

16 Doctrine Commission of the General Synod of the Church of England, 1995, *The Mystery of Salvation: The Story of God's Gift*, London: Church House Publishing.

The Roman Catholic rite

The *Order of Christian Funerals* (1990) was the result of 20 years' work. It is a resource rather than one rite to be performed in all circumstances. It contains 47 prayers for the deceased, addressed for all sorts and circumstances, such as death by suicide, and 15 prayers for mourners. The liturgy includes the potential for lay involvement and aims to facilitate bereavement. It can be a staged funeral, a sequence of separate but related rites and a flexible liturgy, 'attentive to the needs of the family and adapted to local custom'.[17]

The Free Churches

Baptists, Methodists and the United Reformed Church do not regularly use set forms of worship, although their ministers use texts for the occasional offices such as the funeral. The Baptist Union of Great Britain (BUGB) issued its service book in 2005, *Gathering for Worship: Patterns and Prayers for the Community of Disciples*. It is not mandatory, so is used patchily. The section on funerals is entitled, 'Confronting Death – Celebrating Resurrection', signifying the recognition of the pain of bereavement together with the hope in Christ. There are two patterns of funeral rite: the first begins with a service in church followed by a committal; the second begins with a committal followed by a service of thanksgiving. Within each are a variety of provisions, minimal prayers for those near to death, varying funerals: for a child, a suicide, an adult, for multi-stage rites of death and bereavement, and a rite for the burial of ashes. Baptists have reservations about praying for the dead.

The Methodist Church has the *Methodist Worship Book* (1999), which has a range of separate services, such as 'Prayers in the Home or Hospital after a Death' and 'A Funeral in a Church, a Crematorium or a Cemetery, leading to Committal'.[18] There is a liturgical feel to the services, with texts from the patristic and medieval prayers of the Christian Church.

The United Reformed Church (URC) has pastoral offices in the second volume of *Worship: From the United Reformed Church* (2004). There is a range of services and staged rites from which the minister may choose. The final comment in the Introduction states: 'There is always more to do

---

17 Geoffrey Steel, in Jupp and Rogers (eds), *Interpreting Death*, p. 174.
18 *The Methodist Worship Book*, 1999, Peterborough: Methodist Publishing House, pp. 433, 502.

than read from "the Book".'[19] Paul Sheppy, a Baptist minister, who has written in this area of ministry, comments: 'All three books unapologetically offer Christian funeral rites; how well they adapt to the funerals of those without faith or to mourners of different faiths or none is problematic.'[20]

A funeral is a rite of passage in which emotions are expressed – sorrow, relief, anger – depending on the nature of the death. A ritual is a deliberate repeated pattern of activity of symbolic meaning, which may help the needs of bereaved people, psychological, social, spiritual and practical.[21] Liturgy is 'the work of the people'. Rituals change; for example at one time funerals involved wearing black but this is now no longer always the case. The Dutch anthropologist Arnold van Gennep understood that ritual was needed to achieve the traumatic change at a death. He noted this as three stages: pre-liminal, liminal and post-liminal. These can be encompassed in the funeral service, liminal is defined as 'relating to a transitional change; a boundary or a threshold'. In Britain these stages may be a service in the crematorium taking 20 minutes, in a church about an hour, followed by either a short litany at the crematorium and later words at the burial of the body, or burial or scattering of ashes.

We can apply van Gennep's stages to the Anglican *Common Worship* funeral service.

The pre-liminal stage enables the bereaved to acknowledge the reality of the death and to begin to separate from the dead loved one. The material in *Common Worship: Pastoral Services* (*CWPS*) provides for prayers in the home. In some parts of the country the coffin stops there before going to the church. There are prayers for receiving the body at the church before the service, when the family may put a 'pall' – the cloth covering the coffin – or a Bible or cross on the bare coffin, for others it may be symbols of the deceased's life. There is here a note of the bleak reality of death: 'To commend him/her to God ... to commend his/her body to be buried/cremated', and in one of the prayers of commendation the theme of transition is definite: 'Go forth from this world ...'

The liminal stage of the rite involves the transition from the sorrow and pain of the bereaved to a life without the loved one. This may be through

---

19 *Worship: From the United Reformed Church*, 2004, London: United Reformed Church, pp. 189–250.

20 Paul Sheppy, 2008, 'Free Church Liturgies', in Peter. C. Jupp (ed.), *Death Our Future*, Peterborough: Epworth, pp. 179–89.

21 Ewan Kelly, 2008, *Meaningful Funerals: Meeting the Theological and Pastoral Challenge in a Postmodern Era*, London and New York: Mowbray, p. 7of., has a useful list of funeral rituals.

the address, a thanksgiving remembering the reality of the unique life, the bereaved and their needs in the sight of God, not that 'time heals', which suggests speed and a moving on without the loved one, rather, as pointed out by the sociologist Tony Walter, the funeral is the beginning of a process of relating to the dead in new ways. A second place in the service where a transition is recognized is in the intercessions. *CWPS* recognizes the differing grief of those mourning, influenced by the type of death and the need for prayers in public recognition and comfort of the bereaved.

The post-liminal stage is concerned with the reincorporation of the bereaved into society, through living without their loved one. This can remind the other mourners of their role in sensitive care of those close to the deceased over what may be a lengthy time. In Britain many of these rituals are compressed into little more than a single service, so the movement of the funeral has to signal the shape of changes in the lives of the nearest loved ones.

Through the centuries the purpose of funerals has been influenced by, and influences, the cultural context in which it is set. With the demise of religious beliefs and the gradual reacceptance of acknowledging death, there has been a greater variety of funerals available. In the preparation of a Christian funeral and the service, a theology of incarnation emerges and a theology of hope in an afterlife.

Questions for reflection and response

- Do some research on the Doom paintings and the theology that undergirds them.
- Choose a period of history to demonstrate the changes in funeral practices, giving reasons for these.
- What different theologies might underpin cremation and burial?
- Think about the comment that modern funerals allow the bereaved to create their own funerals. What are your thoughts about this?

Reflection on insights from Scripture and the tradition

What do we know about funerals in the Scriptures, and what insights emerge? In the account of the raising of the son of the widow of Nain (Luke 7.7–11) the word *soros* is used, meaning an open coffin. Touching a corpse brought ritual impurity (Num. 19.11, 16), Jesus bypassed these laws in an act of compassion. When Jesus is called to help Jairus, he is delayed and then told Jairus' daughter is dead. He goes to the house and finds a commotion, loud weeping and wailing (Matt. 9.18–26; Mark 5.22–43; Luke 8.40–56). There is flute playing as part of mourning (Matt. 9.23). Jesus takes the girl's hand.

Lazarus is buried in a rock tomb, a natural cave with shafts either vertical or horizontal (John 11.1–44). His body was bound with winding strips around the hands and feet; a napkin, literally a cloth for wiping perspiration, covered the face. It is suggested that only the faces of the poor were covered in this way.[22] Mary suggests the body would stink when Jesus asks for the tomb to be opened. The putrefaction suggests that Lazarus' body was not embalmed, and it was the fourth day. In popular Jewish thinking this was the day of the absolute dissolution of the life. The face was unrecognizable with certainty. The body bursts, and the soul, which had until then hovered over the body, departed.

Jesus' burial

Burial was normally on the day of death. The bodies of criminals – Jesus was counted as such by the Romans – had to be buried before sundown. However, the Romans often left them to decay, or be eaten by vultures, as a public warning to potential dissidents. The Gospel accounts are not consistent; for example the day of Jesus' burial had to be quick because of the Sabbath and the Passover – were these consecutive or the same day (Mark 15.42–47; Matt. 27.57–61; Luke 23.50–56; John 19.38–42)? Who took the body down and pleaded with Pilate – Joseph alone (Synoptic Gospels) or Joseph and Nicodemus (John 19.39)? Luke records that the women watched Joseph take the body towards the tomb, then they left to get spices and ointments to anoint the body after the Sabbath (Luke 23.56).

For the Jew, burial was an act of piety; it must be done (2 Sam. 21.12–14; Tobit 1.17–19; 2.3–7). The poor were buried in the earth, the rich in caves that were sealed, the bones retrieved after a year and kept in an ossuary. The bodies of the rich were wrapped in linen cloth. Linen was a symbol of immortality at this time; it came from flax, which, grown in the earth, was considered life-giving.[23] The linen was bought, or possessed, by Joseph. This was an embalming, the layers of linen interspersed with a vast amount of myrrh and aloe spices brought by Nicodemus, 'according to the burial customs of the Jews' (John 19.40). The rock tomb was new,

22 C. K. Barrett, 1965, *The Gospel according to St John: Introduction with Commentary on the Greek Text*, London: SPCK, p. 337.

23 R. J. Karris, 1993, *The Gospel according to Luke*, The New Jerome Bible Commentary, London: Geoffrey Chapman, p. 720.

one Joseph had for his own burial, a sign of his wealth. It was in a garden (John 19.41) near the place of crucifixion. The tomb was sealed with a rock and later a watch put on it (Matt. 27.62–66).

The Scriptures depict an attention to detail: a ritual of public mourning practices, including wailing, a speedy burial, depending on wealth, the poor directly in the earth, the wealthy in rock tombs or a cave, wrapped in linen and embalmed.

Insights from other faiths

The Abrahamic faiths

Jews bury their dead as soon as possible after death. Historically this reflects living in a hot country where the body quickly decomposes. Today the custom remains of having the funeral close to the death, though not on the Sabbath or a Jewish holiday. Jewish tradition believes that the soul is immortal, though for many liberal Jews immortality comes through the action of the descendants not the immortality of the soul. Many synagogues have memorial plaques; the deceased's memory lives on through giving money and donating their clothes to a charity. Among Ashkenazi Jews there is a tradition of naming children after the deceased. Actions like these can help the mourner and provide release of emotions, therefore being therapeutic. These occasions demonstrate the reality of death and loss, the pain of what is gone, yet the refusal to fall into hopelessness.

Cremation was legalized in Britain in 1884. In the Orthodox community cremation is not permitted. It is allowed in the Liberal and Reformed communities. However, there are secular Jews, who will seek the ancient tradition of a burial.

The deceased may be wrapped in his or her prayer shawl (*tallit*), then placed in a plain coffin. Elaborate coffins are not common, since all are equal in death. The chief mourners are the parents, spouse, children and siblings of the deceased. In traditional communities an everyday garment of each of the chief mourners is cut – tie, shirt or blouse – 'a biblically sanctioned action that allows lacerating feelings of grief (or rage) to find a safe outlet in the presence of death'.[24] Flowers are not customarily part of the Jewish funeral; mourners overcome feelings of helplessness by contributing towards a charity. The funeral service is short and dignified, usually with an address stating the good qualities and achievements of

---

24 Howard Cooper, 2013, 'Reflections on Jewish approaches to death, grief and mourning', in Stephen Oliver (ed.), *Inside Grief*, London: SPCK, p. 108.

the deceased. The liturgy includes the words, 'The Eternal has given and the Eternal has taken away: may the name of the Eternal be blessed' (Job 1.21).[25] At its heart is the traditional prayer, the Kaddish, which, though not mentioning death, is ingrained in Jewish consciousness. Rabbi Cooper states:

> at the graveside all present are encouraged to fill the grave with earth; the hands-on physicality of this can have a powerful impact, as the sight and sound of the earth hitting the coffin makes the finality of the event of death psychologically real.[26]

On returning to the prayer hall, seated mourners say traditional words of hope, that they will be 'comforted with all the mourners of Zion and Jerusalem'. The mourners are greeted individually with the words, 'I wish you long life.'

In Islam, immediately after death, the body is laid on a flat board with feet together, arms to the side, eyes closed and the chin wrapped in a cloth to prevent the mouth opening. The body is washed to cleanse it from impurity, and to prepare the deceased for what awaits him or her. Reading from the Qur'an and chants often accompany the washing. The washers clean themselves three times, before washing the deceased. The water may be mixed with perfume or herbs. The body is cleansed in parts, so that at no time is it entirely visible and is saved from the shame against which the deceased cannot defend him- or herself. This washing must be done by Muslims of the same sex as the deceased, at the mosque, or at the home if the person dies at home, before being shrouded in pieces of white linen. Some Muslims lament loudly, others try to accept and contain grief.

Burial takes place to allow the soul to travel speedily to paradise. In the local mosque, funeral prayers take place, if possible on Friday, the day of prayer, as early in the service as possible. These are preceded by a short ritual to say farewell, pray for the deceased and join in ceremonial forgiving of sin. The cloth covering the face is laid aside. Some crowd around the body at this point to touch and kiss the face before burial. The imam asks, 'Was this a good or bad man/woman?', and all present answer, 'Good'. Burial takes place by men only. The dead are believed to remain in the grave to await judgement. North African women mourn in white, Middle Eastern in black, and Turkish in subdued colours. Women

---

25 Jewish Funeral Service, 2009, *Forms of Prayer V: Funeral Service*, London: Movement for Reform Judaism, p. 19.

26 Cooper, 'Reflections on Jewish approaches to death', p. 110.

are separated from the men at the funeral, since it is thought their weeping will upset the dead.[27]

Family and community members follow the funeral procession to the graveyard, where a final prayer is said. At the burial, the body in its shroud is taken out of the coffin and put in the ground facing Mecca. There are no headstones; all graves look the same, Muslims are equal in death.

The Eastern faiths

Hindus see death as a natural process in the existence of the soul, which makes several reincarnations on the basis of karma. The greater the karma, the better. Hindus cremate the body at death.

In the East, mourners take up residence in the courtyard of the house of the bereaved. Funeral rituals last for 12 days, during which time the family and guests sleep on the floor and eat only vegetarian food. Prayers are said, chants sung, and there are readings from the holy books. Friends join after ablutions at sunrise and at sunset. They visit the body in the house, which is shrouded in a white sheet on the floor with face uncovered. The sons in white sit on stools, bare-chested with the sacred thread diagonally across. They are then ritually shaved.

The following day a group constructs the bier, others prepare meals for all the guests, the family priest and the sons prepare the body. The latter are dressed in white. They wash the body with perfumed water, then oil and anoint it. Finally, with the face uncovered, they wrap it in muslin and place it on the bier. It is tied there and decorated with flowers, marigolds and jasmine and carried to the courtyard. The widow wipes out her wedding mark, *sindoor*. She and other close female relatives will wear a white sari for a year after the death and shave their heads, apart from a small tuft. There is much wailing, as all come and see the body for the last time.

Then the bier is carried in procession to be cremated at the burning *ghat*, where the pyre is lit by the eldest son. Close relatives wait until they hear the skull crack open, so that the spirit can depart. Mourners chant and wail encouraging grief. At a further ceremony the ashes are scattered in the water of the River Ganges. Beggars are fed as a tribute to the deceased. Those who can afford it prefer to fly the bodies back to India, since it is very difficult to carry out the rituals mentioned above in

---

27 G. Jonken, 1997, 'The many facets of Islam. Death, dying and disposal between orthodox rule and historical convention', in Colin Murray Parkes, Pittu Laungani and Bill Young (eds), *Death and Bereavement across Cultures*, London and New York: Routledge, p. 165.

a country like the UK where the rituals are not known by nurses when a person dies in hospital.

For Buddhists, death is regarded as of major significance, for the deceased and the bereaved, marking the transition to a new mode of existence. At death the karmic forces that the dead person accumulated during his or her life become activated and determine the next rebirth. Death is a powerful reminder of the Buddha's teaching on impermanence in life. The funeral is presided over by monks and is a cremation. There are many cultural variations.

Questions for reflection and response

- Explore the understanding that, for the Jew, burial was an act of piety (2 Sam. 21.12–14; Tobit 1.17–19; 2.3–7).
- Biblical readings from *Common Worship* for a funeral service are:
  - John 6.35–40; John 11.17–27; John 14.1–6
  - Romans 8.31–39
  - 1 Corinthians 15
  - Revelation 21.1–5
  - Psalm 23.

  Choose one of these readings and explore how you would use it to preach the gospel and integrate statements about the deceased's life.
- Why are rituals significant in a funeral service?
- Collect some funeral service sheets. Assess and comment on them as an aid to the bereaved.

Reflections on cultural context in dialogue with Scripture and the tradition

The context of funerals has changed substantially in the last 150 years, leading to a variety of services, from the Book of Common Prayer with its emphasis on sin and redemption, to a humanist celebration of life in a decorated coffin. These changes have been wrought by the creation of local authority crematoria, urbanization, increased longevity, the experience of the devastation of war, the growth of the funeral business, commercialization and the decline of religious faith.

Today the philosophy of postmodernism is dominant. It is defined as threefold: the collapse of metanarratives, a culturally held consensus; the autonomy of the individual, making one's own world of meaning; and a divide between the public and the private. In the past the Christian meta-narrative or story was seminal to beliefs held, with authority given to Scripture and clergy as the interpreters. This is no longer so. For some Christians there are fewer absolutes and more questions, arising from the complexity of our world, particularly the insights of science. The research into the worship and reflective habits of the population in Kendal discovered that although churches having a higher or external authority are out of step with popular culture, other spiritual activities are attracting people, which enable individuals to search for meaning in their own experience.[28]

Postmodernism has had a profound effect on the ritual and words around funerals. The Scriptures witness to customs of public mourning over death, rituals and prayers that have informed the funeral rites. There are historical liturgies, still in use, written in an age that assumed the Christian story, the language of a theology of incarnation, community (Trinity) and hope, that are not always understood in our culture. However, it is these very doctrines, which the tradition has proclaimed, that can inform the ways in which as 'ministers' we help Christians who turn to their church in times of bereavement and funerals. Some believe that the funeral needs to uphold the historical tradition and be obedient to the gospel, since salvation is a result of belief, repentance, commitment and faith. Other Christians believe that in the end all will be saved. The tradition is, however, a process that is ongoing as God's people attempt to make sense of their faith in the context in which they live, in other words as they do theology. Can we represent a servant church, which is pastoral, and balance the interests of the deceased, the bereaved, the Church's doctrines and our own theology as Christian ministers, lay and ordained?

Questions for reflection and response

- What effect has postmodernism had on funeral rites? Is this significant to you as a Christian minister?
- Why do bereaved families turn to the Church for funerals?
- What differences are there for a 'servant church' in the taking of a funeral?
- What are the prime considerations in taking a funeral?

---

28 The Kendal Project: Patterns of the Sacred in Contemporary Society, Department of Religious Studies, Lancaster University, 1999–2003. Kendal is a small town in the English Lake District.

Pastoral practice

This chapter is about a Christian funeral. Sometimes we are approached directly by relatives, familiar to us. We are likely to know about the deceased, as a member of the congregation, whose name has been on the prayer sheet, who has been visited and is known. Members of the congregation want a Christian funeral for their deceased loved one. For the older generation this sometimes means the BCP, for others a liturgy from *CWPS*. We are expected, and indeed it is a joy, to respond to those to whom we have been called to minister in our congregations. These will be members of the church by baptism and commitment. Their care at the end of life and through the funeral is what we think of as a 'Christian funeral'.

What is the purpose of the service? Michael Perham states that a Christian funeral seeks to bring a community together:

- to honour a life
- to commend the dead to God
- to give space for grief and yet to move people on
- to express the love and compassion of God to the bereaved
- to proclaim the gospel message of Christ's death and resurrection
- to warn of the inevitability of death and to encourage the bereaved to walk in this life with an eye on eternity
- to take leave of the body and to say farewell; to dispose of the body reverently.[29]

This is rooted in theological beliefs that the individual is precious and significant. People become persons when their uniqueness and distinctiveness is acknowledged and celebrated. Personhood is ultimately established and sustained by God, so we are remembering the dead *before God*, witnessing to a life and giving thanks for it. This is done by being honest; it is essential that the deceased is real for the mourner. If there is no connection with reality because we have eulogized the deceased, then it is unlikely that statements about God will be heard as real either. This needs care and sensitivity, a theology of incarnation. God is our ground of hope. Our hope is in God not because of who I am but because of who God is. The service will vary according to the situation, but it is the same hope in God. Hope is communicated in the words of hymns, readings, prayers and the address. It is important to remember and acknowledge the mourners.

---

29 Michael Perham, 2000, *New Handbook of Pastoral Liturgy*, London: SPCK, p. 195.

Grief at the loss of a loved one is a natural part of being human. We acknowledge loss while offering an assurance that life will continue.

The service in church

The service has six sections: Gathering, Readings and Address, Prayers, Commendation and Farewell, Committal and Dismissal.

The Gathering includes the reception of the coffin, if not already in church where the paschal candle is lit beside it; or the coffin is led in by the minister, with words of Scripture, carrying the paschal candle. The candle is a symbol of continuing life beyond death; a white pall can be placed over the coffin by the family; suitable symbols of the life of the departed placed beside the coffin. Water may be sprinkled round the coffin, a symbol of the baptism of the deceased into the life of faith.

A greeting, welcoming those present, enables the minister to bind the congregation together, particularly if the bereaved family are far-flung geographically. An introduction to the service is followed by a hymn in which all can participate. This is followed by prayers of thankfulness to God for the life lived, and prayers of penitence, which may take the form of the Kyrie eleison or short sentences of invitation followed by silence for thoughts. The deceased stands under the judgement of God and some of the bereaved have a sense of guilt. Thoughts and prayers may be about forgiving the deceased, or about forgiveness for the guilt of omission. This is reconciliation with the past, followed by an absolution, then the collect.

A choice of readings is found in denominational service books. This can be followed by Psalm 23. The address or sermon follows. It is helpful if this weaves the gospel into the story of the life of the deceased, so that a Christian life can be seen within the greater story of the Scriptures and God's relationship with us. It is a demanding task, since the minister needs to be real about the deceased and yet speaking to the bereaved, who may be fragile and hurting. Michael Perham states that the minister speaks for God, as spokesperson for the congregation, 'trusted with articulating what the mourners are thinking ... charged with saying enough to allow people to have their own thoughts and do their remembering ... speaking for them from inside their grief and speaking to them from outside in the name of God and of the Church'.[30] The prayers follow: thanksgiving for the deceased, prayers for the mourners, prayers for the congregation to live in the light of eternity, followed by the Lord's Prayer.

---

30 Perham, *New Handbook*, p. 200.

The following section of the service is the commendation and farewell. The minister stands beside the coffin; the family can be invited to participate, placing hands on the coffin. This is followed by silence and the prayer of commendation. This can be an alternative time for the sprinkling of the water of baptism. If the coffin is to be buried in the churchyard, the coffin can be taken out at this point for the committal, and similarly with the crematorium, if the congregation are attending and it is geographically near. The committal consists of words of Scripture, a text and prayer. Finally comes the dismissal – a blessing for all present. Dependent on the wishes of the family, though unusual unless High Church, the funeral is in the context of a Eucharist, saying goodbye to a Christian within the declaration of the death and resurrection of Christ and the communion of saints. Perham suggests, 'A funeral Eucharist is a powerful Easter liturgy.'

My youngest sister died nine days before Christmas, leaving a bewildered husband and a teenage daughter. Although she was popular and we knew that her friends and work colleagues would want to attend the funeral, her three sisters realized that her husband and daughter could not cope. The pastoral need was paramount. We arranged a quiet unannounced Christian funeral service two days before Christmas in the church where she had worshipped. We then went to the crematorium. In the middle of February we held a service of thanksgiving: her daughter and friends played wind instruments, a group from her choir contributed, and teachers who were colleagues gave a tribute. There were hymns, poetry, a family tribute, prayers and a retiring offering divided between the church and Cancer Care, followed by a display of family photos and nibbles in the village hall. The church was packed: it was truly a celebration of her Christian life.

Questions for reflection and response

- From experience, what would you hope to establish in an initial visit to a bereaved Christian family?
- Answer the following questions in your journal at a quiet time. Notice your own emotions while you answer them:
  - What does 'death' mean to you?
  - Who would you like to take your funeral?
  - Who would you like to be present?
  - What would you like said?
  - What do you believe about the afterlife?
- What theology underlies the Christian funeral service?

- What, do you think, is the function or usefulness of
  (a) a funeral in church?
  (b) a cremation service?
  (c) a thanksgiving celebration?
  Whose 'needs' are most served at funerals?

Further reading

Mark Earey, 2012, *Worship that Cares: An Introduction to Pastoral Liturgy*, London: SCM Press.

R. Anne Horton, 2000, *Using Common Worship Funerals*, London: Church House Publishing.

Hugh James, 2004, *A Fitting End: Making the Most of a Funeral*, Norwich: Canterbury Press.

Ewan Kelly, 2008, *Meaningful Funerals: Meeting the Theological and Pastoral Challenge in a Postmodern Era*, London and New York: Mowbray.

5

Liturgy, Theology and Funerals for the Non-Churched

Said a father to his daughter, 'You are always late, you will be late for your own funeral!' The daughter responded, 'Yes I hope that I am.'

The chapter begins with the challenge brought by a family who are unfamiliar with the Church, yet ask for a church funeral. Theological reflection follows. A recent report on types of funerals and changes in funeral practice is considered, and the opportunities for Christian ministry to the non-churched. This includes the importance of grief. Scriptural insights come from the idea of the 'outsider', the non-Jew in the Hebrew Scriptures. In the New Testament the 'outsider' is included. The non-churched can be thought of as outsiders, though known and loved by God. Scripture and cultural context are brought together in critical dialogue, leading to a theology of grief, of vulnerable incarnation, a merciful God and pastoral sensitivity in working alongside the bereaved in preparing for a funeral.

Pastoral circle

Pastoral practice: co-constructing a funeral

Experience – theological reflection: non-churched asking for a funeral

Cultural context: research by Co-op Funeralcare; significance of grief

Scripture and tradition: The outsider, Jesus' attitude

Scripture/cultural context; theology of grief; vulnerable: incarnation and God

Experience

> Trevor came into the hospice as an emergency. His breathing was laboured. He was in a small ward with the curtains round him. Either side of him were his two daughters, each talking on their mobiles about their dad's condition. As chaplain I was asked to help. I went and sat with the family and tried to initiate a conversation.
>
> An hour or so later, Trevor died. I was able to make little contact with the family. Having spoken my condolences to them, I left them to their grief and to one another.
>
> Later that day I received a phone call from the funeral directors asking if I could take the funeral, since the family did not know anyone else. I obtained the family's address and phoned them to arrange a meeting. I went to see them the following day – a conversation developed.

Reflection on experience

As chaplain of the hospice I had no chance of getting to know Trevor. Experience told me that he was dying, but I could not force Christianity – he was vulnerable, I wanted to respect him and his family. I have found that on such occasions there is an opportunity simply to be silent with the family, and pastoral, praying if it feels appropriate, while recognizing that the public are not familiar with dying and death and may never have seen a corpse.

I knew that God was present; I prayed within myself for Trevor and committed him to a merciful and loving Creator God.

On visiting the family at home I asked Trevor's wife to tell me about her husband.

Trevor's wife said: 'He was a bugger. I'm glad to be shot of him.'

His daughter said: 'Mum, you can't just say that – you have to give the vicar some help about Dad. We want a decent funeral.'

Eventually the mother and daughters decided that they wanted some music to listen to, a hymn, 'Jerusalem' ('everyone knows it'), 'Abide with me' and the Lord's Prayer. A work colleague, a volunteer in the chaplaincy team, later rang me and said, 'Old Trevor was a right so-and-so. There will be a crowd at his funeral, since the standard of his work was greatly respected in his trade. But ... I want to suggest to you, since you are taking the funeral, that his colleagues had no time for him. He was a cheat and always got the job by undercutting them. And his wife ... well, he treated her like dirt, never gave her a birthday or anniversary present in his life.' I had been warned, and wondered what on earth I was going to do at the funeral, which was to be in a chapel in the grounds of the local authority's crematorium.

Funerals are difficult occasions. Despite having no church connections, people in their hour of need turn to the Church's ministers and chaplains, who are seen as a safe pair of hands, providing some form of ritual, and holding together the emotions of the occasion. It is easier for a hospice or hospital chaplain to do this than ministers in parishes or other communities, since 80 per cent of visits requested by relatives following a hospice or hospital admission are from the non-churched.

Trevor was a skilled craftsman creating marquees used for weddings and other celebrations. I thought of marquees as something like large tents, which led me to think of Paul, a tent-maker by trade. Within the funeral I talked about Paul, known through his letters, a challenging character, sometimes benign, at other times angry, a working man whose hands, and probably eyes, bore the marks of his trade. Pride in his work was important to Paul, as to Trevor, and the beneficiaries of both appreciated their skills. Links between the stories of the two men were made. I mentioned that Paul had a commitment to a wider vision of building a community of peace and justice across racial divisions, of helping people to appreciate one another.

Questions for reflection and response

- What else could have been said within the funeral given the hospice experience and the conversations in the home?
- Weigh up the different reasons you think that people, who have no church connections, look to the Church for help with a funeral. Are they wise to do this?
- Are churches wise to take on the responsibility of a funeral of non-church people? Can this be mission?
- What is the aim of a funeral with non-church people?

Reflection on cultural context using insights from the social sciences

In Chapter 4 I indicated the context of funerals and the extensive changes that have occurred; I continue to illustrate this with a report from one of Britain's largest funeral companies, Co-operative Funeralcare.

Co-operative Funeralcare are responsible for about 100,000 funerals a year. Their study reflects comments from staff and clients from 550 of their establishments, published in a booklet, *The ways we say goodbye: A study of twenty-first-century funeral customs in the UK* (2012).[1] The main message is that the 'twenty-first-century funeral is undergoing funda-mental change. Traditionally viewed as a time of mourning, the ceremony is now increasingly a celebration of a person's life' (p. 2). It continues: 'What many people are celebrating is the uniqueness of the individual: their character, their passions and interests, the thing that made them unique.'

The content of funerals is changing: choosing a theme, which may be a mixture of traditional or contemporary, words, music, coffin and hearse. Two in three funerals that Co-operative Funeralcare arrange are classed as 'traditional', that is, they follow the established rites of a religion, led by a religious minister at a place of worship. There are 'contemporary' funerals with an element of religion, perhaps a hymn, a prayer, or the services of a minister of religion, but there is a personalization and a celebration expressed through music, words, flowers or coffin decoration. Just over 10 per cent of funerals are classed as 'humanist', which may be led by a humanist officiant, or family and friends of the deceased.[2] The booklet states that people don't just want religion spoken about. The funeral is more an occasion. This does not resonate with my own experience. There is a deep sense of loss at a funeral, and the expression of grief is important. If the deceased is a young mother who died of breast cancer, leaving a distraught husband and children, there is a sense of anger at being cheated of life and concern for the future of the children. A fatality caused by a drunken driver creates anger and sometimes a search for revenge.

The funeral service

The report states that religious music is declining and that secular choices are increasing. These are songs the family associate with the person, such as 'My way', 'Angels', 'Wind beneath my wings', 'Simply the best', 'Danny

---

1 www.co-operativefuneralcare.co.uk.

2 Jane Wynne Willson, 2006, *Funerals without God: A Practical Guide to Human-ist and Non-Religious Funeral Ceremonies*, London: British Humanist Association.

Boy' and the use of live music such as bagpipes, Spanish guitars and jazz bands. The eulogy plays a significant part, often given by a member of the family, or the leader of the occasion. Co-operative Funeralcare has a guide to eulogies, *Well Chosen Words*.[3] The range of poems has been extended and orders of service often include photos and stories of the deceased and refer to the ceremony as a celebration of a life. In my experience 'a celebration of life' is for remembering with thankfulness the life now physically gone, but with memories and influence continuing, at an occasion later than the funeral, which is a time when loss and grief are foremost in the minds of the bereaved, faced with the reality of the coffin. This later occasion is sometimes called a 'memorial service' and may not be in the context of worship. For non-believers it makes sense to create a ritual conveying life-values reflecting the memories of the deceased by family, friends and workmates.

Black remains a colour for funerals, though other colours are emerging; for a younger person, relatives may ask the congregation to wear the favourite colour of the deceased. At the graveside, earth was thrown, symbolic of our origins and destiny, today petals are thrown, music is sometimes played and balloons, bubbles or doves released. It is interesting to ponder the meaning given to these very different rituals. The ashes of the deceased can be scattered, buried or kept; a recent option is using them in a piece of jewellery. Some ashes are never collected, an interesting comment on attitudes to death.

Funeral services within the Church

The funeral service within Anglicanism is called an 'Occasional Office'. Michael Perham notes that in a normally law-abiding church, driven by pastoral concerns those conducting funerals depart from the legal provisions more than on any other liturgical occasion. He reasons that 'both the Book of Common Prayer (1662) and the Alternative Service Book (1980) are light years away from where most mourners are'.[4] The BCP is austere. The Introduction of *Common Worship Pastoral Services* states that church liturgy needs to embody flexibility, adjusting to different pastoral situations while reflecting the dependability, consistency and stability that is implied by the long history of the Church, its worship,

---

3 www.co-operativefuneralcare.co.uk/writingatribute.

4 Michael Perham, 1997, 'Anglican funeral rites today and tomorrow', in Peter C. Jupp and Tony Rogers (eds), *Interpreting Death: Christian Theology and Pastoral Practice*, London and Herndon, VA: Cassell.

traditions and buildings.[5] This suggests it is possible to adapt the funeral service as a pastoral act. Tess Ward suggests that Anglican clergy (her own tradition) humanize the service and adds that this can enrich and renew the strong heritage of tradition.[6]

Non-church and traditional funerals

Tess Ward has addressed the issue of non-church people and church funerals, stating that the non-churched invite a priest, attracted by the church tradition and the expression of spirituality, but find a traditional church service does not express their spirituality and may be too impersonal. Spirituality is a word used in many diverse contexts. In its broadest meaning it is about 'the driving force within an individual', 'what motivates people'. It is a strong dimension in religion, but is not limited to religion. Christian congregations are often uncertain of the word 'spirituality', thinking that it is New Age. Ward adds that today people want a funeral to be chiefly about the deceased and may turn away from the Church because they do not think it is possible to be personal and religious.[7] There is misunderstanding here. For those unfamiliar with worship, the use of theological language can get in the way of the prime concern of a funeral, which is pastoral. Ward suggests the use of alternative imagery, particularly in prayers, such as natural images, those from our daily experience such as day and night or coming home after a day's work, and the elements. The concept of God is intangible and beyond our understanding. Therefore we use metaphor to speak of God. Ward refers to story and human metaphors. She cites some of the best-known parables – the prodigal son, the good Samaritan – and the phrase in the Eucharist, 'he opened wide his arms on the cross', which is meaningful to many. These tell of God's love stretching out to us through the light and darkness of our lives.

A funeral in the twenty-first century has to carry more shock and grief than in previous generations. In the past the dying were surrounded by family, visited by neighbours and friends. This is now no longer so, due to geographical mobility through educational opportunity and work. The family might have had little contact with an elderly relative in a home, resulting in a sense of guilt at not keeping in regular contact.

---

5 *Common Worship: Pastoral Services*, 2000, London: Church House Publishing, p. 3.

6 Tess Ward, 2012, *Alternative Pastoral Prayers: Liturgies and Blessings for Health and Healing, Beginnings and Endings*, Norwich: Canterbury Press, p. xi.

7 Ward, *Alternative Pastoral Prayers*, p. 233.

The Church and its ministers can offer a 'package' to the bereaved, collaborating with the family to prepare the funeral. They can lead the funeral itself and follow up in a way which recognizes the nature of grieving. This strength of the Church is significant, since today the public are not at ease in anything connected with death. Funeral and memorial services provide clergy with opportunities to work with families to plan and 'perform' rituals of great psychological and spiritual significance. Time spent in discovering the family's 'religious language' and involving them as fully as possible in the service can change an ordeal such as a funeral into a moving experience; it can also build a relationship of trust that will facilitate later pastoral care if that is helpful in the situation.[8]

Questions for reflection and response

• Comment on an aspect of Co-operative Funeralcare research.
• What does the Church and its ministers have to offer the non-churched in the area of funerals?
• Write a prayer for a bereaved person who is not a Christian.
• Research praying for the departed (history and present-day views). Where do you stand on this issue?

Reflection on insights from Scripture and the tradition

Many funerals, particularly in the Anglican tradition, are for non-church people. These people might, by some, be considered as outsiders because they are not familiar with Christian worship.

The Hebrew Scriptures

Who were the 'outsiders' in the Scriptures and how were they treated by God's people? In the Scriptures there was considerable interaction between the people of God and the surrounding nations due to the trade route of the Fertile Crescent. The prophets understood those who conquered God's people, the Philistines, the empires of Assyria, Egypt and Babylon, as God's agents of punishment. The prophet Isaiah speaks of Cyrus, the conquering leader of the Persian Empire, as 'a shepherd, the servant of God, anointed' (Isa. 44.28; 45.1). Cyrus, a non-Jew, allows

---

8 Alan Billings, 2002, *Dying and Grieving*, London: SPCK, p. 59.

the exiled Jews to go home (Ezra 1.1f.). The Jews, God's chosen people, were called to be 'a light to the Gentiles and the glory of my people Israel'. Their mission was a witness to God and to non-Jews.

The New Testament

Shepherds were told of the birth of Jesus (Luke 2.8f.), yet shepherds were considered unclean because their job prevented them from keeping the strict requirements of the law. There were disciples who were considered 'outsiders' to orthodoxy. Jesus called Matthew, a hated quisling, a tax-collector, to be a disciple. When criticized for eating with Matthew and his friends and of being a drunkard himself (Matt. 11.19), Jesus said: 'Those who are well have no need of a physician, but those who are sick. I have come to call not the righteous but sinners' (Matt. 9.9–13; Mark 2. 13–17; Luke 5.27–32). On meeting Zaccheus, another tax-collector, and inviting himself to dinner, Jesus is accused of being 'a guest of one who is a sinner'. Jesus says: 'Today has salvation come to this house, because he too is a son of Abraham. For the Son of Man came to seek out and to save the lost' (Luke 19.1–10). Jesus told the temple authorities that the tax-collectors and prostitutes would enter the Kingdom of Heaven before them (Matt. 21.31). There are accounts of Jesus healing those with leprosy and those 'possessed', all ostracized, made outsiders of the community because of their 'medical' condition. Jesus welcomed those at the edges into his Kingdom; his was an inclusive ministry.

Jesus' encounters

The evangelist of the Fourth Gospel uses dialogue between Jesus and certain individuals on matters of faith: Nicodemus on 'rebirth' and 'being born again' (3.1–10); with the woman of Samaria he talks about 'living water', sustaining life (4.5–15); with Martha he discusses the nature of resurrection life (11.20–28). Jesus begins with the experience of an individual, accompanying them and helping each to have a clearer vision of the presence of God in their lives. In the Synoptic Gospels Jesus encounters a rich young ruler concerned about inheriting eternal life. The young man's wealth prevents him from discipleship; Mark's Gospel says, 'Jesus looking at him, loved him' (10.21), and Jesus lets him go (Mark 10.17–22; Matt. 19.16–23; Luke 18.18–24.) He allows the young man to be responsible for his own life, and walk away from the good news. Jesus does not judge, condemn, or manipulate, he allows the young man to be himself.

The walk to Emmaus is another incident of encounter. Jesus accompanies two distraught travellers on a journey, listens to their experiences and their disillusionment with the events of the Passion. He talks with them, helping them to see another point of view. It is only in his homely, familiar action of breaking bread that they recognize Jesus (Luke 24.13–31). These are stories beginning with present experience, accompanying, listening, journeying, dialogue and symbolic action, a model for meeting the non-churched.

Questions for reflection and response

- How did outsiders influence Jesus' ministry?
- Think of the composition of your church. Is it exclusive in any way? Why?
- Write a paragraph about those who are excluded by your community. How would Jesus have helped them?
- Plan a Bible study on the rich young ruler (Mark 10.17–22). How might Jesus' attitude to the young man help when preparing a funeral with the non-churched?

Reflection on cultural context in dialogue with Scripture and the tradition

The changing nature of society – the loss of local women who could be called on to lay out a body, the growing individualism, the demise of Christianity – means that many people are not familiar with what to do when a loved one dies. They want a 'decent' end, ritual and a space in which to express their emotions, but do not know where to turn. In the past it would be the Church, but the Church, according to Co-operative Funeralcare's research, is not seen as 'personal' or 'flexible'. The Church is seen as imposing its liturgies and theological language, which do not make sense to many. There are debates within the Church about a funeral for those on the edge of the Church, thought of as non-churched.

Grace Davie sees de-Christianization as an inevitable consequence of modernity; Christianity has 'mutated'. Davie developed the concept of 'vicarious religion', which she relates to churches holding part of a 'collective memory' for the community as a whole, in four ways. Churches and church leaders perform ritual on behalf of others; they believe on behalf of others. Church leaders and active Christians embody moral codes on behalf of others. Churches offer space for the vicarious debate of unresolved social issues. She notes Europeans may not practise religion on a daily basis but recognize its worth at critical times in the life of the community, such as at the mourning and articulation of grief. They then instinctively turn to the Church, its officials, symbols and liturgy to help them understand and articulate the sacredness of what has happened.[9] Her research is conducted chiefly in Britain, Scandinavia and France.

The story of Jesus is about those on the edge whom the religious leaders considered outsiders yet to whom Jesus openly ministered. It is about how Jesus encounters and ministers. Within sections of the Church, questions are being asked about the non-churched and funerals, yet this is an opportunity to challenge the myths they have about the Church being not of their 'spirituality', nor 'personal'. Dave Tomlinson says, 'It is a sad fact that many people will never appear in church because they feel judged by those of us who call ourselves Christian. Meanwhile, Christ's arms remain open to all.'[10]

Churches, in revising funeral rites, can offer flexibility, in that the aim of the service is pastoral. Its ministers are called to reflect the attitude of Jesus in responding to need. Scriptural insights into the nature of God in Christ, being alongside, accompanying, compassionate, non-judgemental and challenging give me clues when being with the non-churched. It is in these incidents that we witness a theology of grief, of vulnerable incarnation through presence and encounter of God who is immanent. It is these doctrines that guide our witness and work with the non-churched who come to us for help with funerals.

Questions for reflection and response

- How can ministers make accessible funeral rites?
- What gospel principles guide the making of a funeral for a non-church family?
- Is the Church's history in public services and liturgy an asset?
- Make a theological defence of the criticism that the Church is not 'personal'.

9 Grace Davie, 2000, *Religion in Modern Europe: A Memory Mutates*, Oxford: Oxford University Press.

10 Dave Tomlinson, on the Ronnie Biggs funeral he conducted, *Church Times*, 17 January 2014.

Pastoral practice

Throughout this chapter I continue to use the word 'minister' to refer to the person, lay or ordained, who is taking the funeral service. Historically the Church controlled the content of the liturgy. It is now being recognized that the funeral is a pastoral service and as such it belongs to the bereaved as a pastoral response, and not solely to the liturgy of the Church. It therefore makes sense to work alongside the bereaved in creating the funeral. Underlying this ministry is a theology of incarnation, of incarnate presence, which is inevitably risky and vulnerable.

Who approaches the Church to conduct a funeral?

Reasons are diverse for choosing a church funeral: the bereaved may have previously been to a church funeral and found it helpful. They may have passed the church and been impressed by the care taken of its building and grounds. The bereaved may know a neighbour who is friendly towards them and attends the church. Clergy are occasionally seen as a profession for which one pays: we are hired to do a job. A family may think that they have little faith, but believe the clergy to have great faith and need that faith on this occasion. It may be the bereaved were inarticulate at the death and were 'bounced' into a church funeral by the funeral directors, at a time of shock not knowing alternatives to a church. This I think was the case with Trevor's family.

The Church of England as the state church has a parish system. This means that it is expected to conduct funerals for all living in a geographical area, for those with little faith, nominal faith and no faith. It is very disconcerting and harmful to the Church if the priest refuses a family who live in his or her parish, because he or she does not know them. If the funeral is of such a family, the minister may feel the funeral is a burden, extra work, yet it is an exciting opportunity to share God's love, implicitly by the attitude towards the family, and explicitly by the funeral 'liturgy' and the words used. The temptation is to evangelize, but this would be taking advantage of vulnerable people. We are not there to sell the gospel, but rather to be present, to listen, enable, interpret, to reflect a theology of incarnation, presence and encounter. Neither are we taking God to folk; God is present, since it is God's created and redeemed world, though those to whom we minister may not recognize this.

What do bereaved people want from the Church?

The bereaved may see it as their right to have help from the Church – in some ways in our agnostic age this is a good sign. They certainly want some sort of ritual or rite of passage, a decent ending, something in contrast to the '20 minutes only' at many crematoria and the impersonal celebrant on the rota. Some might see a church service as an insurance policy to heaven for the deceased. Others believe that they will receive care and personal attention from ministers as professionals. Yet others seek help because they have no experience of what is appropriate at a funeral, even though they may have attended one, and they want 'to do it right by their loved one'. Some relatives do not feel confident enough to plan a funeral and look to those with experience and training in public ceremony, such as 'ministers'.

The bereaved will have some beliefs about life and its meaning. These will be individual, depending on their experience. Sunday congregations will also have many and varied beliefs! Some beliefs may be negative – of a vengeful, damming, judgemental God – or from childhood, the old man in the sky who intervenes for his own people and not for outsiders, underlying what we as ministers say is a different theology of God. Many who never darken the door of the church building have beliefs in an after-life. My cousin Colin, a hard-nosed, beer-swigging long-distance lorry driver, says, 'We're too amazing to be snuffed out at death.' My agnostic nurse niece Katie, when preparing a dead body, says that 'something has happened, they are "not there"', and 'we always talk to the person while washing their body'.

How can we interpret what people are saying?

The bereaved are approaching a Christian minister saying that they are not religious but are spiritual: 'Dad would never miss *Songs of Praise* on the telly', or 'He was a choir boy when he was young.' Are we then simply functionaries of a rite of passage? There is a gap between their beliefs and ours, particularly in the language used. Our words need to be care-fully thought through. The bereaved may want a celebration of life, grief swallowed up in thankfulness, but that is not in the long term appropriate, for grief must be recognized. Many say they do not know any hymns or prayers, including the Lord's Prayer, yet I have folk asking for traditional hymns like 'The old rugged cross' and 'Abide with me'. There is a balance to be achieved between pastoral and theological issues, being compassion-ate to relatives and keeping our integrity as ministers of the gospel. Several different positions can be taken.

Judgemental

If neither the deceased nor the relatives asking for a funeral come to church, is judgement appropriate? Here are some illustrations. A fellow priest refused to take a funeral since neither the deceased nor the relative attended the church, although both lived in his parish. His comment was that they were simply 'using him'. Perhaps they were, but are we not here to serve? A mental health chaplain refused to bury someone who had committed suicide; he commented to other patients, 'We know where she is now ... in hell.' Dave Tomlinson was judged by conservative members of the Church of England because he officiated at the funeral of Ronnie Biggs, the great train robber. Questioned he said, 'No human being ... is entirely good or bad. Jesus stated that he didn't come for the righteous; he came for sinners. He hung out with the unsavoury people in society, he ate and drank with prostitutes and publicans.' Michael Perham asks if we should make a judgement on people – surely that is for God alone. Those who argue for two orders of service, one for Christians and one for others, involve judgement; surely no pastor would seriously want to take that action. Perham therefore suggests a Christian funeral for all, and let people appropriate it at the level of which they are capable.[11]

A 'secular' funeral

As requested by the relatives, we may take a funeral but not mention the name of God, knowing that God is present through ministers. Is this selling out on the Christian tradition, which we represent, or enabling the family to be honest and not hypocritical in what they say? If we are concerned, is it more honest to suggest the phone number of a humanist minister? Are we, in working with a family to create a funeral, remembering that the modern rites from the major denominations talk about using their new liturgies flexibly, coming alongside a family and in a small way reflecting a theology of immanence and incarnation?

Integrate as required by the Church

Integration can happen with the set service. I am most familiar with the Anglican *Common Worship: Pastoral Services*, a set liturgy with its orthodox prayers and formality. It is not about letting go the deceased, but rather remembering them. We pray for the dead not to change God's mind

---

11 Perham, *New Handbook*, chs 25 and 26.

concerning their destiny, but because there is a continuing relationship of love with those who have gone before us. Emphasis is on the bereaved, as much as the departed. Do we then respond pastorally to the bereaved on their terms, beginning where they are? Helping to create a funeral with relatives may be a therapeutic and encounter role reflecting Christ.

The funeral begins the cathartic process of grief. However, at the service there will be diverse mourners present: those there at the death, others who visited the chapel of rest, others who have not seen the deceased for some time. The needs of all of these people are to be recognized. At some funerals there is family division, for example when a divorced partner appears, having seen the notice of death and funeral in the local paper. This can be difficult for the celebrant, particularly if she did not know of the existence of this person; often a previous partner is mentioned during the meeting with the family while preparing for the funeral, and the celebrant is therefore aware and if necessary can talk to this person to avoid a potential disturbance.

Funeral preparation

The initial visit to the bereaved is to build a relationship. It is helpful to visit the bereaved in their own home, where they are likely to feel more relaxed. The contact is vital; it may be the first time the minister has met the family and is an occasion to build trust and relationships. The minister is the face of the Church for the bereaved, so may like to say a prayer for the wisdom of the Spirit before going into the house.

The bereaved may be numb with grief and shock. They don't know what is expected of them or how to arrange a funeral. It may be that they are apprehensive at the visit of a church representative and fearful they will be emotional at the meeting and cry. They may fear demands the Church will make of them. It may be a blended family, or members who are not speaking to one another; in that case care is needed. It is essential to be alongside, reflecting the theology of incarnation.

Unlike other professionals

We are not present at the meeting with the family in a professional role, but as fellow human beings. The role comes later, in leading the service. We meet the family to talk person to person, to befriend. The focus is the bereaved, getting their names right and using them, their relationships with each other and the deceased. Alan Billings comments: 'It is ... the evident humanity of the clergy or lay visitor that is valued rather than any expertise.'[12] At this emotionally charged occasion it is important for the minister not to hide behind glib words, clerical gear or badge of office, or even to give the impression of busyness and lack of time, which may diminish the significance of the mourners' pain. There is the need of an unhurried and supportive presence. This is spiritual care. It is important to be alongside the bereaved in their grief, their journey and life story. This is likely to make us feel vulnerable. Bruce Rumbold, an Australian pastoral theologian, notes that in a hospital situation, establishing a relationship with a patient, the minister must become vulnerable, running the risk not just of professional inadequacy but of personal helplessness so that change may happen; if the minister is not open to change, neither will the patient be.[13] I believe that this is also the case in working with the bereaved. As Christians, we believe that 'the Word became flesh and dwelt among us', choosing to share our human vulnerability, just as Jesus wept with Mary (John 11.35) and on the cross cried out, 'My God, my God, why have you forsaken me?', the lament of a human desperately alone using the psalms of lament. It is a theology of vulnerable presence.

This visit is initially to recognize the grief of the bereaved. Emotions may be of sadness, anger, blame, or of feeling cheated. The minister may bear the brunt of this anger against God, as God's representative. Allowing this to be expressed is to recognize the importance of the bereaved. It is a time of waiting and cannot be bypassed. This giving of unhurried, supportive, acceptance of emotions is a Christlike characteristic; here is a theology of grief.

The next task is to begin working together on the funeral, so that the family 'own the service'. Ewan Kelly calls this 'co-constructing'.[14] It suggests mutuality, though in some ways it is not, since the bereaved have asked for the help of a professional, as they feel they do not have the skills themselves to construct a funeral. There is an imbalance. Bruce Rumbold calls it an 'asymmetric mutuality', Alistair Campbell 'a mutuality of need'.[15] The minister has experience to bring to the task: experience of conducting funerals, of pastoral encounters, including reconciling

---

12 Alan Billings, 2002, *Dying and Grieving: A Guide to Pastoral Ministry*, London: SPCK, p. 50.

13 Bruce D. Rumbold, 1986, *Helplessness and Hope: Pastoral Care in Terminal Illness*, London: SCM Press, p. 39.

14 Ewan Kelly, 2008, *Meaningful Funerals: Meeting the Theological and Pastoral Challenge in a Postmodern Era*, London and New York: Mowbray.

15 Rumbold, *Helplessness and Hope*, p. 103; Alistair Campbell, 1986, *Rediscovering Pastoral Care*, 2nd edn, London: Darton, Longman and Todd, p. 100.

skills, and theological skills. All these gifts, given through vocation and training, are invested in the minister by the bereaved. These the minister may contribute to the conversation. There is the danger here of the use of authority and power: the model is of Jesus who had both. The Scriptures state, 'he taught them as one having authority, and not as the scribes' (Mark 1.22), at healings, 'They were all amazed, and they kept on asking one another, "What is this? A new teaching – with authority! He commands even the unclean spirits, and they *obey him*"' (Mark 1.27). Jesus' authority was used, but with the marginalized and the powerless he did not use it to manipulate but to empower those who came to him; it was 'power for rather than power over'.[16] Theologically this is about the humility of Christ. The minister needs to be prepared to be alongside and help the bereaved put the story of their deceased into the larger picture of the Christian story, using Christian language if it seems helpful for them.

Invite the family to talk about their loved one, using the name by which the person was known, perhaps a pet name. Gather information about the deceased, without being shocked, and give opportunities to express emotions freely: to talk, cry, rant if necessary. This may be a unique occasion for the bereaved in which openly, yet in a safe place, to express their real emotions. It is important to allow silence, so that the bereaved will trust you with their secrets. Ian Ainsworth-Smith and Peter Speck highlight trust:

> Many bereaved people are frightened by the intensity of their feelings, and the presence of other people whom they trust, coupled with a sensitive and calm leadership of the ritual, can enable them to feel safe about expressing feelings at the funeral.[17]

Ask to see photos and receive memories; it may be possible later to do research using Facebook. Listen with all the senses to verbal and non-verbal language, write down the phrases of the mourners to include in the tribute as triggers for recollection. It is important to listen to 'the bass clef', what is not said but is present – family differences, desires of the deceased for the funeral, reconstituted families, responding to needs, ritual and its significance – remember this is a once-only occasion. Through stories told by the family, get a rounded picture of the deceased; touch on working life, hobbies, interests and family life; allude to the shadow side. Help people to make their sense of the death and the 'now'– not providing

---

16 Kelly, *Meaningful Funerals*, p. 133.

17 Ian Ainsworth-Smith and Peter Speck, 1999, *Letting Go: Caring for the Dying and Bereaved*, London: SPCK, p. 99.

answers, rather helping them to understand their questions better. This is in a real sense 'doing theology'. This may be the anger of the cutting off of a young life, which raises questions of why there is suffering when many believe in a good God – the question of theodicy. The existence of God may be raised, and the belief in an afterlife. This shared authorship of the funeral service reflects the way Jesus in his ministry encountered people, journeyed with them and helped them to theologize. Kelly comments that for church members and non-church people alike, the 'presence and involvement of a church representative embodies the presence of Christ'.[18] Billings states that today few people accept beliefs because some authority such as a minister, church or sacred text tells them; beliefs will be tested against personal experience.

> If pastors are to speak about a Christian understanding of death their authority will not derive from their position as pastors or even from the hallowed tradition of the church; people will listen to see whether what the pastor says has been tested in the fire of personal experience and/or whether it resonates with the listener's experience.[19]

Check the practicalities of the service – the date, time, place, church/crematorium, burial/cremation. Talk about the purpose of the service (see p. 117) which is a rite of passage and helps formalize the new social status of the bereaved. Discover how the family would like to participate in the funeral service; make some assessment of their pastoral needs; reassure the bereaved that the funeral of their loved one will reflect their wishes. Finally, leave a folder of resources, which could include biblical material, particularly the psalms of lament, and prayers, music, songs, hymns and sample service sheets, for them to look through.

The folder of resources

It is useful to include a list of suggestions of how the family could be involved in the funeral:

- Production of the service sheet, including choosing music and/or hymns for the congregation.
- Young grandchildren may like to draw a picture or write a letter or poem to put in the coffin.

---

18 Kelly, *Meaningful Funerals*, pp. 118–19. Chapter 6 resonates with my own practice and is well worth reading.
19 Billings, *Dying and Grieving*, p. 69.

- An overnight vigil of family members around the coffin in church. This will be supported by church folk allowing space, stillness and the lighting of votive candles. This was done locally when two popular young motorcyclists were killed. Their friends came in for short periods through the night, joining the family.
- Provide coffin-bearers.
- Give out service sheets.
- At the beginning of the funeral service close relatives can be invited to come and light a candle, a symbol of Christ, the light of the world, the light that lights everyone who comes into the world (John 1.3–5), or place a flower on the coffin, a symbol of beauty yet impermanence.
- Give a tribute.
- Read a poem or piece from the Bible.
- At the committal the immediate family could encircle the coffin and touch it, taking leave of their beloved, which is a highly symbolic act.

A caveat here – a family offered to do the service sheet. They were not church people though they wanted hymns. They put the words on the service sheet. One hymn was 'Abide with me'. I did not have time to check the words and from somewhere eight verses were found, many of which were dubious in their theology; their choice of 'All things bright and beautiful' included the verse about 'the rich man in his castle, the poor man at his gate'. Leaving materials for the family to look through gives a reason for a second visit.

A second visit

This may seem excessive in terms of time, but is well worth it, demonstrating to the family our concern and care for them. A visit is preferable to a phone call, but the latter may be necessary because of time restraints. A funeral is a deeply human event. Discuss if the deceased stated wishes for the funeral. In law the deceased's wishes have no legal standing but if these wishes are ignored by the living relatives it can later cause rifts in the family.

This visit is to look at the details of the service and the choices and suggestions of the bereaved. Co-authoring is about creating a unique partnership. It is empowering the bereaved at a time of great vulnerability; it is to facilitate and enable choices without being a barrier, to assist and guide a liturgy. As far as possible allow the family to choose material, words and music that reflect what they believe and are honouring to the deceased. To some extent this is dependent on the time allocated for the service.

Indicate to them an outline of the structure of the service (see Chapter 4). Check at what point the family come into the church, for example will the coffin be in before them or will they follow the coffin? Co-creating does not mean that anything goes. The minister has a contribution of the Christian metanarrative to make, if this is appropriate for the family. It may be that the family have chosen readings or hymns that could be used as a basis for insights into faith. At a recent funeral, the bereaved had chosen 'The Lord's my Shepherd', allowing me to pick up the theme of 'green pastures' and 'the shadow of death' and say a few words about the deceased living in 'Suffolk, sheep country' and her journey through difficult times, the death of each of her two husbands. If a family member is giving a tribute, ask them to write it down, since, in the emotion of the day, they may not be able to speak, and you can read it on their behalf. Get the person to limit it to five minutes. The use of Scripture or non-scriptural readings will depend on the choices made by the family. Although ministers would prefer Scripture, for some on the fringe Scripture may have no authority, they may not know who Paul was. So, if choosing, perhaps use a modern version or paraphrase, such as *The Message* or *Good as New: A Radical Retelling of the Scriptures*.

If there is an opportunity to say a few words – preach. It is important to remember the bereaved and the planning conversations with them. The bereaved are vulnerable and need words of comfort. Evangelism is not appropriate. It may be a message of hope to comfort and strengthen the family. What are we hoping for? Reasons vary. It may be to convert, or win members for the Church; to teach and help folk understand better; to build on an implicit spirituality, cultural Christianity or folk religion that has never been fully understood, explored or expressed; to be alongside the bereaved and offer our humanity, which for us as Christians is rooted in an incarnational Christology.

Prayers are appropriate when taken quietly, giving plenty of spaces for silent thought for the deceased, since everyone will have been in a unique relationship with him or her. These are words of thankfulness but need also to include prayers of penitence. The deceased stands under the judgement of God. Some of the bereaved have a sense of guilt: forgiving the deceased, forgiveness for guilt of omission, reconciliation with the past. In this way it is remembered that nothing we say or do will shock God. We are accepted as we are and can be changed. There will be thanksgiving for the life of the deceased, prayers for those who mourn, for all present, for readiness to live in the light of eternity; there may be a collect and the Lord's Prayer. These prayers need not necessarily be addressed to God, if that is not likely to be helpful to the family; their beliefs need to be respected, though they have come to you for help as a Christian minister. Prayers may be in the form of a meditation; they should be real, acknowledging the situation, being honest about the reality of pain and suffering, God with us in the present situation sharing our sorrows. We know that, as praying ministers, resurrection underpins our hope.

The funeral service

Help people to feel at ease in the service by welcoming those present – family, friends, work colleagues. Mourners are disoriented at funerals, and they may be unfamiliar with worship and don't want to do the wrong thing. The minister is their security. This can be assured at the beginning by explaining the purpose of the service, giving clear instructions to stand or sit, using the familiar name of the deceased, allowing space for memories, using triggers – words, symbols, gestures – introductory prayers with time for silence, so that mourners can think and give thanks for their memories. As ministers we need to face our own feelings of mortality, of grief – don't deny them. We must remain calm but not uninvolved; this needs experience. A gentle reminder here: we should not be tempted to take the funeral of one of our own loved ones, since it prevents us from beginning grief; it is much better that this is in the hands of another.

Whatever is said at the funeral, those who are nearest to the deceased are likely to be so distressed at seeing the coffin that they will take in little of the words of the service. However, they will be aware of the care that has been taken in preparation for the funeral; the listening ear that has been given to them during the preparation. At the funeral itself they will be aware of the reality and accuracy of the description of their deceased loved one; the tone of voice, the humanity, sensitivity and gestures of the minister; the pace of the occasion, that it gives space and silence for contemplation to acknowledge this final physical parting; they may remember the 'pictures' painted of the naturalness of death and the acknowledgement of their grief and need of comfort. As for those journeying to Emmaus, it was the presence of Christ that mattered. Ministers today are the representatives of Christ.

A touch, a handshake as people leave, sometimes a hug or an arm may be appropriate. Warmth communicates to people and is remembered. After the service you may be invited back to the house – if you go, don't stay too long, it is a special time for the family.

Difficult funerals

The greatest asset to help a bereaved person is a human befriender to listen and be alongside.

A sudden death may be a result of a heart attack or an accident in the home; there are 3,000 accidents annually in the UK. The husband of a friend had a heart condition, which was monitored, but he had a fatal heart attack overnight. She woke to find him dead beside her. This has taken her years to get over. A sudden death may be an undiagnosed or an unusual medical condition. On these occasions involvement will mean sitting with the person, allowing them to cry, sob, rant. Sitting will be in silence, and when the bereaved is able to speak it is the minister's job to listen while she repeatedly goes over the incident to make some sense of it. It is important to be aware of the safety of this person; to keep promises of visiting, and to encourage them to have some nutrition. The whole process is likely to be very repetitive, over a considerable period of time. The funeral must be realistic of the suddenness of the death.

A road accident may be the result of a careless or drunken driver, or joy-riding. If the accident is at Christmas time, bereavement will be compounded by delay until after the New Year celebration, because crematoria and coroners are not available. There is likely to be police involvement, and this may delay the reception of the body by the family, which may be too distressing to see. The bereaved are likely to be overwrought. A husband and wife I knew reacted very differently to the news of the death of their daughter who was about to be married, killed by a joy-rider mounting the pavement on which she was walking. The wife came to church, a non-churchgoer, with a neighbour who was a church attender, and suddenly went to the front and took over the service, becoming increasingly distraught and incomprehensible. The priest took her up to the altar and put her arm round her in comfort. Her husband simply locked himself away and then went on long walks alone. In these situations the anger and unbelief will take a considerable time to abate, if it ever does. The funeral needs to be real, expressing anger yet gently offering comfort. The use of parts of Job would be appropriate.

Dealing with a violent death is a daunting task. It might come through terrorism or war. These situations seemed remote, but have become increasingly near through the country's involvement in major wars abroad. There may be no identifiable body, which makes the situation more difficult. With a murder, the bereavement time will be extended due to time taken by police investigations, coroners, pathology, prosecution, trial, appeal, retrial. In domestic violence, the bereaved is often responsible for the death. In the UK, two women are killed each week in this way. Nevertheless the deceased needs a sensitive funeral, and human sinfulness needs to be recognized.

Suicide leaves many questions for the bereaved. Was it the intention of the deceased? Could the death have been avoided? Those left may feel guilty. Could they have prevented the death; sometimes they feel they might be the cause. Suicide was decriminalized in 1961, traditionally deemed *felo de se*, literally 'a felon of himself'. Some Christians still see suicide as sinful and believe the Church should withhold a normal funeral and insist on burial in unconsecrated ground. Certainly this was the case in the Book of Common Prayer (1662), but in recent years attitudes have changed, so that the emphasis is on the mercy and love of God, which is dominant at the funeral. A charity for those bereaved by suicide is www.uk-sobs.org.uk.

Aftercare following the funeral

It is important for the minister to be realistic about the aftercare to provide. Whatever is promised it is important to fulfil. The minister should suggest ringing the next of kin a month after the service and arrange, if the bereaved would like this, to make a visit. After the funeral there is much to do, such as dealing with the deceased's clothes, letters and other sentimental belongings. This is hard and often needs support. Many have friends and family who support. If there is a person left on their own, it is important to recognize they may need more help.

Following a visit, introduce the bereaved to a befriender. It is important that a church has a team of befrienders who could visit regularly, particularly if the bereaved is someone on their own. The team will need teaching on models of grieving, preparation, regular supervision by the minister, material about confidentiality. If the person's need is beyond them, they will need the address and phone number of the local Cruse to suggest. Many churches have a regular group for those who are bereaved, and there are sensitive booklets to help the bereaved (see Chapter 3 and p. 200 for suggested reading). The key help is, however, that of a listening, caring person.

Being human: some examples

The place of the funeral may evoke memories. Recently I buried a woman who was a few days under 90. Her first husband of 30 years and the father of her children was buried in the churchyard. After several years she married again. This husband also predeceased her. Subsequently a granddaughter of 19 was buried there. She had moved after the death of her first husband, but wanted to be buried with him. It was therefore a very emotional occasion for the returning family.

Recently I visited a family about the death of their elderly mother. I knew there were two sons and a daughter, but one son was missing. Those present told me of a rift in the family; all they knew was that the missing son could not cope with death and was deeply distressed, though he had asked for the hymn 'All things bright and beautiful' for the funeral. I asked if I could phone this son and was reluctantly, and apologetically, given his number, but warned that he was likely to be abusive. Later when I rang him, I offered my condolences, thanked him for his choice of hymn, stated that his brother and sister had told me about his mother, and I wondered if he might have a memory that I could include. He was not able to give me one, but explained the possible reason for the rift and then thanked me for ringing. It seemed that the call had in some way helped him to realize that his grief was real and that he was important and his contribution was acknowledged.

On one occasion a brother and sister in their thirties said that they wanted to ask me a favour. Their mother had only been able to eat ice cream near the end of her life, and she had died on Red Nose Day wearing a plastic red nose. Their childhood memories were sitting watching *Crackerjack* with her and yelling out 'cabbages'. She loved life, and in her memory please could they give out wrapped choc-ices as people left the crematorium?

Self-care of the minister

After the service the minister needs time to 'potter'. Funerals are emotional occasions, and the role of leading the funeral is a challenging one. Reflection on the funeral is useful, such as asking questions like 'How are the bereaved?', as well as 'How was the funeral?' The service is usually a team effort – organist, curate, churchwarden, steward – and they are a safe forum to reflect on the funeral with, honestly and openly. This may be a continuing to struggle with a theology of suffering or of the absence or presence of God, and how to create more meaningful funerals. As ministers of the gospel our theology needs to inform and shine through ministry to the bereaved.

Questions for reflection and response

- How does theology inform a funeral service?
- Research the place of ritual within funerals. What part does ritual play in funerals that you take? How significant is it?
- Check out ten gravestones illustrating a difference in the age at which they were erected in the churchyard. Write down the dates of death, the sex and role of the deceased. What are the words on the gravestone? What does this information tell you of attitudes and beliefs about death?
- What today are the expectations in the community in which you live of a church funeral?

Further reading

Colin Murray Parkes, Pittu Laungani and Bill Young (eds), 1997, *Death and Bereavement across Cultures*, London and New York: Routledge.

Tony Walter, 1990, *Funerals and How to Improve Them*, London: Hodder and Stoughton.

Jayne Wynne Willson, 2006, *Funerals without God: A Practical Guide to Humanist and Non-Religious Funeral Ceremonies*, London: British Humanist Association.

6

Looking to the Future – Post-Funeral Support

Grief is a natural phenomenon that occurs after the loss of a loved one.
Stephen Schuchter and Sidney Zisook[1]

A case study begins the chapter, looking at a woman's journey through bereavement and reflecting on it theologically. This chapter examines post-funeral support through the Christian year and the ongoing care of the bereaved in a society that appears to want to marginalize and forget the existence of death. The needs of the bereaved following the funeral are examined. The cultural context is Western society's expectations of impatience with the bereaved and insistence that they 'get on with life!' Scriptural insights are examined through concepts such as covenant, comfort and compassion. When the context and Scripture are brought together theological insights emerge that can be reflected in appropriate pastoral care.

Pastoral circle

Pastoral practice:
occasions for bereaved
to remember

Experience – reflection:
one for ongoing care of
bereaved

Cultural
context:
dimensions of
bereavement

Scripture and
tradition:
relationship and
covenant

Scripture/tradition
and context:
theology of
relationships – Trinity

---

1 Stephen Schuchter and Sidney Zisook, 1993, 'The course of normal grief', in Margaret S. Stroebe, Wolfgang Stroebe, Robert O. Hansson (eds), *Handbook of Bereavement*, Cambridge: Cambridge University Press, p. 23.

Experience

> Janet was married to Geoffrey, her childhood sweetheart. They were devoted to each other, both worked, and their leisure time was spent together. They had an adult son and grandchildren, and a daughter who was engaged to be married. Geoffrey had a rare ongoing medical problem, which was monitored by the hospital and controlled by medication. In the summer they had a memorable holiday, swimming and walking together. Geoffrey was full of energy and healthier than he had been for many years. The last day of the holiday he had a blip, his knee causing discomfort.
>
> Returning home Geoffrey made an appointment with his GP, who knowing the medical history sent Geoffrey to Accident and Emergency. His consultant was called and he was admitted. Tests began, but before he could be moved to a specialist hospital he was dead from a rare leukaemia. Janet was devastated.
>
> After the funeral she lived on her own for the first time ever. Her bereavement was complicated and long. She was hospitalized and placed on an 'At Risk Register'. The support from the Well Being team was magnificent, visiting her regularly and giving her a round-the-clock phone number for emergency use. Gradually Janet made progress, until one day she was introduced to Together, a local church-run group for the bereaved.

Reflection on experience

Follow-up after a bereavement is not always available. Locally our mental health team has been renamed a Well Being team, releasing users from the stigma which exists within mental illness. A large percentage of both men and women will at some point in their lives seek professional help for stress and depression, often following bereavement in which they have not adequately grieved. In Janet's case, living alone for the first time had taken its toll on her resilience and well-being. Church bereavement groups may have a major contribution to make to care in such cases. The following conversation relates to Janet and her daughter.

Janet: 'I have been invited to go to a church-run group called Together for those who have suffered a bereavement. I've been several times now.'

Daughter: 'But you don't go to church, so why go? Perhaps they are trying to convert you.'

Janet: 'No, I don't think so. It is at the church where they did your dad's funeral – the one with that nice vicar.'

Daughter: 'So what happens at Together?'

Janet: 'Well, we just sit and chat about whatever we like. Sometimes we talk about our bereavements, but only if we want to. On occasions someone gets tearful, but Judy the leader always puts out a box of tissues in case. Judy makes the tea and provides the cakes. The church room is part of the church itself, so if we want to be quiet, anyone can wander into the church.'

Daughter: 'Oh, is that all?'

Janet: 'Well, I meet people like me, who are now on their own and feel lonely. And I have met Linda.'

Daughter: 'What is so special about Linda?'

Janet: 'Linda has invited me round to hers for a cuppa, and she is a dressmaker like me, so she is going to help and encourage me in making designs for your wedding dress.'

Daughter: 'Great, Mum, I'm so glad.'

The Church has a heritage of buildings and committed members. Judy is trained as a Reader in the Anglican tradition and has personal skills, listening and being alongside those in need. Through the group, Janet has met others in a similar situation to herself. The result is that she does not feel so alone in her loss. She has also made a friend to talk and relate to, who has a hobby like her own. She is able to network. The Church in this instance is able to offer pastoral care, available to a particular group of people. It is 'earthing' the theological concepts of presence, incarnation and the Trinity.

Judy has been available to listen to Janet, alongside her as a caring presence. This follows the model of Jesus, who came among us and shared our human experience. Like us, he was 'greatly disturbed in spirit and deeply moved, weeping at the death of Lazarus' (John 11.33, 35) and reaching out to the bereaved (Luke 7.11–17). 'He went' to help the daughter of Jairus (Mark 5.21–42; Luke 8.41–42, 49–56) and the centurion's servant/son. This is the theology of incarnation.

Janet was helped by others in the group who had been bereaved as she had and this helped her, since they understood her experience 'from the inside'. Others knew the pain of waking up in the morning without the loved one present, of the aloneness of widowhood. They knew the desolation and unbelief of bereavement. This created a 'fellowship of sharing'. This is a relational theology, paralleled by the relationship within the Godhead that is the Trinity.

Questions for reflection and response

- Should the Church be doing more to help the bereaved? What else could be done?
- Make a list of all the church-based post-bereavement groups that you know. Find out who runs them and the content of them. If you can, attend one of these. Get to know how members of the group are helped by the gathering.
- How important is it that the church does not use a group like Together for evangelism?
- What theology underlies a group like Together?

Reflection on cultural context

Cultural expressions of loss

Mexicans celebrate 'the Day of the Dead' in honour of their ancestors. *El Dia de los Muertos* was originally celebrated by the Aztecs throughout August. The Spanish conquerors in the 1500s saw the ritual as sacrilegious and wanted to make it Christian. They moved the event to All Saints' Day/All Souls' Day, 1 and 2 November. The festival honours and remembers loved ones who have died, believing that the souls of the deceased return each year to visit the living. On All Saints' Day, children are remembered; their gravestones are decorated with toys and balloons. All Souls' Day remembers deceased adults; they are honoured by the building of altars, lovingly decorated with flowers, candles and photos. Family members gather at the graveside and have picnics, serving the favourite foods of the deceased; they tell stories and remember the times they shared with their loved ones. The ritual is rooted in pride. The family want to create the most welcoming homecoming for their loved one and to reassure them they will never be forgotten. Similarly in the rural areas of Hong Kong, the whole community, on the same day, meet, tend the grave, talk and picnic with their ancestors.

The Maori give full voice to a loss, within a community that has been Christian since the nineteenth century. The traditional ways of mourning commemorate the dead before a Christian burial. Following a death, Maori shout, cry and chant for three days and nights, expressing their grief in a very voluble way to the dead person whose spirit they believe is still present. Emotions include criticism of the dead, who may be taken to task for sins of commission and omission. This ceremony is called *tangi*. Distant relatives, including non-Maori, bring small gifts of food or money to the mourners. They greet the dead person first, then everyone present, in the traditional way by touching their nose to each side of the other person's nose. After three days the Christian priest conducts a funeral and inters the body in a Maori cemetery, which has a fence around it decorated with traditional Maori symbols.

Some of our European neighbours fix photographs on to the gravestones of their deceased, keeping their memory alive. Welsh-speakers have a cultural practice of remembering their dead on Palm Sunday, translated as *Sul y Palmwydd* in the *Church of Wales Book of Common Prayer*. It is more commonly known as *Sul y Blodau*, which means Flower Sunday.[2] It is the day when families, who have moved away, return to visit their kin and to tend and put flowers on the graves of their loved ones. There is here a sense of community, since all will have someone whom they have lost.

Western developed countries

The sense of community has been lost. This is evident in funeral aftercare, noted in the profound changes during the last century in Chapter 3. In the twenty-first century there are few cultural norms for the bereaved, it is a journey into the unknown. Bereavement is individual since it is related to the unique relationship of bereaved and deceased, but it is useful to have some idea what to expect. When working with small groups of bereaved relatives at the hospice, there was always a sigh of relief when one person stated that they had 'seen' their dead relative and thought that they were going mad until others reflected on similar experiences (see p. 76). Some visit a Spiritualist church, hoping to contact their deceased. Most Christian denominations quote Deuteronomy 18.11 against this. The subject must be approached pastorally and thoughtfully with the vulnerable bereaved.

There are many variables in bereavement

Variables in bereavement affect its depth, intensity and length. The circumstances of the death make a difference, particularly if the death was sudden or traumatic. Culture and religion also affect the nature of bereavement. Ewan Kelly suggests that there are four dimensions of bereavement: the psychological, spiritual, social and practical.[3]

---

2 Hugh James, 2004, *A Fitting End: Making the Most of a Funeral*, Norwich: Canterbury Press, p. 152.

3 Ewan Kelly, 2008, *Meaningful Funerals: Meeting the Theological and Pastoral Challenge in a Postmodern Era*, London and New York: Mowbray, p. 31. I have developed Kelly's four dimensions of bereavement from my own experience.

The psychological dimension of bereavement

The work of Freud, Colin Murray Parkes and Elizabeth Kübler-Ross is well known. Parkes' research on widows in London noted the long-lasting depression following bereavement. However, when Burgoine used the same questionnaire to compare widows in London and the Bahamas, she found that the latter who expressed their grief more fully suffered less depression.[4]

I have found in teaching that the work of Bill Worden and Margaret Stroebe is helpful. Worden proposed the thinking that grief is a process and not a fixed 'state'.[5] People need to work through their reactions in order to make a complete adjustment. He drew on Freud's concept of grief work, Bowlby's attachment theory, developmental psychology, and Engel's concept of grief as an illness. Worden recognized that humans have, and are, narratives/stories – we are made up of all the people, events and places we have experienced in our lives. However, change and re-creation is necessary for each of us as we build on previous memories and incorporate new experiences, such as the death of someone close. Change requires redefinition of ourselves and our 'world' in an ongoing creation story. Grief and loss in bereavement are significant parts of our life story and common to all humans. Worden understood grief as a process of re-visioning the world, ourselves and our place within the world. He thought of grief as having four overlapping tasks:

1 to accept the reality of the loss
2 to experience the pain of grief
3 to adjust to an environment in which the deceased is missing
4 to let go, that is, to withdraw emotional energy from the relationship with the deceased and to redirect the energy. (I do not forget the deceased, rather the influence of the person on my life is integrated into memory and my story of meaning.)

---

4 E. Burgoine, 1988, 'A cross-cultural comparison of bereavement among widows in New Providence, Bahamas and London, England', paper read at the International Conference on Grief and Bereavement in Contemporary Society, London, 12–15 July.

5 J. W. Worden, 1991, *Grief Counselling and Grief Therapy*, 3rd edn, London: Tavistock Cinic.

Worden's grieving process

TASK	DESCRIPTION	CHALLENGES
1 To accept the reality of the loss – the deceased will not return. Reunion is impossible.	Intellectual and emotional acceptance of the loss.	Acceptance may be resisted by denying the fact of the loss; denying the meaning of the loss; and denying that death is irreversible. Worden states it is common for people to hope for reunion or assume that the deceased has not gone – but the illusion is short-lived.
2 Work through the pain of loss.	Experience the painful feelings.	Suppressing pain prolongs mourning. Expressing pain is difficult in some cultures that are uncomfortable with the expression of feelings.
3 Adjust to environment without the deceased.	Adjust to changes in circumstance, role, identity, self-esteem and personal beliefs.	Depends on relationship with deceased and roles of that person. Involves developing new skills – this may lower the self-esteem of the bereaved, who may feel inadequate for these tasks.
4 Emotionally relocate the deceased and move on with life.	Find a place for the deceased. Let go of emotional attachment with the deceased and invest in the present and future including new relationships.	Not give up the deceased but find an appropriate place for them in their emotional lives; the deceased continues to be important but enables the bereaved to carry on living effectively.

Margaret Stroebe likens grief work to a set of scales, as people search to maintain and establish balance or equilibrium in their lives following loss.[6]

Stroebe model of the grief process

LOSS ORIENTATION	RESTORATIVE ORIENTATION
Grief work: facing emotions. Focusing and dealing with some aspects of the loss. Crying. Looking at photos.	Adjusting to change. Learning new skills. Adapting to daily tasks. Consciously choosing to avoid triggers of grief. Suppression.
TIME 'IN' GRIEF Crying. Remembering. Sorting emotions out. Talking to friends about the death.	TIME 'OUT' FROM GRIEF Forgetting about loss – sometimes feeling guilty when the person remembers again. Being absorbed in everyday, ordinary life.

Gradually with use these theories have become more nuanced. There was a tendency to make authoritative claims about what was, and was not, healthy grieving. Descriptions of grief became prescriptions. It is realized that these models of grief are simply observations and not rigid definitions. On one occasion I gave Janet a diagram of a spiral that showed grief as a pattern of returning to earlier phases of grief, then moving forward again, but that the movement was a process towards an accommodation with grief. I liken it to the tide coming in, the waves roll up the beach and then recede, but next time they move they come further forward. At the early stages Janet did not believe this was possible, but kept the diagram and some months later said how useful it was.

The spiritual dimension of bereavement care

The spiritual is that aspect where the bereaved attempts to make some meaning out of their loss. Often this begins with anger, an emotion reflected in the psalms of lament:

---

6 Margaret Stroebe and Henk Schut, 2000, 'The dual process model of coping with bereavement: Rationals and description', *Death Studies* 24, pp. 197–224.

Rouse yourself! Why do you sleep, O LORD?
Awake, do not cast us off forever!
Why do you hide your face?
Why do you forget our affliction and oppression?
For we sink down to the dust; our bodies cling to the ground.
Rise up, come to our help.
Redeem us for the sake of your steadfast love.
(Ps. 44.23–26)

God seems absent and unable to help. The story of Job also reflects this anger with God. Sometimes there is blame. The wrestling with meaning is emotional and existential. For the psalmist, and many others, it is also physical. These questions of meaning are common among the bereaved and are present in other situations of loss. Gradually meaning begins to make sense. Janet said that after several months of being supported and listened to she was beginning to realize that she was a person in her own right and not an appendage of her late husband.

The social dimension of bereavement

The social dimension of bereavement concerns accepting the reality of the death within a paradox of the dead 'being present'. The deceased is a part of the bereaved's story. This involves the bereaved talking about their loved one. The journey through grief is both internal and external. Janet lives on her own. She has begun to talk to her late husband. This may seem strange, but this aspect of her grieving has been a great strength to her, enabling her 'to move on'. She feels that he is close to her, 'watching over her' and 'caring for her'. These are her words. Is this an expression of afterlife? In psychological terms she is externalizing her grief. The telling of memories of the deceased is important and changes with time. My late father, Alf, told jokes based on puns. We discovered he learnt them from the *Readers Digest*! Now, ten years after his death, when anyone in the family tells such a joke, we all laugh and say, 'Sorry, Alf.'

Western society has certain expectations about bereavement, an impatience, an attitude of 'get on with life!' This is evident within the family and in situations such as work. The same memory is repeated by the bereaved person. Others get tired of listening and ignore, switch off or avoid the person. After a few months following the death there is an expectation that the bereaved will have moved on and have returned to a pre-mortem state. This, however, is not possible. We are irrevocably changed by the death of someone close. A bereaved person does not 'get over it'. Death changes the person for ever, but in some way she must learn to live without the deceased.

There is also abnormal grief, for example when a bedroom is left untouched as a shrine. Help is needed and can be given if sought.

For some, after the initial grief, gradually there is a liberation, a freeing from the previous life, and a new person comes into being. This can happen when one of the partners in a long-term relationship is the dominant one. An elderly cousin and her husband were about to celebrate their fiftieth wedding anniversary when he died after a short illness. Their single daughter Lesley, a civil servant, lived with her parents. Dolly did not know what she was going to do without her husband. En route to the funeral there was laughter and tears as she and I remembered my uncle's life. Harry had been a civil servant all his life. He was meticulous. The story was that everything in the house had to be done in triplicate! He was an avid gardener and a keen member of the Royal Horticultural Society. No pets were allowed in his garden. He was not an adventurer, so had never flown. I suggested to my aunt that she might now have the opportunity to do the things she had always wanted to do, but not been 'allowed' to do. She amazed her daughter and me. Within months, at 80, she had booked to fly to Canada to visit relatives, bought a dog and then took in a lodger.

The practical dimension of bereavement

The practical dimension of bereavement is particularly acute for older people who lose a partner and are left on their own, even if they have adult children, since these are likely to have their own children and live at some distance. A widow may have learnt to drive, but her husband insisted on driving, so she needs to regain confidence on the road. There are tasks that widows may find difficulty in tackling – taking the car for a service, cutting a high hedge, or family finance. An elderly widower may never have learnt to use the washing machine or change a double duvet, not know how to cook an egg, let alone prepare a balanced meal. These can be tasks that weigh heavily on a person in the early days of bereavement since they are the stuff of everyday life.

Each of these four dimensions of bereavement we've looked at can be helped by church ministers.

The bereaved remembered

Sometimes a will states specific desires: money for a stained-glass window, for example. This will need to be created and permission given for its inclusion in the church. Other requests include a scholarship or a financial gift for the purchasing of books by local schoolchildren, a tree planted in a place of significance to the deceased in a local park, a named park bench, or the body, or parts of it, given for medical research or organ donation. Gravestones with a personal design say a lot about the values of the bereaved. These may be in a churchyard, cemetery or as plaques in the crematorium, and set up some months after the funeral.

Many have no permanent physical memorial created by themselves or their family. Reference to them is found in the registers in the church-yard or crematorium and the death certificate rather than gravestones. Incidentally, researching the genealogy of the family has now become a popular hobby. All the above are ways in which the bereaved can be involved and may be ongoing ways in which the process of their bereavement is helped.

Organizations that hold regular occasions for the bereaved

Hospices have an annual 'Light up a Life' celebration at Christmas. Relatives donate and write a card in memory of their loved one, which is placed on a decorated, lit Christmas tree and dedicated at an outdoor carol service. This occasion recognizes losses, particularly felt at Christmas when there is an empty chair. Many hospices have a regular service in which those bereaved recently are welcomed back. Usually there is a ritual of some kind, the invitation to come and light a candle and name the deceased, or to come and receive a seed or a bulb, reminding people of the long process of new life emerging. On these occasions relatives often meet other visitors they have known at the hospice and are able to share experiences of their grief and feelings, so supporting one another. Some funeral directors now have similar services.

Public occasions to help the bereaved

Flowers and teddy bears are laid at the scene of road accidents, loss of life through fire, or a murder. These are rituals that have emerged and display a powerful message to the bereaved that they and the deceased are remembered by the neighbouring community.

There is an annual national remembrance service at the Royal Albert

Hall, London, on the Saturday evening before Remembrance Sunday, the nearest Sunday to 11 November when, in the UK, the war dead and those bereaved are remembered. On the Sunday, at war memorials throughout the country, services are held with the laying of poppy wreaths, the keeping of a two-minute silence for the dead of the two world wars and the major conflicts since. The nation's tribute at the Cenotaph in Whitehall is centred on the two-minute silence from 11 o'clock, followed by the laying of wreaths by members of the Royal Family, leaders of the political parties, the Armed Forces and the Commonwealth nations, a service led by the Bishop of London and a march past of those involved in the various wars.

Questions for reflection and response

- Comment on the statement, 'in the twenty-first century there are few cultural norms for the bereaved.'
- Reread Worden's 'grieving process'. Comment in the light of your experience.
- Comment on 'the deceased is part of the bereaved's story'.
- List support sources you know of for the long-term help of the bereaved.

Reflection on insights from Scripture and the tradition

Integral to both Testaments is the concept of covenant. It is a complex idea, but in essence it is about relationship, between God, who is other, and individuals/the community. Possible origins are those with Abraham, but of greatest significance is the one with Moses, sealed in the responsibilities of keeping the Ten Commandments. The covenant reflects mutuality and trust, yet it is with partners of very different 'weight', God and frail humanity. Initiated by God, it was a call to enter into a relationship. 'I will be your God, and you shall be my people' (Jer. 7.23; 31.33). Israel repeatedly broke the covenant and cried out to God in anguish, illustrated in the psalms of lament. God was constant in faithfulness to them, through the upheavals of their history. The prophets challenged Israel to return to God and finally looked for a new covenant, written on the heart (Hos. 2.19–20; Jer. 31.31–34). There are parallels here with the process of bereavement, a situation when some bereaved believe that they are deserted by God, but God is constant, desiring a relationship. The covenant relationship was expressed as a particular option for the poor and those at the margins of society, particularly widows. Today the bereaved may be ostracized and marginalized in our society. The Shema, at the heart of the Jewish faith, is of love of God, a relationship that brings a person into relationship with their neighbours (Deut. 6.4–9).

The New Testament

In the New Testament, Jesus' ministry was one of healing, bringing about a greater wholeness to the dis-eased. These are acts of compassion. In bereavement ministry, the minister comes alongside the one whose life is 'in pieces', so that the awakening process of healing and reintegration may begin to happen. There are examples in the Scriptures where Jesus heals from alongside the one needing help, at the pace of the person. Jesus takes a blind man from the glare of publicity, puts saliva on his eyes and lays hands on him. Jesus asks him if he can see. The blind man responds, 'I can see people, but they look like trees walking.' Jesus lays his hands on the man again and his sight is restored (Mark 8.22–26). A deaf man with a speech impediment is brought to Jesus. Again Jesus takes him away from the crowd. Jesus 'put his fingers into his ears, and spat and touched his tongue', healing him (Mark 7.32–37). The physical contact of touch (Matt. 8.1–4; Mark 1.40–45; Luke 5.12–16) is significant, as are those who want to touch Jesus (Matt. 14.34–36; Mark 6.53–56).

The healings of Jesus are expressions of the activity of God incarnate in covenant relationship with his broken people, bringing healing and new life. The sick were considered outcasts from society. Jesus commented on the visiting of the sick and stated that 'as you did it to the least of these, who are my family, you did it to me' (Matt. 25.40). The healings can be seen as metaphors of ministry with the bereaved, being alongside, listening to the cries of brokenness and lament, gradually, with appropriate touch, when words break down, silence, healing of new life. In response to the questioning of the Sadducees, Jesus said, 'God is not a God of the dead but of the living, for all live to him' (Luke 20.38). To Martha, sister of Lazarus, Jesus said, 'I am the resurrection and the life' (John 11.23f.). The new life is a quality of life in the present.

At the Last Supper Jesus spoke of a new covenant. He broke bread, asking the disciples to do it in remembrance of him (Luke 22.20). Offering wine, he spoke of the blood of the new covenant, 'poured out for many for the forgiveness of sins' (Matt. 26.27–28; Mark.14.24; Luke 22.20–21). Theologically in the Eucharist or Holy Communion, we remember again Christ's life, death and presence with us now, through the Spirit, in resurrection.

Within the Orthodox Church there is a marking of the soul on its journey, *Panikhidi*, on the third, eighth and fortieth days after the funeral, in
which psalms are chanted with short anthems, and those present pray,
'With the Saints give rest, O Christ, to the soul of thy servant where there
is neither sickness nor sorrow, but life everlasting.' Some believe that
during the first three days the souls of the dead grieve for their loss of life
and roam the earth. Then, grief over, they are escorted by their guardian
angel to appear before God, spending the next five days seeing the souls
of the elect in heaven. After a second appearance before God, the next
month is spent viewing the torment of the damned. Following this the
souls appear for judgement.

Insights from other faiths

The Abrahamic faiths

Within Judaism there are marked rituals of grieving, *shiva*. Following the
funeral, a symbolic meal is eaten including a boiled egg as a symbol of
the continuing of life. During the first seven days of mourning the family
stay at home, wear no leather shoes and sit on low stools, the *yahrzeit*
candle constantly alight. The Kaddish prayer is recited daily. The family
stay within the house; the community support the bereaved in appropriate ways, bringing food, being with the family with their condolence and
memories of the deceased. Some families cut short this time, and Rabbi
Cooper states his sadness at this: 'Whatever is evoked by a death is held
within the ritualized framework of the tradition, and for that week-long
period there is nothing else to focus on.'[7] The living have time to confront
their loss within a loving and supporting community. In the month following the funeral, *sh'loshim*, the bereaved return to work, but do not
take part in parties or celebrations or buy new clothes. In the next ten
months the community regards the bereaved as a 'mourner', who traditionally attends the synagogue weekly to recite the Kaddish to remember
the dead; and the community remembers them. Around eleven months in
the UK, mourners and friends revisit the cemetery to set a tombstone to
formally mark the grave. The name inscribed on the stone is read out in a
service with an address given to recall the deceased. It is both honouring
the deceased and a comfort to the bereaved who attend the ceremony. On
the anniversary of the death a *yahrzeit* candle is lit at home, as at the death
itself, and the Kaddish said for the final time.

7 Howard Cooper, 2013, 'Reflections on Jewish approaches to death, grief and
mourning', in Stephen Oliver (ed.), *Inside Grief*, London: SPCK, p. 111.

Losses are real and lasting. As Freud wrote, 'We will never find a substitute (after loss) ... And actually, this is how it should be, it is the only way of perpetuating that love which we do not want to relinquish.' From that time, whenever family or friends visit the grave, they place a pebble on the grave as a remembrance of a life.

Liturgically on four occasions in the year the dead are remembered, when Jews mourn losses in their history. *Tisha B'Av*, literally 'the ninth day of the Hebrew month Av', is a fast day concluding a three-week period of mourning for the destruction of the First and Second Temples. Rabbi Cooper says:

> the final destruction of the cultic centre in Jerusalem by the Romans catalysed a revolutionary era of diasporic Jewish religious creativity ... authority passed from a hierarchical priesthood to an egalitarian rabbinic leadership ... the losses ... are still remembered with sadness by traditional Jews.[8]

The book of Lamentations is chanted in darkened synagogues with a plaintive melody. It is communal mourning, remembering historically the cost of faith to Jews, yet there is hope, since it is this day rabbinic legend states the Messiah will be born.

The second communal day of mourning is *Yom HaShoah*, Holocaust Memorial Day, inaugurated in Israel in 1953, remembering the loss of 6 million Jews. There is no one service, but those who have lost family and friends join with other Jews, the *yahrzeit* candle may be lit, memories read, poems, prayers and the Kaddish prayer recited.

At Yom Kippur, the Day of Atonement, acts of confession and remission of sins are made. Many bereaved people remain with feelings of guilt over the death of a loved one. This occasion is for all Jews a time of repentance (*teshuva*), a healing process, recognizing and confessing wrongdoing and taking steps not to repeat it. Prayer is called 'the cry from the heart'. For the bereaved this may include being angry with God and blaming God for the death. The help of a rabbi may be used.

Islam is widespread across the world, existing in Islamic states and as communities of faith in many countries. In some ways it is death and mourning practices today that unite Muslims in a common past. These practices include the care of the bereaved. Young women wear funeral clothes for three months after the funeral, older women for a year, marking them out for care and compassion. On the third, seventh and fortieth days after death men gather at the mosque to pray for the dead, while

8 Cooper, 'Reflections on Jewish approaches to death', pp. 113f.

women prepare sugary dishes. The story of Muhammad's birth is read aloud, and tears are shed. On the first anniversary of the death, a ceremony is held to place a stone on the grave.

Muslims who die away from their country of origin want their body returned to their 'home'. A lined casket is expensive, as is the cost of flight. In doing this the 'exiled' family feel even more foreign. They are bound only by their faith, which may then become more important to them and be observed more carefully.

The Eastern faiths

Hindu observance varies according to caste, region and finance. Rites at death and beyond are a sacred duty and in accordance with the Scriptures, together with acts of piety and charity to ensure the peaceful repose of the departed soul.

Buddhism emphasizes impermanence, the cycle of birth, death and rebirth. The Buddha recognized that the impermanence resulting from suffering characterized human life; only by the loss of attachment to the self through a series of rebirths could enlightenment and freedom be found. Theravada Buddhists believe in instant reincarnation: *The Book of the Dead* proposes that the art of living well and the art of dying well are one and the same. Buddhists teach that acceptance is a good thing, for it will be followed by rebirth in an endless cycle until you can break free.

Questions for reflection and response

- How does Mark 8.22–26 model a process of bereavement care?
- Comment on the concept of covenant as helpful post-bereavement.
- Choose a psalm of lamentation (see Index). Comment on its usefulness in helping the bereaved.
- Judaism has marked rituals of grieving. What does Christianity offer?

Reflection on cultural context with insights from Scripture and the tradition

Despite the taboo on any conversation about mortality and the increase in the medical advances that have extended life and denied death, there is a growing awareness that each of us has to accept our mortality, as we experience the deaths of those close to us and those we love. The psychologists have increased our understanding of bereavement, its individuality, process, factors affecting it and the necessity of appropriate grieving. We have become aware of how we affect one another's lives and the possibility that our deceased loved ones may be part of our ongoing story. This is a challenge to the individualism of Western society and our limited concept of society. Expressing emotion in public is an accepted part of the social ritual in many cultures. In Northern European societies, death is viewed as a private event, and people are inhibited, if not prevented, from sharing their grief with the community. 'By keeping death away from the home, absolving themselves from all other rituals related to the handling, laying out and dressing of the body, Westerners have succeeded in "distancing" themselves from death.'[9]

Thinking about the four dimensions of bereavement – the psychological, spiritual, social and practical – it is notable that the process of bereavement depends on the encouragement and support of individuals and groups around the bereaved, but this is frequently lacking in a driven, materialistic, individualistic society. Bereavement today is a journey into the unknown, with few signposts.

In contrast, the Scriptures are dominated by the concept of covenant, the relationship between God and all humanity, expressed in concern, particularly for those at the margins of society. In Western societies it is the bereaved who are frequently in this marginal group. The Scriptures reflect Jesus' ministry to those living with dis-ease, as are the bereaved. His is a ministry of coming alongside, being with, and listening to, the distressed. He brings healing and new life. This was subversive, challenging much of the history of his own people and a factor that led to his death. Concern and continuing care for the bereaved is a subversive activity today in that it is not a feature of our culture. Society is looking at 'what next', 'the 'future', rather than the influence of the past on our present. The Christian Scriptures lead to a theology of incarnation, of attributes of God in covenant, and in the Trinity as witnessing to our need for relationships.

Questions for reflection and response

- How is a death in your street or neighbourhood acknowledged?
- Find out what you can about 'death cafes'. Comment on them as an ongoing aid to bereavement.

---

9 Pittu Laungani and Bill Young, 1997, 'Conclusions: Implications for practice and policy', in Colin Murray Parkes, Pittu Laungani and Bill Young (eds), *Death and Bereavement across Cultures*, London and New York: Routledge, p. 231.

- As a Christian, write a letter to a neighbour who has recently been bereaved, offering condolences.
- Comment on our need for relationships. How is this a theological concept.

Pastoral practice

Our pastoral practice derives from our theology. In the incarnate Christ we see the attributes of compassion, comfort, forgiveness, healing/wholeness and of presence. There is a theology of relationships expressed in covenant and the doctrine of the Trinity. These insights are reflected in appropriate pastoral care and in personal and communal occasions, such as annual celebrations in church. It is important to point out that there is not often any difference between the bereavement of Christians and non-Christians; Christians experience the same range of emotions, despite, or maybe because of, hope in an afterlife. I have met Christians embittered by a particularly difficult loss, whose faith is badly dented and for some lost. These people feel that their experience of death cannot be held together with their understanding of a loving God.

At Easter in many churches, particularly on Holy Saturday, when we experience and live in the numbness and shadow of the death of Christ, we remember our own parting from loved ones and our broken, sinful relationships. On Easter Day we remember the resurrection hope that 'nothing can separate us from the love of God that is in Christ Jesus our Lord' (Rom. 8.38–39). In some churches the names of the deceased are read out at some point during the Easter period. Invitations can be sent, for example to those known to the church whose funerals were held in the church. There is here a theology of presence.

All Souls' is another annual remembrance of the dead. Many churches have services on this occasion. Invitations can be sent to the relatives of those whose funerals have occurred during the year. The service will include a reading out of the names of loved ones who have died. While the reading of names is made, the congregation could be invited to bring a photo or piece of memorabilia of the deceased, for those present to see and share. It is helpful to have a theme for the service, with ritual acts, so that those attending may remember their own particular grief and be united with other bereaved people by a common action. This emerges from a theology of relationship of covenant and Trinity. I have invited folk to come, receive a tea-light, light it and place it in a sand tray. On other occasions everyone was given an apple and invited to look at the bruised skin and think about their battered, bereaved life and the new life of the seed within the apple. One year a piece of rosemary was given to each person, since rosemary speaks of remembering. Another year I thought of the changing season of nature paralleling those of our lives, and each person was offered a spring bulb. In these ways the church helps the dead to have an ongoing relationship with family and wider community. Having refreshments, before or after the service for All Souls', enables bereaved folk to talk with others – they may not know each other and may have never met before but they share bereavement and the loss of someone dear to them. It means that they realize that they are not alone and can be united with those who have gone before us in the body of Christ.

Remembrance Sunday has already been mentioned as an annual occasion for remembering.

Many churches have a regular time for the bereaved to meet. In one of the churches in our rural benefice this is monthly and called Comfort Corner. It is simply a time to come, to share with one another and have a cuppa and a piece of cake. In other churches there is a weekly coffee morning. On these occasions, the time is enabled by a member of the ministry team, who is present and has pastoral skills to be alongside and listen to the bereaved. The bereaved share with others present and, as in the experience at the beginning of this chapter, network and are comforted by others. If there is any formal content on these occasions, it is important that this reflects the needs of those present. The Church is present as the enabler and incarnates the presence of a loving and vulnerable God. In my experience several widowers, who were of retirement age and not churchgoers, began coming to the church following a church funeral and were accepted and welcomed by the church community. Other churches run a lunch club to which many on their own through the death of a partner attend. This is important particularly at Christmas, since immediate family may live at a distance.

Churches often have a weekly pew sheet, which includes for prayer, with the permission of the relatives, the names of those who have died. They are prayed for during the intercessions at the Sunday service. The bereaved who attend find this helpful; it also means that the church community knows and can have a role in being alongside the bereaved.

Visiting the bereaved

The long term follow-up of a bereavement is in the care of the church's pastoral team. Reflections on this are included in Chapter 3. It is important that ministers are supported and receive some supervision within the context of confidentiality. Bereavement is very varied. Some people simply get on with life, not acknowledging the death, as a father whose daughter was killed in a road accident, who did not mention her name again. Grief in this situation may be buried and can lead to resentment, which can be psychologically harmful. Others can feel comfortable in grief and do not want to move on. Most handle grief with the help of family and friends who are willing to listen. For others, having someone outside the family, who relates well and is skilled at listening, is helpful in reflecting an incarnational theology and relationality in the theology of Trinity. Grief's length and processes are varied.

The minister needs to remember that he or she is a guest in the bereavement, which is shared; the theology of covenant and Trinity. An essential is to listen, to be alongside in presence and comfort. It is important to keep promises to visit, and to ring before visiting. Listening intensely, often to the same repeated account, is important – bereavement can be a slow process.

Near the beginning, if the person is living on their own for the first time, the nights and mornings are difficult times. Suggestions can be made: having a warm drink last thing at night, thinking and recording in a diary something lovely seen or heard that day. The bereaved get stuck and numb, not feeling able to do anything, so that ordinary household chores mount up. It is useful at night to think of one task to do first thing in the morning, and, having done it, to be pleased about it. Doing some sort of physical exercise is important – simply a walk down the road or a little weeding in the garden. If the person is severely depressed and you are told by the person that he or she has a lot of pills and feels that life is not worth living – address it, don't leave it. Help them to think about the effect the action of taking the pills would have on those left. Don't tell them – sensitivity is important. If there is a real danger, stay with the person, and if necessary tell someone else, such as a doctor. This only very occasionally happens.

Judaism is wise in having markers during the first year of bereavement. This is the time of anniversaries – of the death itself, of the birthday, of a wedding anniversary, of the first Christmas and holiday without a loved one. Some churches send a card on the first anniversary of the death.

Help with practical issues is important for the bereaved at the early stages; it may be that someone known to the visitor, maybe within the church, could help.

Caring for the bereaved is challenging; agree the next visit at the end of each. Remember that the aim is to help the person find new life in whatever way is important to them. Jesus said, 'I came that you might have life and have it to the full' (John 10.10).

Questions for reflection and response

- What theology underlies your pastoral practice?
- Comment on the practice in some churches of praying for the dead.
- How can the pastoral visitor pace him- or herself?
- Why is the care of the bereaved both a privilege and demanding?

Further reading

Mark Earey, 2012, *Worship that Cares: An Introduction to Pastoral Liturgy*, London: SCM Press.

Hugh James, 2004, *A Fitting End: Making the Most of a Funeral*, Norwich: Canterbury Press.

Ewan Kelly, 2008, *Meaningful Funerals: Meeting the Theological and Pastoral Challenge in a Postmodern Era*, London and New York: Mowbray.

Tony Walter, 1999, *On Bereavement: The Culture of Grief*, Maidenhead: Open University Press.

7

Resources for Pastoral Carers

In our own woundedness we can become a source of life for others.
Henri J. M. Nouwen[1]

This chapter begins with a case study, reflecting on its implicit theology. I look at the cultural context of postmodernism and attitudes to faith and spirituality. The scriptural resources are examined: Jesus' ministry, his need of withdrawal for prayer and companionship in the work of the Kingdom as a model for our own ministry as pastoral carers. Context and Scripture are brought together, leading to a theology of presence, incarnation and Trinity, informing practice. Suggestions are made for resourcing pastoral carers. There are questions for the reader to reflect on experience, and suggested reading.

This chapter is intensely personal. Illustrations have emerged that have challenged the theology I hold, a theology that continues to be in process.

Pastoral circle

Pastoral practice: resources for pastoral carers

Experience – reflection: a patient becomes a carer

Cultural context: postmodernism attitudes to faith and spirituality

Scripture and tradition: Jesus' need for withdrawal

Scripture/tradition and context: theology of being human, presence, incarnation and Trinity

---

1 Henri J. M. Nouwen, 1994, *The Wounded Healer: Ministry in Contemporary Society*, London: Darton, Longman and Todd.

Experience

Karen, a colleague, and I entered the hospice in which we worked, to be told that one of our elderly patients had died peacefully during the night. We discovered that Miriam's body was in the hospice mortuary and asked the nurses if we could go in and say goodbye. There was surprise. The nurses had laid out Miriam's body – it waited collection by the funeral directors. What more was there to do? Miriam was, after all, dead.

The mortuary was quiet; Miriam looked at peace. The nurses had placed a rose on the pillow beside her. She had worn herself out caring for Daniel her husband, who had died in the hospice earlier in the year. She was left alone and had died alone. Miriam and Dan had no children; a baby had been born to them, but lived only a few hours, and Miriam was unable to conceive again. She had a relative in the area, but who never visited their home, or either of them in the hospice. Despite a sad, hard life Miriam was always cheerful and her room full of laughter. She cared for everyone, taking a great interest in all the staff and their families. She appreciated all that was done for her. Nurses would search for knitting and sewing needles lost in her bed, and there were gales of laughter when the lost objects were found on her bedside cabinet.

Karen and I wanted to thank God for this amazing woman who had, through her life and her dying, selflessly reached out to others. We wanted to give thanks for all she had taught us simply through being Miriam. We stood either side of her bed and took her hands. Together we said the grace and a prayer committing her to the love and mercy of her Creator.

Reflection on experience

Miriam was a patient yet cared for the staff in extraordinary ways. She was in the hospice at the same time as my youngest sister, who had terminal cancer, although they never met. Somehow Miriam discovered this fact. It was near Christmas, and she gave me a letter she had written:

A few words at Christmas for Marian. We all need a shepherd to guide and care for us, especially when we are overcome by events we never expected, well we have Marian an ordained shepherd who is always with us to help when we really need help. There may be many times when our shepherd needs someone to give comfort and care and we do not know of this, so just to put our hands together, and share in kind thoughts will, I hope, help to brighten those dark days that are never very far away. Miriam speaking, I am sure, for all the sheep and lambs.

At Christmas Miriam gave me a gift that she had made for my sister and attached to it was a note:

A small token for Marian's sister, to stand her cup of bedtime comfort on. For every stitch in the tray cloth I have sent up a word or two, to help the 'Chief Shepherd' in his care of you. All blessings and love to you 'little lady', we are there beside you. Miriam.

Those letters are a treasured possession and brought tears to my eyes. The words reveal a deep humanity, which, despite and maybe because Miriam herself was suffering, she was able to stretch out beyond herself to the needs of my sister and me. I was attempting to preserve a professional role as hospice chaplain. Miriam saw, beneath this, a human suffering on a different journey, one of anticipatory grief for my sister's imminent death. It revealed a simple and yet profound faith and trust in God, 'the Chief Shepherd', in Miriam's words. Patients unwittingly resource us and care for us. Shepherd is a biblical metaphor (John 10.11) and was later a metaphor used of the pastoral carer. The latter use of the image was often criticized as being too 'soft', yet thinking of biblical shepherds, it was one of toughness, danger and vulnerability. Who was the pastoral carer in this experience?

I remember another occasion when as a hospital pastoral worker I had been the only member of the team on call for the whole weekend. It had been busy. The task in the late afternoon of Sunday was to take communion to those who had requested it but could not get to the chapel service. The last visit was to an elderly bed-bound woman. I was exhausted and longed for my bed. At the end of the brief service she said to me, 'Could you spare a minute?' I groaned inwardly. 'Please sit down. I would like to pray for you,' she said. I was humbled and touched. Who was the pastoral carer?

My years as a hospice chaplain were formative in my Christian experience. Friends could not understand how anyone could work full-time in a hospice; I experienced and learnt so much from being with patients, their relatives and staff about what it means to be human, and about God. It was an immense and humbling privilege.

Questions for reflection and response

- What theology underlies the 'happenings' with Miriam?
- Explore the idea of 'professional' in being a 'minister' in a situation where you are with the elderly, those dying with a terminal illness or the bereaved.
- How is your humanity shown with 'patients'? Is it permissible to cry or laugh? Share something of your own story.
- Comment on a theology of the 'ministry of presence'.

Reflection on cultural context

Characteristics of twenty-first-century society

Previous chapters have explored something of the cultures of the world in which we live. In the developed world it is one in which individualism is significant, human and personal rights matter. 'There is no such thing as society, only families,' said Margaret Thatcher.

The economies of the West have been in recession; cuts in public services have been made, resulting in great discrepancies in wages and the rise of foodbanks on which many families depend. Advertising that tells us the possessions we need to be fulfilled and happy has proliferated. There are slogans from the supermarkets – 'You shop and we'll drop.'

Communication systems, mobile phones, smartphones, iPads and emails have created instant accessibility. TV and radio have vast networks of equipment and reporters, so that we can witness, almost instantaneously, what is happening in our own country and across the world: disasters, court trials, sport fixtures, governments and politics.

The technology that has created communication systems has been working in the field of medicine with the manufacture of imaging equipment and other diagnostic tools such as X-rays, ventilators and dialysis machines. Drug research and production has increased medications to ease pain and vaccines have eradicated and controlled disease. The result has been an extension of life and a growing population. Technology has eased housework, allowing women to express themselves, use their gifts and work outside the home. However, technology has also enabled the creation of weapons of mass destruction, with an increase in acts of terrorism and a multiplicity of civil wars, the horror of death, displacement and millions of homeless refugees.

Postmodernism has defined our society. There is a decline in the meta-narrative that holds people together. Authority in political leaders, in texts, in holy Scriptures are questioned. Church attendance is in decline, though there are experimental groups that show growth. Groups such as the Mothers Union and Women's Institute have ageing memberships, yet are looking outwards to support and help women in the developing world. There is a searching for meaning in life, for answers to existential questions – a spiritual quest – but this interest in different kinds of spirituality does not fit easily with the narratives and creeds of existing established institutions. Life is lived in the paradox of a growing interest in spirituality and at the same time a decline in institutional churchgoing.

Stress

Secularism has undermined the old world-view that traditional religions took for granted and that placed God at the centre. Now in Europe and North America the assumption is that the universe, humans and future history can only be understood in terms of the disciplines of modern science. One of the results of the emphasis on materialism and achievement is burnout and stress. It is as if, 'we are always doing something, talking, reading, listening to the radio, planning what next. The mind is kept naggingly busy on some easy, unimportant external things all day'.[2] This burnout is across the professions, including the Church, as seen in such books as *Clergy Stress: The Hidden Conflicts in Ministry*.[3] Stress can be a particular challenge to those working mainly in the area of death, dying and bereavement, yet Christians have resources that can challenge stress. This is the subject of this chapter.

Questions for reflection and response

- Write a list, in order of importance to you, of ten characteristics of twenty-first-century life.

---

2 Brenda Ueland, quoted in Julia Cameron, 1995, *The Artist's Way: A Course in Discovering and Recovering Your Creative Self*, London: Pan Macmillan, p. 87.

3 Mary Anne Coate, 1989, *Clergy Stress: The Hidden Conflicts in Ministry*, London: SPCK.

RESOURCES FOR PASTORAL CARERS

- Where and why are some Christian churches bucking the trends of decline?
- Write a short questionnaire on spirituality to give to ten church people and ten non-church people, to discover what people understand by spirituality. For example, you could make a list – e.g. yoga, meditation – and ask people to tick which activity they consider spiritual and why.
- Why is stress pertinent to ministers of faith, lay and ordained?

Insights from Scripture and the tradition

The Hebrew Scriptures

There are several occasions when individuals are 'stressed' and in their anguish they are met by God. Jacob, fleeing from his brother Esau's threat to kill him, stops for rest (Gen. 27.41–43; 28.10–17). He dreams of a ladder stretching from earth to heaven, with angels ascending and descending and hears, 'Know that I am with you wherever you go, and will bring you back to this land: for I will not leave you until I have done what I have promised you' (Gen. 28.15). Jacob recognizes the holiness of the place and sets up a marker stone. Years later, having prospered in exile, Jacob decides to return and be reconciled with his brother. Nearing home, yet fearful of the future meeting, he sends his household ahead (Gen. 32.22–24). Alone, at the brook Jabbok, he wrestles with an unknown assailant (Gen. 32.24–30). At daybreak Jacob discovers he wrestles with a God who is always present to bless. The story is told by Rachel Naomi Remen. Paralleling it with an experience of her own, she says: 'Perhaps the wisdom lies in engaging the life you have been given as fully and courageously as possible and not letting go until you find the unknown blessing that is in everything.'[4] In Jacob's emotional stress, alone, he finds God is present, ready to bless; something as pastoral carers we need to remember.

Elijah flees Jezebel's anger and threat to kill him after his defeat of the prophets of Baal on Mount Carmel (1 Kings 18.20–40; 19.1–20). On his journey, Elijah is fed and nourished. Finally at Mount Horeb, after wind, earthquake and fire, there is 'a sound of sheer silence' (1 Kings 19.12). What a wonderful image – sheer silence! God's presence speaks in reassurance that Elijah is not alone. God has appointed a new king and prophet who will continue Elijah's work. There are times when pastorally there are challenging situations, such as being with the anger of a bereaved

---

4 Rachel Naomi Remen, 2000, *My Grandfather's Blessings: Tales of Strength, Refuge and Belonging*, London: Thorsons, pp. 25–7.

person as she blames God for her suffering and weeps. We may want to escape from this situation. T. S. Eliot wrote, 'humankind cannot bear very much reality'. We need to care; and not to care, to have a certain detachment, and when we are silent and listening not feel guilt that we not doing enough. When the calm and the silence follow, we intuitively know that the mystery we call God is present in the situation. Elizabeth Kübler-Ross said, 'Learn to get in touch with the silence within yourself and know that everything in this life has a purpose.' The psalmist says, 'Be still and know that I am God' (Ps. 46.10). This is the grace of the present moment.

The New Testament: Jesus taking time out

Jesus shows his need for 'taking time out' for stillness. Luke tells the story of the boy Jesus, at the age of 12, staying in the Temple, listening 'and asking them questions' (Luke 2.41–52). When found and questioned by his anxious parents, his response was 'Did you not know that I must be in my Father's house?' Through his listening in the Temple, Luke says, 'Jesus increased in wisdom and in years, and in divine and human favour' (Luke 2.52). Later in Jesus' ministry, on entering the Temple, which was being used as a market for buying sacrificial animals, Jesus said, 'My house shall be called a house of prayer for all the nations, you have made it a den of thieves' (Mark 11.17).

Following the decisive experience of his baptism, Jesus is driven out into the wilderness, 'and the angels waited on him' (Mark 1.13). This must have been a period of intense loneliness. Wilderness is a metaphor in the Scriptures, of the desert experience, of waiting on God and as the place where God might be found, yet also a place of wrestling with the demons of self-will. In the wilderness Jesus wrestles with the calling he believed he received at baptism.

Throughout Jesus' ministry, we discover 'in the morning, while it was still very dark, he got up and went out to a deserted place, and there he prayed'. Sometimes the writer states 'a lonely place' (Mark 1.35; 6.30; 7.24; Luke 5.16; Matt. 14.23). Jesus taught, 'Come unto me, all of you who are tired and bear heavy loads, and I will give you rest' (Matt.11.28). Jesus knew his need for silence. He is our model; if he knew this need, how much more, as pastoral workers, do we? On one occasion, after the news of John the Baptist's cruel death, Jesus says to his friends, 'Come away to a deserted place all by yourselves and rest a while' (Mark. 6.31). The disciples too needed silence. Mark adds to this account, 'For many were coming and going, and they had no leisure even to eat.'

There are insights in William Vanstone's book, *The Stature of Waiting*, of the dignity of Jesus' waiting while being handed over to those who arrested and tried him. There is patience and passivity, vulnerability and powerlessness, which was to become, in the crucifixion, part of God's redemptive creative presence in the world. In bereavement care there are some glimpses of this waiting. Vanstone comments:

> waiting can be the most intense and poignant of all human experiences – the experience which, above all others, strips us of affectation and self-deception and reveals to us the reality of our needs, our values, and ourselves.[5]

Jesus partying

There are many accounts, particularly in Luke's Gospel, of Jesus at meal times, partying! We are told of the rejoicing when the 'bridegroom' comes; Jesus at leisure, at playtime. There is a wonderful children's book called *Jesus' Day Off*, which shows the playful Jesus.[6]

In Proverbs 8.27–31 Wisdom is present at creation. The New Jerusalem Bible translates verses 30–31:

> I was beside the master craftsman,
>   delighting him day after day,
>   ever at play in his presence,
> at play everywhere on his earth,
>   delighting to be with the children of men.

For the words 'master worker' the NRSV has another reading, 'little child'. We are all called to be children of God.

Play is a theme taken up by the writing of a thirteenth-century Béguine mystic, which gives insight into the relationship of the believer and God using the imagery of a child at play:

> I, God, am your playmate!
> I will lead the child in you
> In wonderful ways
> For I have chosen you.
> Beloved child, come swiftly to Me
> For I am truly in you.

---

5 W. H. Vanstone, 1982, *The Stature of Waiting*, London: Darton, Longman and Todd, p. 83.

6 Allan Nicholas, 1998, *Jesus' Day Off*, London: Hutchinson Children's Books.

Remember this:
The smallest soul of all is still the daughter of the Father,
The sister of the Son,
The friend of the Holy Spirit
And the true bride of the Holy Trinity.

God leads the child he has called in wonderful ways
God takes the soul
To a secret place,
For God alone will play with it
In a game of which the body knows nothing.
God says: 'I am your playmate!
Your childhood was a companion
Of my Holy Spirit'[7]

We are all called to be 'children of God'.

Jesus reiterated the commandments

The commandments are enshrouded in the Shema. Jesus said of the commandments, 'The first is "Hear, O Israel: the Lord our God, the Lord is
one; you shall love the Lord your God with all your heart, and with all
your soul, and with all your mind, and with all your strength." The second
is this, "You shall love your neighbour as yourself"' (Mark 12.29–31).
Jesus links love of God, neighbour and self: a reflection of the Trinity and
of community. In 1965 Harry Williams wrote of how he could only speak
of things proved true in his own experience: 'must we not therefore look
for God in what we are, in the whole kaleidoscope of our personal experience? And in this sense would it be wrong to speak of a Theology of the
self?'[8] This was important in the 1960s. However, it is not the final word.
Jesus spoke of following him as denying ourselves: 'For those who want
to save their life will lose it, and those who lose their life for my sake, and
for the sake of the gospel, will save it' (Mark 8.35). This seems to indicate
that the self, created in the image of God (Gen. 1.26), is the work of God,
and we find our true selves in God. God is at the centre.

---

7 Sue Woodruff, 1982, *Meditations with Mechthild of Magdeburg*, Santa Fe, CA:
Bear and Co., pp. 47, 54.
8 H. A. Williams, 1965, *The True Wilderness*, London: Constable, pp. 8–10.

Hope in God

The hope in God is not only for this life, but for the next, whatever that life is. Paul comments: 'If for this life only we have hoped in Christ, we are of all people most to be pitied' (1 Cor. 15.19). The promise of the ascended Jesus was 'remember, I am with you always, to the end of the age' (Matt. 28.20). These two statements are encouraging to those called to be pastoral carers.

Insights from other faiths

The Abrahamic faiths

In the esoteric Judaism of the Kabbalah, the Deep Self is named the *Neshamah*, from the root of *shmhm*, 'to hear or listen'. The *Neshamah* is 'She Who Listens, the soul who inspires or guides us'.

In the Islam of the Sufi mystics we find the work of Rumi (1207–73). His poetry and writings have inspired many.

Kahlil Gibran (1883–1931), though not a Muslim, was influenced by Christianity and Islam's Sufi tradition. He stated: 'You are my brother and I love you when you prostrate yourself in your mosque, and kneel in your church and pray in your synagogue. You are one, sons of one faith – the Spirit.'[9] Gibran's work has a great deal to say on inner stillness and the grace of the present moment.

Questions for reflection and response

- Why is 'wilderness' such a powerful metaphor of the Christian journey of faith?
- What might a 'theology of play' look like?
- Discuss the idea of Jesus' experience of 'withdrawal' as a model for bereavement ministry.
- Einstein said, 'The most beautiful thing we can experience is the mysterious.' Comment.

---

9 Alexandre Najjar, 2008, *Kahlil Gibran: A Biography*, London: Saqi Books, p. 150.

Reflection on cultural context in dialogue with Scripture and the tradition

The first section of this chapter indicated the kind of society in which we live. It is materialistic, pluralist and secular, but above all it is self-absorbed, dominated by an ethic of self. This is at variance with the Scriptures, which write of humanity made in God's image and likeness. God is at the centre, a God whose spirit is in the hearts of all peoples. Paradoxically, the 'self' is significant, individuals matter to God, but a theology of self is limited if it does not understand the grace of God as the creation and bedrock of the self. Humans are recognized by Jesus as body, mind and spirit. Twenty-first-century society is interested in existential questions, though dismissive of metanarratives and the authority of Scriptures and tradition; the spiritualities that have emerged are individualistic and self-driven.

Theology of Trinity

The existence and significance of society is played down in the Western world today. This is unlike the Scriptures, which witness to all as children of God and advocate a new commandment to love the neighbour, whoever that neighbour is. God enters into a covenant relationship with Israel; Christians become part of the body of Christ. This relates to the belief in God as Trinity.

Theology of presence

These dominant differences might suggest that Christianity is not of this world, but rather is concerned with the next world, 'pie in the sky when you die'. However, this belief is challenged by the coming of Jesus and the doctrine of the incarnation (John 1.14). Jesus shows us human potential and possibilities, yet he gets tired, is tested, needs to discover the purpose in his life, enjoys life and parties, belongs to a culture and a tradition that gives his life meaning yet challenges how the Jewish religion of his day is practised. Because of this he becomes vulnerable to the authorities, for example healing on the Sabbath (Mark 3.1–6), driving the market traders out of the Temple (Mark 11.15–19). The faith of Jesus is concerned particularly with those on the margins of society, whom he gets alongside, demonstrating a theology of presence (Luke 19.1–10).

Theology of hope

In previous chapters there is an acknowledgement of the significance of scientific achievements, particularly those of medicine, which have extended the lifespan and eradicated many of the diseases and epidemics of the past. This is praiseworthy, but can lead to a hubris that dominates thinking and to a belief that death itself can be conquered. For many, life today is driven, whether it be to attain fame, position or possessions, so much so that stress and burnout are real health issues, in addition to the social implications of adding to dissatisfaction in relationships, wanting more and wanting perfection, which in turn can lead to marriage breakdown. Jesus shows vulnerability in his life and particularly in his dying (Mark 15.34). In his resurrection, however, we understand this mystery as an act of God giving new life and hope. It could be said that the Scriptures challenge the ideas of life in the West today, that they are indeed countercultural and show a different way to live.

Questions for reflection and response

- What are the dangers of following a spirituality that is individualistic and self-driven?
- Examine the idea that at present we have lost belief in society. Why is a concept of society so important theologically?
- Today individuals seek perfection, for example in a marriage partner. How does this 'fit' for bereavement ministers with Jesus' statement 'be perfect as your heavenly Father is perfect', that is, complete/whole (Matt. 5.48)?
- Comment on the statement that Christianity is countercultural. Give examples of your point of view.

Pastoral practice

Our practice derives from theology: our reflection on things of God leads to changed practice. It is emotionally demanding to care for the dying and the grieving, to be available to those who are searching for answers to sickness, premature deaths and terminal illness. Jesus, in being touched and healing a woman with a menstrual illness, knew that power had gone out of him (Mark 5.25–30). Those working in pastoral care in this area can soon become exhausted, since this is a costly ministry of incarnation and presence. What then can sustain and nurture the emotional, physical, social and spiritual elements of our lives, as we repeatedly enter into such relationships of need?

Inner stillness: a theology of presence and incarnation

Pastoral ministry is predominantly about listening and presence, and to do this we must have developed an inner silence. Listening attentively demands the whole of us. On one occasion, in a hospital, I was called to a cot-death in which the police were involved, leaving the parents of the child acutely distressed. As I listened to their story of anguish, a thought kept popping into my head, and I tried desperately to ignore it. I just about managed. Later I brought to mind the thought. The dead baby's name was Katie, and she was a thriving redhead of a few weeks old; it was a parallel to my niece, recently born, whom I had not yet seen. It could have been my niece being talked about.

Acute listening includes the establishing of relationship, the engagement with another in grief, the hearing of a story, repeated several times, a companioning, supporting a person confronted with death, loss and aloneness. In this situation I may be touched, moved and overwhelmed. It is incarnational. Sometimes the only thing to do is to put an arm round the person, to weep with them and be silent. The issue of touch is a hard one; perhaps it is easier for me as a woman. It is easier in a public place. The vulnerability of the bereaved is paramount. I can and do, within myself, hand the person over to God. As a pastoral carer it is important in prayer regularly to place people whom we are working with before God, and as C. G. Jung says, 'to explore daily the will of God'. Being alongside I realize that the grief belongs to the one bereaved and at some point it needs to be handed back to them, though it is usually a long process to enable them to receive their grief and own it. To know ourselves as carers is an essential part of the process of containing another's suffering.

After a funeral, which is a demanding ritual of pastoral care, I need space and time on my own, but try and arrange a future time, when I can meet with other members of the church team – in Anglicanism, the Reader, who helped with the funeral service, the organist and a verger – to reflect together. This is a great help in my self-awareness and aids my ongoing journey into the mystery that is God. On these occasions I am aware of the significance of 'being' and 'waiting'. When I get it wrong by my openness and availability, as I do, then I need forgiveness, to confess and apologize. I am mindful of the part of myself that is gratified when what I have done is affirmed. The ego challenges, and hubris is a danger. It is also a challenge when identity is tied up with activity, overloading a day with responding to another's needs, when it is my day off! Here there is a potential threat to my health, if my identity is tied up with my role rather than who I really am, a human with all the human needs for forgiveness, love and recognition.

Theology of God's love

When years ago I came across the book *Mister God, This is Anna*, a particular incident in the story became memorable. Anna is a child who is a runaway from an abusive family. She is noticed sitting on a kerb one night shivering by a young man called Fynn, who takes her home to his Irish mother. With Anna, Fynn learns about God. In one such conversation Anna says:

> 'Fynn, Mister God doesn't love us.' She hesitated, 'He doesn't really, you know, only people can love. I love Bossy (the cat) but Bossy don't love me … I love you Fynn, and you love me, don't you?' I tightened my arm about her. 'You love me because you are people. I love Mister God truly, but he don't love me.' It sounded like a death knell. 'Damn and Blast,' I thought, why does this have to happen to people? Now she's lost everything. But I was wrong. She had got both her feet planted on the next stepping stone. 'No,' she went on, 'no, he don't love me, not like you do, it's different, it's millions of times bigger. You see, Fynn, people can only love outside, and can only kiss outside, but Mister God can love you right inside, it's different. Mister God ain't like us, we are a little bit like Mister God, but not much yet.'[10]

Professional needs

Our own spiritual growth is at the heart of ministry. It is easy to be self-deluded about myself. I cannot know myself completely. It is only as I reveal myself to another that I can know more of who I am. Here the insight of the Johari Window is helpful, conceived by Joseph Luft and Harrington Ingham which I have adapted.[11]

---

10 Fynn, illustrated by Papas, 1974, *Mister God, This is Anna*, London: Collins, p. 41.

11 Joseph Luft and Harrington Ingham, 1955, 'The Johari Window: A graphic model of interpersonal awareness', *Proceedings of the Western Training Laboratory in Group Development*, Los Angeles: UCLA.

The Johari Window (adapted)

1 Free or public area The part known to you and to others, the area of mutual sharing and interaction.	2 'Blind' area Known to others, but you yourself are unaware of it. It includes gestures, tone of voice and good traits of which you are ignorant.
3 'Hidden' area Known to you but not shared with others. You might wish to keep some parts hidden.	4 'Unknown' area An area where your creative talents and abilities as well as your fears and limitations lie, which you do not know about and others have never seen, yet are a part of all of us.

The four boxes represent the Self.

1 The free or public area: you can aim to enlarge this area.
2 The blind area: you make this area smaller by getting feedback from others. Working with a group helps.
3 The hidden area: it might help relationships if more of you were known and shared, which can be done by self-disclosure.
4 The unknown area: meditation and relaxation may bring some of these into awareness.

The more your 'free self' coincides with your 'whole self' and the more you share of yourself with the world, the better you communicate your true self to others and the less tension there is within yourself. There are ways to do this through going to a counsellor. For most of us in the Christian Church, it is through having a spiritual guide or director. Within spiritual guidance, with the help of an experienced director, I am able to see and accept more of myself. More importantly I am able to catch glimpses of myself in the light of God, as a child of God. My guide is a Roman Catholic nun. We meet every two or three months. Most Christian denominations have a spirituality group, who train and have a list of recommended directors. The advice is to try a director and see if there is a chemistry between the director and directee; if not, ask for someone else. However, it is important to have a director who is prepared to be challenging.

A further necessity is to have supervision of the pastoral work that you do.[12] I had a supervisor when working at the hospice, who was outside the hospice. We met every month. I chose a person involved in education, who had managerial skills, was theologically well versed, supportive and a priest. My supervisor helped me to 'reframe' the work I was doing, to sort out what it meant to be a Christian within a team of other professions in a secular environment. Supervision helped me to decide on my priorities at work and set goals.

Prayer: theology of relationships, Trinity

What other aids are needed in our pastoral practice? We are part of the 'body of Christ' and need companions on the spiritual journey. Belonging to a Christian congregation or group where we are ministered to is essential.

There are other spiritual resources, such as booking in regularly to a retreat, or a day away in a monastic house simply to be cared for and to have space to reflect and pray.

Resources of prayer

There are many ways of praying. Trying a new way to pray is refreshing and renewing. The Benedictine way is the regular reading of a piece of Scripture and stopping when a phrase or word challenges or captures our imagination and repeating that phrase or word, allowing God to speak to us through it. Ignatius suggested entering, in imagination, into a biblical scene, through our senses; seeing the people in the incident, smelling the rustic smells, tasting the dust blown up or the water beyond the boat and hearing Jesus turn and speak to me. What does he say? Can I hear and obey?

At night I find another Ignatian way of praying helpful. Ignatius suggests discerning and then holding what gives you life, the examen. One group have adapted an incident that emerged from the Second World War.[13] Thousands of children were orphaned and left to starve. Those rescued and placed in refugee camps had lost so much that they could not sleep at night. They feared waking up and finding themselves orphans again;

---

12 Michael Paterson and Jessica Rose (eds), 2014, *Enriching Ministry: Pastoral Supervision in Practice*, London: SCM Press; Jane Leach and Michael Paterson, 2009, *Pastoral Supervision: A Handbook*, London: SCM Press.

13 D. Linn, S. F. Linn and M. Linn, 1995, *Sleeping with Bread: Holding what Gives You Life*, Mahwah, NJ: Paulist Press.

nothing reassured them, until someone had the idea of giving them a piece of bread with which to sleep. Holding this bread they slept; through the night it reminded them, 'Today I ate and I will eat again tomorrow.' The suggestion is that before sleeping I light a candle and become aware of God's presence of light and take about five minutes of quiet to answer two questions: 'For what moment today am I most grateful?' and 'For what moment today am I least grateful?' Then offer it to God. Letting go of the day, required throughout the spiritual life, is a spiritual task, knowing that, in good times and bad, God is there and all is well; Ignatius called it 'holy indifference'.

Meditation is a way of praying, such as using the Jesus Prayer, 'Lord Jesus Christ, son of the living God, be merciful to me a sinner', and continually repeating it. A breathing meditation is a slow in-breath using the words 'The Lord is my shepherd', and a slow out-breath with the words 'I shall not want'. Or use a biblical symbol, such as a lit candle, an ear of wheat, a seed, and 'experience' it in silent contemplation. It is helpful to have an object such as this in each room of your home.

In a way, prayer can be called 'a waste of time'; in the eyes of Western culture it is just that, since everything we do must be productive. In prayer we are simply offering ourselves and those for whom we have a concern into God's keeping and seeking God's direction.

Care of the body

In the section above on the Scriptures I mentioned leisure and play. I am body, mind and spirit. I need exercise of some sort to keep fit; as my doctor sister reminds me, 'the body is the temple of the Holy Spirit'. Walking with others, with the dog or on one's own and taking in the infinite variety of nature, or going to the gym and swimming – all these help us to keep fit in body.

Walking itself can be an exercise in meditation, simply using one of the senses to observe the Creator's created world. A student of mine thought that this was a stupid exercise but tried it. On the street she passed an elderly man, who asked her what she was doing. She responded that she had been asked, simply and in silence, to enjoy the created world but that she could see no point in the exercise. 'But you yourself are part of the beauty of creation,' he said and walked on. She returned later to the group of other students, stunned.

Care of the mind

The mind needs feeding and this will be different for each of us: reading a novel, visiting the theatre, seeing a film, reading a piece of challenging theology. I enjoy poetry and particularly that of Rumi:

The Guest House

This being human is a guest house
Every morning a new arrival.
A joy, a depression, a meanness,
some momentary awareness comes
as an unexpected visitor.

Welcome and entertain them all!
Even if they're a crowd of sorrows, who violently sweep your house
empty of its furniture,
still, treat each guest honourably.
He may be clearing you out
for some new delight.
The dark thought, the shame, the malice.
Meet them at the door laughing,
and invite them in
Be grateful for whoever comes,
because each has been sent
as guide from beyond.[14]

To each of us this poem will mean something different, since we are each unique, created in the image of God. Henri Nouwen had some wise words to say about being ourselves.

Often we want to be somewhere other than where we are, or even to be someone other than who we are. We tend to compare ourselves constantly with others and wonder why we are not as rich, as intelligent, as simple, as generous or as saintly as they are. Such comparisons make us feel guilty, ashamed or jealous. It is very important to realize that our vocation is hidden in where we are, and who we are. We are unique human beings, each with a call to realize in our own life what nobody

---

14 Jalaluddin Rumi, 2004, *Essential Rumi*, trans. Coleman Banks with John Moyne, A. J. Arberry and Reynold Nicholson, San Francisco: HarperCollins.

else can, and to realize it in the concrete context of the here and now. We will never find our vocations by trying to figure out whether we are better or worse than others. We are good enough to do what we are called to do ... be yourself![15]

The poems of Rainer Maria Rilke (1875–1926) and Mary Oliver, a modern poet who writes out of her own suffering, are a resource of challenge and feeding. I enjoy studying myths and have become interested in the work of the hospice medical director Michael Kearney and the mystic writer Henri Nouwen.[16] The model of the 'wounded healer' is explored by both: in Greek mythology, that of Chiron; in the Scriptures the Suffering Servant of Isaiah and the Passion of Jesus. For me there are parallels between Chiron's story and the Jesus story. There are the 'archetypes' in Isaiah, the so-called 'Suffering Servant songs', suggesting that the Messiah was 'wounded', as was Chiron. Stories grew around Jesus' birth as they did around Chiron's conception. Jesus, fully human, comes to be seen as fully God. He is sought out for healing. In his presence people find their wholeness and healing: 'your faith has made you whole'. One interpretation of the cross is that 'by his stripes we are healed', he bears the wrong done to him in human acts of betrayal, jealousy and miscarriages of justice; Chiron too is 'a wounded healer', his wound a result of intervening in an attempt to bring peace. Jesus says on the cross, 'today you will be with me in Paradise'. At death he descends into Hades, 'he descended to the dead' (Apostles' Creed; 1 Peter 3.18; cf. Acts 2.24–31; Eph. 4.9), as did Chiron. In resurrection, Jesus is transformed, and this wounded healer ascends to God to intercede for us. Jung states:

> In any on-going analysis the whole personality of both patient and doctor is called into play. There are many cases which the doctor cannot cure without committing himself ... the doctor is effective only when he himself is affected, 'only the wounded physician heals'. But when the doctor wears his personality like a coat of armour, he has no effect.[17]

---

15 Nouwen, *The Wounded Healer*.

16 Michael Kearney, 2000, *A Place of Healing: Working with Suffering in Living and Dying*, Oxford: Oxford University Press, and 1996, *Mortally Wounded: Stories of Soul Pain, Death and Healing*, Dublin: Marino Books.

17 Carl G. Jung, 1983, *Memories, Dreams, Reflections*, London: Flamingo, pp. 155–6, quoted in Kearney, *A Place of Healing*, p. 91.

Play renews

May I return to play? This is about getting so totally engrossed in an activity that we forget time. We are all creative people, created in the image and likeness of God our Creator. There are a myriad ways to create, improvising a piece of music, composing, writing poetry or a story, creating a meal, drawing or painting a picture, making a piece of furniture, making a tapestry, sailing, designing and creating a garden, decorating a room, building a boat ... try it![18] Losing myself in creativity is a way of being restored. Mary Daly said, 'It is the creative potential itself in human beings that is the image of God.' The Victorian poet William Blake wrote, 'I myself do nothing. The Holy Spirit accomplishes all through me.'

A favourite story brings to a conclusion this chapter. It concerns an elderly peasant, a man of the land. Each day he would go into his local church alone and sit for a time before the altar, which had on it a crucifix. One day the priest's curiosity got the better of him and he asked the peasant what he was doing in the church. 'Just being,' he said. 'I look at him and he looks at me and we are happy in one another's company.' We know the sustaining power of the Spirit in our lives.

Questions for reflection and response

- How do you pray? Try a different way.
- How important is supervision to pastoral work?
- Jot down a typical week's activity and note where there is lack of balance.
- Can creativity be the work of God in us?

Further reading

Jane Leach and Michael Paterson, 2009, *Pastoral Supervision: A Handbook*, London: SCM Press.

Henri J. M. Nouwen, 1994, *The Wounded Healer: Ministry in Contemporary Society*, London: Darton, Longman and Todd.

Michael Paterson and Jessica Rose (eds), 2014, *Enriching Ministry: Pastoral Supervision in Practice*, London: SCM Press.

---

18 Julia Cameron, 1993, *The Artist's Way: A Course in Discovering and Recovering Your Creative Self*, London: Pan Books.

8

Joining Up the Dots

A man was travelling alone through the Himalayas. The scenery was spectacular but isolated from human habitation. Suddenly he came across a bare hut surrounded by growing vegetables tended by an old man. Each acknowledged the other and conversation began. The traveller asked, 'How do you live in such poverty, with so little?' The old man responded, 'But you have so little – just your backpack.' The traveller replied, 'Oh yes, but I'm only on a journey.' 'So am I,' replied the old man.
Traditional

We use a personal experience to begin our theology. It is one where autonomy and forgiveness are seen as key concepts. The tasks of a pastoral situation emerging from theology are illustrated from Richard Osmer, an American Christian educator. The cultural context recounts the emergence of a challenge to the dominant medical model within certain hospitals, which encourages patient autonomy and planning their end-of-life experience. Scripture is indicated that challenges and informs the initial experience. Context and Scriptures are brought together to inform and guide an emerging theology that in turn guides our pastoral practice. In this chapter the content will be subservient to the journey we have travelled through the book and to the question of what we have learnt together.

Pastoral circle

Pastoral practice: of presence and journeying with

Experience – reflection: reactions to a dying woman – autonomy and forgiveness

Cultural context: challenge to the medical model

Scripture and tradition: autonomy and forgiveness are key issues

Scripture/tradition and context: theology of relationality, Trinity and of forgiveness

Experience

Angie, my sister, was a patient in the hospice in a shared ward. Her medical condition was variable. This was her second brain tumour, and it had proved too difficult to operate. Her family knew that time was short. Angie had been a keen member of the local choral society and sung with my other sister and me. Our conductor called the three of us The Beverly Sisters.

On the last occasion she had attended the rehearsal she had asked the conductor if we could sing a chorus from a work we were preparing for Lent. It contained the words from Revelation 21.4, 'God will wipe every tear from their eyes. Death will be no more; mourning and crying and pain will be no more, for the first things have passed away.' It was a poignant moment, sitting next to Angie. I thought that we were singing it with and for her.

When the hospice music therapist realized Angie's love of music, and that music could give relief to her pain, he asked her if she would like something played and what it might be. She chose the spiritual 'Swing low sweet chariot, coming for to carry me home', a song our mother often sang around the house.

My local sister and I believed Angie was helped by the security the hospice offered, by pain relief and by the staff's care. She seemed to understand and answer in the affirmative when we asked her about staying. We also knew that Angie's teenage daughter, who was taking external exams, and her husband had both already found nursing Angie at home difficult, even with support. We believed that they would find the last part of the journey and Angie dying at home impossible. Another sister, who lived 300 miles away, a five-hour journey, thought that Angie wanted to die at home and pressed for that to happen on her regular visits.

Reflection on experience

Throughout this book I have used experience to begin a chapter. This is one of the methodologies used by pastoral theology. It roots a situation in the reality of life. Anton Boisen began a method of training for ministry called Clinical Pastoral Education (CPE). Boisen believed that carefully reading 'living documents' – patients struggling with illness – should become an essential component of a theological curriculum. His main concern was not primarily that students learn appropriate intervention skills, rather it helped them form their own theology from an empirical base.[1] The theology of Boisen's students looked at the experience in the cultural context and then asked what Scripture resonated with the experience and helped to make sense of it theologically. I have used an experience in a similar way.

In the experience at the beginning of this chapter a decision had to be made as to where Angie would die. It was difficult. There were many aspects and people to consider, particularly Angie. She had not been asked her views and now could not speak. She knew the hospice, having been an outpatient. One day at home she had collapsed on the landing across the staircase between bedroom and bathroom. Hospice at Home were called, and they phoned the ambulance. As she was taken into the hospice building she said to my sister, 'I don't think I will come out.'

A major issue was our sister, who lived away and insisted Angie should go home. She waged what can only be described as a 'war' with the medical director of the hospice, over his reluctance to get Angie home. For months after Angie's death she corresponded with the director. Recently, over eight years after Angie's death, we were talking on the phone. My sister is a humanist. She had just seen the film The Railway Man, which concerned the buried, unspoken anger of Eric Lomax, who had helped in the building of the Thailand–Burma railway line. Lomax was singled out by the Japanese for punishment, having been caught secretly making a radio. He was put in solitary confinement and cruelly tortured, but buried the memory. Years later he began having nightmares. The film explores how he discovers that his torturer is still alive and how he pursues him. Armed with a knife and facing his defenceless torturer, he finds that he cannot kill him. Over the following years they become friends. My sister felt that the film was deficient in not showing how they forgave each other to become friends. She told me how she found forgiveness hard and said that she could not forgive Angie's husband, because he did not have Angie home to die. Anger, which needs forgiveness, is not easy to deal with. It can 'eat' a person up inside, and we talked about it.

1 Daniel S. Schipani, 2014, 'Case Study Method', in Bonnie J. Miller-McLemore (ed.), 2014, The Wiley Blackwell Companion to Practical Theology, Chichester: John Wiley & Sons Ltd., p. 93.

Questions for reflection and response

- Why was forgiveness so key in this experience?
- What is meant by forgiveness?
- Think about forgiveness in the Gospels.
- What will a theology of forgiveness look like?

Reflection on the cultural context

Richard Osmer uses the term 'practical' rather than 'pastoral',[2] seeing the four tasks of practical theology as:

- the descriptive–empirical task: gathering information 'that helps us discern patterns and dynamics in particular episodes, situations or contexts'.
- the interpretative task: drawing on 'theories of the arts and sciences to better understand and explain why these patterns and dynamics are occurring'.
- the normative task: 'using theological concepts to interpret particular episodes, situations or contexts, constructing ethical norms to guide our responses, and learning from "good practice"'.
- the pragmatic task: 'determining strategies of action that will influence situations in ways that are desirable and entering into a reflective conversation with the "talk back" emerging when they are enacted'.[3]

This section of my method, *experience*, uses Osmer's interpretative task, that is, the collecting of insights from the arts and sciences that help us interpret. The film, *The Railway Man* led into the discussion with my sister about forgiveness.

The twenty-first century is a period when the science of medicine has increased life expectation through increasingly sophisticated technology and pharmaceutical advances. This has led in the past to the social historian Philippe Ariès using the term 'medicalized death'. I have given examples and evidence of the use of the term. In the UK a measure of a hospital's success is low death rates, indicating that the medical profession

---

2 Bonnie Miller-McLemore (ed.), 2014, *The Wiley Blackwell Companion to Practical Theology*, Chichester: John Wiley & Sons Ltd, in the Introduction writes about practical/pastoral theology.

3 Richard R. Osmer, 2008, *Practical Theology: An Introduction*, Grand Rapids, MI and Cambridge, UK: Eerdmans, p. 4.

often see death as a failure of competence. There is still a taboo on talking about death. I have noticed challenges to this from organizations, and in some hospitals, with patients being asked and informed of their options for treatment, with help to plan their future to include end-of-life care. Medical ethics have emphasized the autonomy of the patient.

The argument has noted that the postmodern society in the West is mobile, pluralistic and secular, losing its cultural roots and cohesion in a religious faith. This is less so in the USA. There is a decrease in traditional religion, Christianity, evidenced by a decline in churchgoing. However, there is an increase in an individual search for meaning in life, seen from the 1960s onwards in the spirituality of the New Age movement and activities such as meditation and yoga. The 2011 Census in the UK recorded a growth in Islam, though there is a paradox here in that there is a growth in fundamentalism in all religions with acts of terrorism such as that of 9/11. I also noted sociological research in Europe that indicated a 'vicarious religion'. It seems as if the need for ritual and symbol, to convey those experiences in life that are too deep for words, are innate in humans. Christian churches have historical resources and can provide these in ministering to the dying, to the bereaved and in funeral liturgies.

The experience in this chapter raises two issues: that of the autonomy of Angie, the patient, in decision-making as to where she wanted to die, and the question raised for our sister by a film, *The Railway Man*, on forgiveness.

Questions for reflection and response

- How does the cultural context relate to the 'Experience' section of this chapter?
- Does the cultural context help in understanding the experience?
- What do you understand by 'vicarious religion'? Is it possible for religion to be vicarious?
- Comment on the statement, 'the need of ritual and symbol ... are innate in humans'.

Insights from Scripture and the Tradition

The task of discerning the Scriptures relates to Osmer's 'normative task' of using theological concepts to interpret situations. Our theology emerges from understanding and interpreting the Scriptures. In each of the preceding chapters there has been a wide-ranging section on the Scriptures. The Bible is at the heart of the Christian faith and of its practice, a primary witness to the apostolic faith, a formative authority in Christian doctrine and ethics.[4] It is central to pastoral theology, but is not unproblematic. The authority of the Bible depends on the Church using it: the Orthodox Churches see the Bible as rooted in the tradition, noted in liturgy and theology; the Roman Catholic Church understands the Bible as the fundamental witness, though interpreted through the magisterium responsible for the teaching of the Church. Within Protestantism, meaning is guided through the work of the Holy Spirit. There is also a tension within Catholic and Protestant Churches between a conservative, sometimes literal/fundamentalist, interpretation and that of a more liberal position that understands the Bible in the context of contemporary culture. Karl Barth said the Bible should be read held in one hand with the newspaper in the other.

Paul Ballard cites several different approaches to the Bible's use in pastoral care. One stresses the 'normality' of Scripture, providing a 'clear Christian framework for pastoral counselling'. A second approach,

> wants to use the Bible to inform pastoral care in a decisive and formative way. But it recognizes the reality of living in the modern world and so hopes to affirm both the challenges of biblical scholarship and the insights and practices of psychology and psychotherapy.[5]

Stephen Pattison describes three approaches: 'the imagist approach' selects themes and images as a model for the pastor – the good shepherd, the wounded healer, the fool (I have used this understanding in Chapter 6); the 'informative approach' as it provides insights that could illuminate the human condition, for example using biblical genres such as the psalms of lament, which I noted may help the grieving process; the 'thematic approach', which uses biblical themes such as creation, sin and redemption (see Chapter 2). These help self-understanding in a world that is increasingly complex.[6] Other factors come into play. There are emergent contextual theologies, such as feminist and liberation theologies. Lastly there is the 'implicit' rather than 'explicit' use of Scripture in many pastoral situations. For example, I noted this when thinking about leading a funeral on occasions when the bereaved and deceased are not religious

---

4 Paul Ballard, 'The Use of Scripture', in Miller-McLemore (ed.), *Wiley Blackwell Companion*, p. 163.

5 Ballard, 'Use of Scripture', p. 165.

6 Stephen Pattison, 2000, *A Critique of Pastoral Care*, London: SCM Press.

(see Chapter 5). The Bible is central to the task of pastoral care in giving resources, but it must be wrestled with as a text from a different cultural context, as interpreted in alternative ways by biblical scholars and as it challenges and is challenged by our contemporary context.

When we engage with the Scriptures in creating theology, we read into the text (*isogesis*) from our own context, for me that of a white, Western, educated woman living in the twenty-first century. I do this without realizing. In return the Bible informs and challenges me. How does the text address me? To know the Bible is not simply a question of content, rather it involves acting upon it, interacting with it, asking questions of it, and the discipline of choosing to be formed and informed by it. It is about the forming of an identity and about being transformed by the Spirit, a process that is continuous throughout our lives.

The test of the authority that is given to Scripture is the discerning of the meaning of the text in the life of the believer and the community of faith. The interpretation of Scriptures will be judged in answer to questions concerning their potential to give and affirm life in all its fullness, to challenge unjust structures that limit life, shown in the life and Passion of Jesus of Nazareth. The Scriptures are to lead readers into all truth, even if that truth disturbs.

I have attempted to select Scripture that has relevance and might give some way of interpreting the experience at the beginning of each chapter. For example, in this chapter, the theological task is looking at the nature of decision-making, autonomy and forgiveness. In the Hebrew Scriptures, humanity is created in the image and likeness of God and given responsibility for the care of the earth and its creatures (Gen. 1.26). Cain asks, 'Am I my brother's keeper?' (Gen. 4.9). There is an implied responsibility here. The prophets appeal to Israel to decide whom they will serve. In the New Testament, an example of autonomy is the story of the rich young ruler whom Jesus loves and lets go; he has made his own decision, and has autonomy to follow his own way (Mark 10.17–22).

Humanity is rarely understood as individual in the Hebrew Scriptures, but as in a collective, covenant relationship with God. The prophets repeatedly challenge Israel for concentrating on worship and disregarding the poor and the marginalized. Justice and mercy is what God requires. Here is a theology of covenant, of Trinity, which is very different from contemporary society with its individualism, though there are some hospitals who take the relatives of a patient seriously and work with them.

In the New Testament, the Sermon on the Mount gives helpful material about forgiveness: 'if you remember that your brother or sister has something against you, leave your gift there before the altar and go; first be reconciled to your brother or sister, and then come and offer your gift' (Matt. 5.23–24); 'I say to you, Love your enemies' (5.44); and, in the Lord's Prayer, 'forgive us our debts, as we also have forgiven our debtors' (6.12). Forgiveness was central to Jesus' ministry. He recognized human frailty and deliberate sin, the need for repentance, a change of direction, which enabled a new beginning. Words of Jesus from the cross were ones of forgiveness: 'Father, forgive them; for they do not know what they are doing' (Luke 23.34). My sister wrestles with forgiveness, though realizing that she needs it.

Questions for reflection and response

- In what sense do the Scriptures advocate personal autonomy?
- Give some examples of autonomy in the Scriptures.
- Why is forgiveness central to the New Testament?
- What are the 'conditions' of forgiveness?

Reflection on cultural context in dialogue with Scripture and the tradition

This section in each chapter reflects Osmer's 'normative task' in that it interprets situations – my section 'Experience' – the Scriptures and the cultural context. Out of the interaction between them emerges a theology that will inform practice. Our practice will use insights from other disciplines but it is distinctive, informed by our faith and rooted in theology. For example, Chapter 3 uses insights from the psychologists Murray Parkes and Kübler-Ross, but it uses them with scriptural insights to emerge creatively in a theology of presence. This is an area of pastoral theology that is still debatable in academic circles of practical theologians.[7]

The origins of pastoral theology in Britain are found in pastoral studies and 'hints and tips' to clergy in training of how to practise their ministry. Emphasis was on how to apply theology, 'neglecting the potential for practice to disclose the theological'.[8] The British and Irish Association of Practical Theology (BIAPT), founded in 1994, is a professional organization bringing together academic practical theologians and practitioners.

---

7 See the reference in 'the question of the place of the humanistic and the secular disciplines in the theological endeavour', Zoe Bennett, 2014, 'Britain', in Miller-McLemore (ed.), *Wiley Blackwell Companion*, p. 482.

8 Bennett, 'Britain', p. 476.

In 2007 BIAPT held, with the Association for Pastoral and Spiritual Care and Counselling, a conference on 'Forgiveness: Psychological, Spiritual and Theological Perspectives'. The journal *Practical Theology* continues to reflect issues of the rapprochement between academic theology and pastoral practice.

In this particular chapter I will consider the psychological aspects of shame and forgiveness, together with the concept of autonomy in relationship to biblical insights that give rise to theologies of presence, forgiveness, humanity and relationality/Trinity.

Pastoral practice

The circle in the diagram at the beginning of each chapter continues in a spiral. This is because the penultimate stage in the diagram of pastoral practice is premised on a theology that is provisional and will need revision, together with a reflection on using the criteria of Jesus: 'I came that you might have life and have it to the full.'

In this chapter, pastoral practice is guided by a theology of the ministry of presence to Angie, and indeed also to the turmoil of her sister's understanding of forgiveness. A theology of forgiveness is needed that will include understanding a theology of what it means to be human, and within a theology of Trinity. It may well give an opportunity to theologize with the patient and her relatives: to help them make sense of their experience and find meaning in lives.

Questions for reflection and response

- What is meant by 'provisional theology'?
- How will Jesus' statement 'I came that you might have life and have it to the full' have any meaning in a situation of terminal illness?
- How might a theology of forgiveness be associated with a theology of humanity?
- What is the connection between a theology of forgiveness and Trinity?

Further reading

Paul Ballard, 2014, 'The Use of Scripture', in Bonnie J. Miller-McLemore (ed.), *The Wiley Blackwell Companion to Practical Theology*, Chichester: John Wiley & Sons Ltd.

Richard R. Osmer, 2008, *Practical Theology: An Introduction*, Grand Rapids, MI and Cambridge: Eerdmans.

Stephen Pattison, 2000, *A Critique of Pastoral Care*, London: SCM Press. Chapters 1, 2 and 4 are useful chapters.

Conclusion

The roots of the West's medical model can be found in Ancient Greece. Healers were competing craftsmen; most were slaves, herbalists, drug-sellers, and sellers of charms and incantations. If patients became 'overcome by their disease' whether terminal or chronic, healers would stop trying to cure and on occasions administer poisons to achieve a pain-less death. The vocation of Hippocrates was to challenge both the practice and belief of his age.

Hippocrates (460–375 BCE) was born on the island of Kos, site of a temple of Asclepius god of healing. He was a physician who became an ambassador for medicine against a strong opposing infrastructure, spending 20 years in prison, during which he wrote medical papers. He believed disease was the result of environmental factors, diet and living habits, not the gods,[9] and considered documentation significant, suggesting physicians record their observation and methods objectively instead of relying on an oral tradition; records could be written to train, leading to 'case histories' that helped predict the development of a disease. He believed that the body contained within itself the power to rebalance the four humours and heal; recovery was about enabling this natural process to proceed, requiring rest and immobilization.[10] He challenged the practice of his day of using poisons since they destroyed life, an end alien to medicine. If Hippocrates was unable to help terminal patients they chose to go to the temple of Asclepius. Some 60 medical writings, known as the Hippocratic Collection have survived, though style suggests several authors

Hippocrates worked using convictions based on what we now know as incorrect anatomy, since it was a taboo to dissect corpses. But for his emphasis on observation, prognosis, methods, the healing power of the rebalancing of nature and his professionalism, including the ethics of the Hippocratic oath, the humane aspect of the medical profession, he is

---

9 *On the Sacred Disease*, quoted in Plato http://classics.mit.edu/Plato/phaedrus. html.

10 The humours do not seem a rational understanding to us but at that time the idea was considered logical.

traditionally regarded as the father of Western medicine, and represents a beginning of the medical model.[11]

Asclepius, Greek god of medicine, was rescued as a baby and carried to Chiron, the wounded centaur, who raised Asclepius and instructed him in the art of healing. Asclepius the healer, in another version of the legend, was himself wounded, and set up a temple at Epidaurus to heal others. The cult of Asclepius existed from 500 BCE–500 CE. It was practised in temples across the ancient world, including Kos, home of Hippocrates. From about 300 BCE pilgrims flocked to the temples, believing an incurable illness caused by the gods needed a divine remedy in a sacred place. Healing was of body and soul/mind, it was holistic; humanity was a unity.

The journey to an Asclepian temple marked initiation into the 'world' of the gods. The journey outwards now turned inwards. The supplicant was welcomed by a guide, fed, rested and taken to wash as ritual purification. Shoes worn in the sanctuary became 'holy'. There was a pile at its entrance for those in need. A particular type of non-venomous snake was often used in healing rituals and slithered freely on the temple floor.[12] Fasting was followed by sleeping stretched out on the earth, in touch with nature, which healed through the gods, in the holiest part of the sanctuary, the *abaton*. In the darkness the sufferer slept and dreamt, or if he remained awake was visited by Asclepius himself. This time was an 'incubation' period leading to an 'epiphany' or revelation. In ancient times dreams were the work of the gods, mysteries of the night; a patient might stay in the *abaton* several days until he was 'visited'.[13] Healing was recorded on a tablet, with the name of the sick person, the disease, how the cure was affected, and an offering of what could be afforded made to the gods; tablets can still be seen.

The symbol of Asclepius is a staff entwined with a snake, symbol of both darkness and light, evil and goodness. The mysteriousness of the

---

11 The Hippocratic oath begins with the words, 'Apollo Physician and Asclepius and ... gods and goddesses', since Hippocrates honoured the gods (www.pbs.org/wgbh/nova/doctors/oath_classical.html). The oath was the rite of passage for medical students from the eighteenth century and was revised in the twentieth century following the betrayal in the Second World War by Nazi doctors. A modern translation is Ludwig Edelstein, 1967, *The Hippocratic Oath: Text, Translation and Interpretation*, Baltimore, Johns Hopkins University Press, pp. 3–63.

12 The serpent appears in Genesis 3; the Hebrews were punished by being bitten by snakes; healing was brought by Moses lifting up a 'bronze serpent' (Num. 21.8–9).

13 Today in Jung dreams are the place of the unconscious mind, free from the rational, controlled conscious mind. In ancient times dreams were the work of the gods (Joseph sagas Gen. 37.5–11).

snake's shedding of skin made it appear immortal, a continual death and resurrection in one life; 'healing is also paradoxical'.[14] In the sculptures of Asclepius, the staff is a branch from a tree with all its potential for nature's mysterious annual rebirth. Today the staff of Asclepius remains a symbol of medicine, on pharmacies, on some ambulances and on medical journals. His method of healing through visualizations, dreams and interpretation appears today in art and music therapy, deep ecology, body therapies, psychotherapies and spiritual practice.[15] Throughout the town of Kos there are depictions of two intertwined snakes, going in opposite directions, considered to be symbols of Hippocratic medicine and that of Asclepius, as complementary models of medical care.[16] Both models regard what is close to nature as significant and that healing is within the patient working together with the doctor. Hippocrates tends to use what we recognize as right-brain activity – rational and logical, the medical model; in Asclepius, emphasis is on the left brain, the imaginative, creative, symbolic and subconscious.

In the second century, the physician Galen (129–216 CE) developed Hippocrates' method, adding his own extensive study and practical experience. His medicine became written texts to be used in Europe until the Renaissance, when Hippocratic methods were revived and expanded. In the Middle Ages, the Islamic world adopted Hippocratic methods and developed new techniques. Galen's synthesis and techniques were used more recently by people like Jean-Martin Charcot and William Osler.[17]

Francis Bacon (1561–1626) read Hippocrates and Galen. He was pioneer of the scientific method, influencing the scientific revolution

---

14 Kearney, 2000, *A Place of Healing: Working and Suffering in Living and Dying*, Oxford: Oxford University Press, p. 60, and, 1996, *Mortally Wounded: Stories of Soul Pain, Death and Healing*, Dublin: Marino Books. Both books illustrate Kearney's use of daydreaming and visualization within the treatment of hospice patients.

15 Visualization is also used in schools, as found in David Hay et al., 1990, *New Methods in RE Teaching: An Experimental Approach*, Harlow: Oliver and Boyd.

16 Kearney, 2000, p.35 noted this when he visited Kos in researching his books.

17 Charcot (1825–93) was a French neurologist and professor of anatomical pathology, referred to as the father of French neurology and one of the world's pioneers of neurology. His skill was clinical and pathological observation, leading to the identity of multiple sclerosis and his understanding of Parkinson's disease. His biographer was C. G. Goetz, 1987, *Charcot the Clinician*, New York: Raven Press. William Osler (1849–1919) was a Canadian physician whose contribution to medicine was to insist that students in hospitals learnt from seeing and talking to patients; he established ward rounds and student residency in the hospital, stating, 'Listen to your patient, he is telling you the diagnosis.' He went to Oxford and was made Regius Chair of Medicine in 1905.

of 1550–1700. He derided the speculative science and philosophy of Aristotle and the medieval period; he called for reform, proposing science should be experimental, practical and inventive, based on first principles of reason through observation, experiment and deduction. Bacon's work was called the 'induction method', reasoning which led from fact to axiom to physical law. He wrote a treatise on medicine, *The History of Life and Death*. In the Preface he wrote of his hope that he would contribute to the common good and through it physicians become 'instruments and dispensers of God's power and mercy in prolonging and renewing the life of man'. He rejected Hippocrates' category of an illness that did not respond to medicine – his advancement of learning was to bring about the restoring of humanity to before the Fall. Physicians were called to fight against death, using the weapons of their research. As Hippocrates, Bacon encouraged the discovery of the context of the patient: the physical home, food, diet, manner of living, exercise and drinking water. He advised, if a cure was not found:

> let [the physician] resort to palliation, and alleviate the symptom without busying himself too much with the perfect cure; and many times ... that course will exceed all expectation. Likewise the patient himself may strive ... to overcome the symptom in the exacerbation, and so by time, turn suffering into Nature.[18]

There was always optimism. Today we are grateful that many diseases have been conquered, but this paradigm shift led to the 'Baconian Project' and to the further medicalization of death. In the Baconian Project are the seeds of eliminating human mortality and vulnerability to suffering by scientific technology. Allen Verhey comments, 'advocacy of science and technology could finally deliver human beings from the death and misery to which nature seems to condemn them, all find a seed in Bacon.'[19]

With the Industrial Revolution (1720–1840/60) and all its achievements, religion was neglected and attention shifted to science. The Deist movement began; God was understood as the great designer of the universe, a machine, no longer personal and caring, rather an object of scientific observation, a hypothesis. There gradually developed an understanding of the designer as absent and many people became indifferent to God; science dominated knowledge. Medicine became mechanistic, medicalized.

---

18 G.W. Steeves, 1913, 'Medical allusions in the writings of Francis Bacon', in *Proceedings of the Royal Society of Medicine 6*, pp. 76–98.

19 Allen Verhey, 2011, *The Christian Art of Dying: Learning from Jesus*, Grand Rapids, MI and Cambridge, UK: Eerdmans, p. 31.

Thoughts

Michael Kearney, medical director of a hospice, uses the Chiron myth, together with Asclepius' dream healing, as a complementary model to the medical model when working with dying patients. He learnt from Cicely Saunders and the hospice movement, which used art and music therapy and meditation. He uses visualization techniques, together with the psychological underpinning of Jung's theory of individuation. Kearney suggests that the integration that can happen is significant to all humans. The medical model with all its achievements in physical health needs to recognize that humans are also spiritual beings, on a journey seeking wholeness. Existential and mental illness with its physical manifestations needs healing; only with the return to the complementary models of Hippocratic and Asclepius can this be found. A Jungian analyst, Albert Kreinheder, used the words of Kieffer:

'the object of healing is not to stay alive ... [it is] to become more whole. Death is the final healing' ... the unconscious leaks through and before long we are almost immersed in the divine. God, as Meister Eckhart envisioned Him, is 'a great underground river', and as we are gently, gradually borne upon its waters, we are supremely content and fully healed.[20]

At the beginning of this book I stated that this is a workbook in which I share my experience of ministry in the area of death, dying and bereavement. This involved suggesting that you the reader were invited to explore your own experience so that together we could recognize the significance of theology in our ministry and that theology would inform and be reflected in our practice. I hope that you have found tools and resources to do this, and I hope that, however inadequate my attempts, you will have been informed and helped to 'assess' your own ministry, and that if you would like to enter into a more personal dialogue then that is possible at dyingtolive.org.uk.

---

20 Albert Kreinheder, 1991, *Body and Soul; The Other Side of Illness*, Toronto: Inner City Books, pp. 108–10.

Resources for the Bereaved

Astley, Neil (ed.), 2003, *Do Not Go Gentle: Poems for Funerals*, Northumberland: Bloodaxe Books.

Atwell, Robert, 2005, *Remember: 100 Readings for Those in Grief and Bereavement*, Norwich: Canterbury Press.

Christian Publicity Outreach in Worthing, UK, have a website to obtain helpful cards for initial bereavement, 'In your constant love', and on the first anniversary of the death, 'Comfort from his love'.

Dying Matters Coalition (www.dyingmatters.org) produces excellent booklets to help and inform relatives and patients about dying, entitled: *Putting your house in order – 5 things you can plan for end of life*; *Five things I want to be remembered for*; *Thinking of you – what to say if someone you know is dying*.

Oliver, Mary, 2008, *Red Bird*, Northumberland: Bloodaxe.

Sheppy, Paul, 2003, *In Sure and Certain Hope: Liturgies, Prayers and Readings for Funerals and Memorials*, Norwich: Canterbury Press.

Sheppy, Paul, 2005, *Cries of the Heart: A Daily Companion for Your Journey through Grief*, Norwich: Canterbury Press.

Stewart, Dorothy M., 2013, *Still Caring: Christian Meditations and Prayers*, London: SPCK.

Tiley Tim Ltd, cards, 33 Zetland Rd, Bristol, B56 7AH.

Bibliography

Aries, Philippe, 1974/75, *Western Attitudes toward Death: From the Middle Ages to the Present*, Baltimore and London: Johns Hopkins University Press.

Ariès, Philippe, 1981, *The Hour of Our Death*, trans. Helen Weaver, New York, Knopf.

Badham, Paul and Ballard, Paul (eds), 1996, *Facing Death: An Interdisciplinary Approach*, Cardiff: University of Wales Press.

Berger, D. and Wyschogrod, M. in Helen P. Fry (ed.), 1996, *Christian–Jewish Dialogue: A Reader*, Exeter: University of Exeter Press.

Billings, Alan, 1992, *Dying and Grieving: A Guide to Pastoral Ministry*, London: SPCK.

Bruce, Steve, 1996, *Religion in the Modern World*, Oxford: Oxford University Press.

Burgess, Ruth, 2013, *Saying Goodbye: Resources for Funerals, Scattering Ashes and Remembering*, Glasgow: Wild Goose Publications.

Davie, Grace, 2000, *Religion in Modern Europe: A Memory Mutates*, Oxford: Oxford University Press.

Davies, Douglas J., 1997, *Death Ritual and Belief: The Rhetoric of Funerary Rites*, London: Cassell.

Davies, Douglas J., 2005, *A Brief History of Death*, Oxford: Blackwell Publishing.

Davies, Douglas J., 2008, *The Theology of Death*, London and New York: T & T Clark

Doctrine Commission of the General Synod of the Church of England, 1995, *The Mystery of Salvation: The Story of God's Gift*, London: Church House Publishing.

Edwards, David L., 1999, *After Death? Past Beliefs and Real Possibilities*, London and New York: Cassell.

Funerals Group Churches (ed.), 2009, *Funeral Services of the Christian Churches in England*, 4th edn, Norwich: Canterbury Press.

Hauerwas, Stanley, 1990, *Naming the Silences: Medicine and the Problem of Suffering*, New York and London: T & T Clark.

Henk, Ten Have and Clark, David (eds), 2002, *The Ethics of Palliative Care: European Perspectives*, Buckingham, UK and Philadelphia: Open University Press.

James, Hugh, 2004, *A Fitting End: Making the Most of a Funeral*, Norwich: Canterbury Press.

Jupp, Peter C. (ed.), 2008, *Death our Future: Christian Theology and Funeral Practice*, Peterborough: Epworth Press.

Kearney, Michael, 1996, *Mortally Wounded: Stories of Soul Pain, Death and Healing*, Dublin: Marino Books.

Kearney, Michael, 2000, *A Place of Healing: Working with Suffering in Living and Dying*, Oxford: Oxford University Press.

Kelly, Ewan, 2008, *Meaningful Funerals: Meeting the Theological and Pastoral Challenge in a Postmodern Era*, London and New York: Mowbray.

Kübler-Ross, Elizabeth, 1970, *On Death and Dying*, London and New York: Routledge.

Levenson, Jon D., 2006, *Resurrection and the Restoration of Israel: The Ultimate Victory of the God of Life*, New Haven and London: Yale University Press.

Magonet, Jonathan, 2004, *A Rabbi Reads the Bible*, London: SCM Press.

Miller-McLemore, Bonnie (ed.), 2014, *The Wiley Blackwell Companion to Practical Theology*, Chichester: John Wiley & Sons Ltd.

Murray Parkes, Colin, Pittu Laungani and Bill Young (eds), 1997, *Death and Bereavement across Cultures*, London and New York: Routledge.

Oliver, Stephen (ed.), 2013, *Inside Grief*, London: SPCK.

Osmer, Richard R., 2008, *Practical Theology: An Introduction*, Grand Rapids, MI and Cambridge, UK: Eerdmans.

Robben, Antonius (ed.), 2004, *Death, Mourning, and Burial: A Cross-Cultural Reader*, Oxford: Blackwell.

Rumbold, Bruce (ed.), 2002, *Spirituality and Palliative Care: Social and Pastoral Perspectives*, Oxford: Oxford University Press.

Rumen, Rachel Naomi, 2000, *My Grandfather's Blessings: Stories of Strength, Refuge, and Belonging*, New York: Riverhead Books, and London: HarperCollins.

Smith, Richard, editorial, 'A good death: An important aim for health services and for us all', *British Medical Journal* 320:7228, 15 January 2000, pp. 129–30.

Verhey, Allen, 2003, *Reading the Bible in the Strange World of Medicine*, Grand Rapids, MI and Cambridge, UK: Eerdmans.

Verhey, Allen, 2011, *The Christian Art of Dying: Learning from Jesus*, Grand Rapids, MI and Cambridge, UK: Eerdmans.

Ward, Tess, 2012, *Alternative Pastoral Prayers*, Norwich: Canterbury Press.

Woodward, James, 2005, *Befriending Death*, London: SPCK.

Wright, Tom, 2003, *The Resurrection of the Son of God*, London: SPCK.

Online Resources

www.rcn.org.uk/_data/assets/pdf_file/0008/372995/003887.pdf (Royal College of Nursing, 2011, 'Spirituality in Nursing Care: a Pocket Guide')

www.dh.gov.uk/publications (End of Life Care Strategy)

www.ambercarebundle.org and www.coordinatemycare.co.uk (Personalized care plans)

www.dyingmatters.org (Dying Matters Week)

www.deathcraft.com (Death cafés)

www.merseyside&Cheshire.cancernetwork (Spiritual care in other cultures)

www.crusebereavementcare.org.uk (Cruse)

www.macmillan.org.uk (Macmillan Nurses)

www.mariecurie.org.uk (Marie Curie)

www.anglicansonline.org/basics/thirty-nine_articles.html (Anglican site)

www.rcn.org.uk/_data/assets/pdf_file/0008/372995/003887.pdf (Royal College of Nursing)

www.ethnicityonline.net

Index of Biblical References

Index of Names and Subjects

Psalms of Lament 21, 85, 135, 137, 152, 156, 191
psychologist 12, 42, 161, 193
psychology xi, 27, 52, 150, 191
purgatory 55, 56, 102

reconciliation, ministry of 34, 118, 139
redemption 22, 87, 115, 191
Reincarnation 25, 26n17, 57, 58, 88, 114, 160
remembrance 76, 156, 157, 162
Remembrance Sunday 155–6, 163
Remen, Rachel Naomi 171, 171n4
repentance 18, 22, 31, 36, 59, 116, 159, 193
Resurrection 21n30, 22, 23, 29, 54, 55, 62, 67, 93, 107, 128, 140, 157, 162, 197
resurrection body 36, 38, 53, 55, 59, 67, 71, 86, 89, 102, 103, 105, 108
resurrection of Jesus 54, 55, 67, 93, 100, 119, 157, 177, 184
Rilke, Rainer Maria 184
ritual xi, 8, 30, 36, 44, 54, 63, 70–1, 72, 78–81, 87, 89, 99–101, 100n3, 104–5, 106, 109, 109n21, 110, 112, 113–15, 116, 123, 125, 127, 129, 132, 136, 148, 155, 158, 160, 162, 178, 190, 196
Royal College of Nursing 44n21, 203
Royal College of Physicians 39
Rumbold, Bruce 135, 135n13&15
Rumi, Jalaluddin 175, 183, 183n14

Sacks, Jonathan 19n26, 24, 27–8
sacramental confession 34
sacraments 36, 103
sacrifice 6, 21, 56, 72, 100
Salvation Army 70, 79
salvation xi, 1, 9n6, 15, 29, 36, 55, 55n40, 56, 68, 86, 90, 107, 107n16, 116, 128
Sanders, E. P 24
Saunders, Dame Cicely 32 n1, 41, 43, 199
science xi, xii, 19n26, 26, 26n38, 27, 27n39, 28, 28n41, 29–30, 29n46, 68, 90, 100, 115, 170, 189, 198

sciences
  biological/social x, 28, 66, 124
  medical x, 1, 11–12, 27, 28, 73, 189
  physical x, 28, 59
Second Coming 54, 86
secular x, xii, 13, 29, 44, 50, 87, 103, 106, 112, 124, 133, 170, 176, 181
secular as research 13, 13n17
servant church 104, 116
Sheldrake, Philip F. 12
Sheol 20–1, 53, 80–1, 83
shepherds 16n18, 127, 128, 139, 168, 182, 191
snake/serpent 4, 17, 196–7, 196n12
soul 4, 7, 15, 17, 23, 37, 52, 53–4, 57, 58, 59, 64, 82, 86, 87–8, 89, 100, 102, 103, 107, 111–14, 148, 157–8, 160, 174, 175, 184n16, 196, 199n20
spiritual body 59, 67, 86, 89
spirituality definition xi, 9n8, 12n11, 14, 38, 44, 44n21, 45, 59, 69, 126, 130, 139, 166, 170, 177, 180
story
  human 4, 44, 50, 63, 73, 78, 81, 92, 97, 118, 126, 135, 150, 154, 160, 169, 178, 179, 185
  of scriptures 15, 16, 17, 28, 68, 85, 99, 107, 115, 116, 118, 130, 136, 171, 172, 184, 192
Stroebe, Margaret 77, 77n14, 145n1, 150, 152, 152n6
suffering 5–6, 6n3, 19, 33, 43–4, 51, 53, 54, 57, 59, 60, 61, 62, 64, 69, 77, 81–2, 83, 84, 85, 90, 137, 140, 143, 160, 168, 172, 178, 184, 184n16, 197, 198
suffering servant 22, 184
suicide 65, 108, 133, 142
supervision 91, 142, 163, 181, 185

taboo 46, 49, 76, 160, 190, 195
technology xii, 3, 29, 169, 189, 198
terrorism 12, 27, 141, 170, 190
theodicy 137
theos 58–9, 58n41
Thistleton, Anthony 81
Tomlinson, Dave 130, 130n10, 133
Tree of Life 17

CPSIA information can be obtained at www.ICGtesting.com
Printed in the USA
LVOW03s0028220115

423772LV00026B/215/P